ALSO BY HAROLD N. LEVINSON, M.D.
A Solution to the Riddle Dyslexia
Smart But Feeling Dumb

HAROLD N. LEVINSON, M.D.
WITH STEVEN CARTER

Phobia FREE

A MEDICAL BREAKTHROUGH LINKING 90% OF ALL PHOBIAS AND PANIC ATTACKS TO A HIDDEN *PHYSICAL* PROBLEM

MJF Books
New York

Published by MJF Books
Fine Communications
Two Lincoln Square
60 West 66th Street
New York, NY 10023

Phobia Free
ISBN 1-56731-318-3

The authors and publishers are grateful for permission to use the material listed below:

Portions of the stories of Susan S. in Chapters 1 and 9, Margarita M. in Chapter 4, Sue S. in Chapter 9, and Anne M. in Chapter 16; the list of guided-missile symptoms in Chapter 19, and the questions about primary medication in Chapter 23 are taken from *Smart But Feeling Dumb* by Harold N. Levinson, M.D. Copyright © 1984 Harold N. Levinson. Reprinted by permission of Warner Books, Inc.

The excerpts from "The Cerebellum" by Ray S. Snider in Chapter 11 are taken from the August 1958 issue of *Scientific American*. Copyright © 1958 by Scientific American, Inc. All rights reserved.

The illustration by Harriet R. Greenfield of the middle ear and inner ear in Appendix B is taken from the May 1982 issue of *The Harvard Medical School Health Letter*. © President and Fellows of Harvard College 1982.

The illustrations of the Blurring Speed Test, Bender Gestalt Drawing Test, and Goodenough Figure Drawings in Appendix B are from *A Solution to the Riddle Dyslexia* by Harold N. Levinson, M.D. Copyright © 1980 by Springer-Verlag New York Inc.

Design by Lauren Dong

Manufactured in the United States of America on acid-free paper

MJF Books and the MJF colophon are trademarks of Fine Creative Media, Inc.

10   9   8   7   6   5   4   3   2   1

Phobia Free *is dedicated to:*
My family
My patients
30 million phobic Americans.

"Sit down before fact as a little child, be prepared to give up every preconceived notion, follow humbly wherever and to whatever abyss nature leads, or you shall learn nothing."
THOMAS HUXLEY

ARE YOU AFRAID OF ONE OR MORE OF THE FOLLOWING?

L X Needles or knives

𝕏 Small enclosed spaces

Heights
Flying or driving
The dark
Loud noises
Needles or knives
School
Motion
Traveling
Suffocating
Small enclosed spaces
Wide-open spaces
Stairs or escalators
Bright lights

Snakes, mice or bugs
The water
Telephones
Sports ?
Choking
Elevators
Bridges or tunnels *Dan*
Crowds *Pc Hi*
X Public speaking X
Sleeping
Germs and diseases
Sex
Buses, trains, or boats

Have your phobias defied all types of treatment, including psychotherapy, drugs, and behavior modification?

Have all phobic theories, books, and explanations left you without meaningful insight into your condition?

Did your phobias suddenly appear or intensify after any of the following: ear infections, mononucleosis, pregnancy, menopause, surgery, sinus infections, drug use, or a concussion?

Do your everyday anxieties often snowball into uncontrollable, long-lasting panic episodes?

Do you feel as though you were born phobic?

Do your phobias come and go for no apparent reason?

Are your phobias or panic attacks associated with any of the following distinct physical symptoms: disorientation, dizziness, lightheadedness, disassociation, floating sensations, loss of balance, fainting, falling or nausea?

Do fears of losing control, going insane, passing out, or dying permeate your existence?

Do you suspect that your irrational fears have a very rational basis?

If you answered "yes" to any of these questions, your phobias may stem from a common *physio*logical problem: an inner-ear malfunction. Even more important, these phobias may be clearly explained and properly treated . . . all for the very first time!

Contents

Foreword

I am very pleased to write the foreword to this most fascinating book. Written in a clear and understandable manner, *Phobia Free* will be very helpful and thought-provoking to both the general population and professionals involved in the field.

Phobias are very common and complex entities that appear in many different ways with different symptoms as well as different causes. As a result, they may not be recognized by the individual or his family or by many professionals. Consequently, they are often not treated or, if treated, are managed improperly.

The pages of this book provide numerous case histories of people with phobias and detail the various problems they have encountered and have overcome by proper management.

The author's concept of the interrelationship between the inner ear, the cerebellum and the brain is unique, though still somewhat controversial, as are many innovations. This concept, however, provides the professional with a means to better understand and treat these problems.

Dr. Levinson's previous work with dyslexia had a particular application to my family. Dyslexia affected my son and two grandchildren. All three were mirror writers (they wrote words and sentences backward) early in their schooling and, therefore, were poor readers and poor learners. Spelling was most difficult for them. It is known, however, that people with this problem often have high intelligence quotients and often overcome their difficulty by intense concentration. This is exemplified by my son, who finished medical school with a high ranking in his class and now practices otology in our group. My two grandchildren, soon to enter high school, are doing extremely well. Even though they are still slow readers, they are doing well because of their intense listening and concentration ability.

The relationship of the inner-ear syndrome to dyslexia and phobias as detailed in this book will be of great interest to all professionals and patients.

> Howard P. House, M.D.
> Otologic Medical Group, Inc.,
> Chairman Emeritus, House Ear Institute,
> and Clinical Professor of Otology,
> University of Southern California

Acknowledgments

Knowledge stems from experience. To the many patients who selflessly shared their experiences in hopes that others would not have to suffer, my greatest thanks.

This book could not have been written without the help of all of the following people: Julia Coopersmith, Herb Katz, Linda Cabasin, Joyce Baron, Selma Henick, Mary Lee, Cathy Ficht, Georgette Lambros, Caroline Chiu, Laurie Lynn, Debbie Wattenberg, Andrew Finkelstein, Joy Levinson, Laura Levinson and my wife, "Diggy." Thanks to all.

My most sincere thanks to Dr. Howard House, who generously donated his valuable time to writing the foreword.

Finally, a very special thank you to Steven Carter. Were it not for his dedication, enthusiasm, insight, and hard work, this book would have taken me countless years to complete.

Introduction

Sometimes the most complex problems have the simplest solutions. An overwhelming amount of clinical evidence now suggests that phobic behavior is one such problem.

The physiological basis of phobic behavior isn't something you will find in any psychological text. Nor is it something your doctor will necessarily know of or understand. In fact, it is something I discovered almost accidentally—and only after twenty years of psychiatric practice.

Yet once this physiological basis was recognized, it was immediately obvious that the psychiatric community, and the medical community at large, had overlooked the most important piece of the phobic puzzle. Today, having treated more than fifteen thousand patients, and having analyzed the appearance and disappearance of a vast array of phobic symptoms, I can share this crucial missing piece with you.

In the pages that follow you will learn the difference between *realistic* phobias (Type 1), *neurotic* phobias (Type 2), and *physiologically determined* phobias (Type 3). Furthermore, you will see how I have been led to conclude that *the vast majority of phobic behavior, including panic attacks, is physiologically determined by a malfunction within the inner-ear system.** Finally, and most important, you will learn that if you are among the estimated 90% or more of all phobic victims whose problems stem from this common inner-ear disorder, the kind of help and understanding you have prayed for is finally here.

*When I say the inner-ear system, I am really referring to the cerebellar-vestibular system (CVS), a complex network comprised of the vestibular system (the inner ear) and the cerebellum. The CVS is discussed in detail in Chapter 11. Note that the inner ear is not to be confused with the middle ear, the small air-filled space between the eardrum and inner ear where our sense of hearing originates.

PART I

THE PHOBICS SPEAK

CHAPTER 1

The Phobic Nightmare

Many books have been written on phobic behavior. Usually the reader is *told* rather than *shown* the cause-and-effect relationships that determine phobic symptoms. But this isn't how I learned about the physiological basis of phobic behavior, and I don't think it's how you should learn.

Both my theories and my treatment approach developed after I had examined, talked with, and listened to thousands of patients—patients suffering from a never-ending variety of phobias. I feel you should have the opportunity to come to the same understanding. After all, it is the real-life experiences of phobics, not the theoretical opinions of experts, that ultimately define phobic behavior.

Though I wish I could take you through twenty years of phobic case histories, this is, of course, not possible. But in this chapter, and in many of the chapters that follow, you will find a wide variety of case histories, ranging from typical to extreme, that will greatly enrich your perspective on this elusive menace we call phobias.

All of the patients whose stories appear in this chapter are Type 3 phobics: phobics whose condition stems from a malfunction within the inner-ear system. As you will see from these stories, there is no typical Type 3 phobic. A malfunctioning inner-ear system can result in a wide variety and combination of phobias. Therefore, your own experiences may be extremely similar to those of some patients and totally dissimilar to those of others. Yet there is something to be learned from every story.

Listen carefully to these Type 3 phobics. Their experiences will help you to better understand your own struggle with phobic behavior. Furthermore, their stories will give you new and valuable insight into helping yourself and others who suffer. With this kind of understanding and insight, you will be well on your way to becoming phobia free.

Deborah H.

During Deborah's first visit to my office, she recalled all of the details of her agoraphobic nightmare:

I do not recall that I suffered from any phobias as a child. They appeared suddenly in my senior year at college. In retrospect, I realize that they occurred during a particularly stressful period. I had recently broken up with a young man whom I loved, and my father had just suffered a nervous breakdown. I felt overwhelmed, and I was afraid that there was insanity in the family.

In order to earn extra money, I found a job in town during school semesters. The first day on my way to work I was riding a bus. As it went over a slight hill, I experienced a weird feeling—a sensation that I was plunging downward in space and toppling over—analogous to the sensation one experiences when riding in a roller coaster as it accelerates downward and then quickly upward. I frantically clutched the arm of a perfect stranger who was sitting next to me and hung on for dear life.

Within a few moments the feeling was gone, but I was quite shaken. Each time I rode the bus, this sensation returned. Eventually I found I could not ride the bus. My mother, not a very understanding person, became angry with me. I couldn't give her any explanation for my feelings.

Gradually this odd and frightening fear of falling extended to other modes of transportation—cars, subways, trains—and to other places—tunnels, elevators, and other crowded or confined places. I felt trapped and out of control. I found I could not be in a building taller than three stories. I felt that I would topple over and plunge down through the floors.

I was referred to a psychiatrist, placed on tranquilizers, and in therapy for several years. Although the doctor helped me to understand myself better and to be more assertive, my phobias persisted. A year after the onset of my phobias, I once again met the young man I had loved. Within a short time we were engaged. With him I felt loved and at peace, and my phobias disappeared. However, constant family pressure and my own doubts as to the suitability of the marriage led to my breaking the engagement. My parents did not think our marriage would work because he was not as educated as I, and I deferred to them.

Afterward, my phobias returned in full force, and I seriously questioned my sanity. My mother encouraged me to take a trip in hopes of raising my spirits. She offered to pay for a vacation to Ocean City with my sister. She thought the change would be good for me. However, on the way there I broke down. I simply couldn't drive across the Bay Bridge. The length and height of the bridge literally paralyzed me with fear.

I was having difficulty overcoming the trauma of the broken engagement, having wild thoughts about the cause of my phobias, and I felt overwhelmed by everything. I kept asking myself over and over: "What's wrong with me? Why am I like this?" I felt like a trapped animal waiting for the Hulk to strike me down. I truly felt as if I wanted to stop the world and get off.

One day I spoke to our neighbor, a doctor, and confided my fears and feelings. He replied, "I don't know what the problem is, but I do know you aren't going crazy!" He recommended that I see a colleague of his, a psychologist, whom I consulted. He used various kinds of therapy—art, music, hypnosis, and even Karma and reincarnation, as well as more traditional approaches. Again, I felt better about myself as a result of my sessions. But none of his approaches helped me to accomplish what I wanted most—to rid myself of those phobias!

I have done everything I possibly could to help myself. I've seen other therapists in hopes of alleviating my condition, but no one has been successful in helping me. In addition, I have read many books about phobias—whatever I could get my hands on—had my eyes checked and rechecked for visual problems that might contribute or cause such feelings; and reiterated words of reinforcement to effect a behavior modification. But nothing has really worked.

Clearly, Deborah is a woman of intelligence and sensitivity whose phobias made her feel dumb, ugly, inadequate as well as fearful and unhappy, influencing and shaping all facets of her relationships and life-style. Deborah is a Type 3 phobic.

Sue S.

When I first examined Sue she was twenty-four years old. She was actually referred to me because of her academic difficulties, but my discussion with her revealed a history of phobias. She told me:

As a child I would not swim in the ocean if there were waves. I felt as if the waves would pull me under and I would not be able to find the top. I would not dive off a diving board. I could not adjust my body to form the correct position for diving. I also feared that I would go too deep and not be able to come up in time.

Many of my childhood dreams centered around drowning. I would dream that I could not find thé surface in time. When doing flips underwater, I often did not know which way was up. In my dream I would not find my way up and would then picture myself drowning. I used to imagine my lungs filling up with water and exploding, creating a very loud noise as they burst. I always had to hold my nose, because I feared that I would impulsively breathe in instead of out while submerged.

I also had fears of new places and transitions. When routines stopped or started again (i.e., school), I would feel sick for days. The sickness would lessen and lessen, but it was always there at first. The way I mentally controlled it was by telling myself, ''Next week I will feel better, and the week after that I will be just fine.'' But the fear of the fear was always with me.

Going to a friend's house was very difficult for me to deal with. At times I was so afraid of going to any unknown place I would imagine that if I went, the friend's mother would murder me. This would leave me in such a state that once I got there I would often ask to leave right away. Many concerned moms often took this personally and would try their hardest to make my stay as comfortable as possible. But often, this was to no avail.

Sleeping over at someone's house was very traumatic. I could not sleep in a bed that was not in the same position as mine. If I did, I would wake up in the middle of the night terribly disoriented and often sweating and on the verge of becoming hysterical. This same feeling would also possess me if my bed was repositioned. I would become panic-stricken if my bedroom was rearranged. So my bed stayed in the same position year after year.

I experienced nightmares several times a week. In fact, this continued until I began my medical treatment. Nightmares centered around being chased and not being able to run; not being able to walk while in the middle of large crowds; falling over and not being able to stand for no reason; monsters; being killed violently; my mother dying; being in an elevator that would turn upside down; drowning; and being lost. As a child, I spent many a night sleeping with my mother.

The worst part of these dreams was the inability to voluntarily awaken from them. In fact, even when I had my eyes open and was walking around, my brain would continue to play the dream. I could still witness the images and hear the sounds, and they would not stop until I shook my head violently. This was still no guarantee that they would not return when I closed my eyes.

As a child I was also terrified if my parents ever left me with a baby-sitter. No matter how kind the sitter was, I would never fall asleep until they returned. I was always sure they would die and that would be the last I would see of them.

I also feared sleigh riding. I was sure that I would run into something and break my neck. Ferris wheels frightened me, though other amusement rides were not a problem.

High places intrigued me, but there was a fear that I would not be able to control the impulse to jump. Tall city buildings seemed warped and tilted if I looked up at them. This perceptual illusion fascinated me. I used to imagine that they would cave in and crush everyone. While walking across bridges that connected buildings, I would feel a pulling sensation to the sides of the structure. It was as though a force was pulling me to the sides to throw me off, making me unable to walk down the middle.

Robert B.

Robert sought my help for various difficulties, including phobias and avoidances. These problems had plagued him for most of his life, making him feel as though he "lived in a well of loneliness for fifty years." He recalled:

I am convinced that no one really understands how I feel. Not that anyone has ever said anything derogatory to me. But the polite smile or the blank, silent look speaks volumes.

Outwardly I may appear calm and in control of the situation, but inwardly I experience many fears and anxieties. I'm fine on a one-to-one basis, but a group of people makes me feel trapped and panicky. If I inadvertently become involved in such a situation, I'm unable to contribute anything worthwhile to the conversation. I sit silently, and if I do comment, what I say seems to come out stupidly and I'm faced with blank, uncomprehending stares. Then I wish the earth would open up and swallow me.

My job creates problems and intense anxieties for me. For this reason, each day is a constant struggle, fraught with many possibilities for error and discovery. As I grow older, the struggle becomes harder and longer, and I pray that I will have the strength and ability to deal with these daily challenges.

Twenty years ago, hoping to overcome my fears and insecurities, I registered for a Dale Carnegie course. But if anything, the course created more problems than it solved. I would get stage fright when I had to address a group of strangers in the class. Frequently, I would forget what I had to say and feel more like a fool than ever. To this day, I deliberately avoid groups of people or crowds.

Susan S.

Seeing Susan's perpetual smile, one would never guess that she was the victim of severe, paralyzing phobias. For many years, Susan suffered from:

- Fear of crossing streets
- Fear of becoming lost
- Fear of riding escalators
- Fear of going on elevators alone
- Fear of driving and being in cars
- Fear of being in New York City alone
- Fear of heights, which resulted in avoidance of bridges, cable cars, etc.
- Fear of water and of drowning
- Fear of thunderstorms
- Fear of traveling

The following is an excerpt from our first discussion:

I was extremely afraid of crossing streets. My mother was still picking me up at school, helping me cross the street, etc., even when I was quite old. When I crossed on my own, I was afraid of being struck by a car because I had no idea where the cars were coming from. I was confused: I didn't know whether to cross the street when the light was red, as my mother told me to do, or to cross when the light was green, as my teacher advised. What I ended up doing was running across the street and praying a lot.

In retrospect, I think my mother was confused, too. I recall that she also had trouble crossing the streets. We'd start crossing, a car would come, she would go back, the car would start, she would go forward, the car would stop—it was like a dance. Whenever a car approached, she would just stop. I did the same thing, I guess, and a couple of times I was almost killed.

When I walked, I always crossed the street at the narrowest place. If it was a quiet street or a narrow one it was okay, but if it was a busy or very wide street, I had a problem. I would simply wait until there were no cars. After I had my baby daughter, I virtually stopped crossing streets. I felt responsible for her, so I didn't go anywhere. I walked around the block or went to the park where I could sit.

I was always very apprehensive about escalators and elevators. My mother was, too. She wouldn't go into an elevator alone. My sister never goes on escalators either, though she insists she's not phobic. With my husband or friends, I would go up the escalator but never down. I was terrified of falling. Actually, I feared that my foot might become caught on the step. I couldn't figure out which foot to step on with first. I would panic, become light-headed. For years my therapist worked with me through behavior therapy and desensitization. I was finally able to go down escalators, but with great difficulty and fear. It created a problem when my husband and I went out. We always had to find an elevator.

I was afraid of riding in an elevator unless someone was with me; I was afraid the door would crush me. It just didn't seem that there was enough time to get safely inside before the door closed. Actually it's always been like that: If I'm with somebody, my husband or a friend, I give them the responsibility of taking care of me and protecting me.

My therapist showed me how to hold the door of the elevator open so that it wouldn't close. I became better as long as I could hold the door open. I felt it couldn't crush me and I would be okay. If for some reason I can't control the door and keep it open until I step in safely, I start to panic and scream; I can't help it. I am also afraid of riding the subway or a train for the same reason: I am afraid of the door closing on me and crushing me.

I was always afraid of becoming lost. When I began college, I generally got lost. Inadvertently, I would take the wrong buses and would have to ask people for directions; it was a nightmare. That's one of the reasons I dropped out of school. I was phobic, particularly about Manhattan: I was, and still am, afraid of getting lost there.

Early in our marriage my husband tried to teach me how to drive and I just couldn't learn. Whenever I was in a car, I believed the other cars would crash headlong into us. I wasn't able to judge how far away the cars were; it's slightly better now, but I do close my eyes and fall asleep. Perhaps it's a way of escaping.

I was also terrified of bridges and looking down. I was afraid of cable cars, too. I wouldn't look down; I didn't want to know that I was that high up—that I might fall off.

Due to all my fears, I became very overprotective of my daughter. I wouldn't allow her to ride a bicycle or roller skate because I was afraid she would hurt herself. It was hard for both of us. As a result, I saw a psychiatric social worker about this problem. Later, I began to see a therapist for behavior modification therapy. After years of my being in therapy, he began to think I might have a learning disability. He had been teaching me to cross the streets, and he came to realize that I had no idea from which direction cars were coming—they could have come from the sky as far as I was concerned.

Mary F.

Mary found help for her phobias almost by accident. She came to my office because her twelve-year-old daughter was having serious academic difficulties. But as I talked to her daughter, Mary began interjecting comments about her phobias.

Commenting on her fear of bugs and stairs, Mary explained:

When I was young, a hornet bit me on the face five times. I think I was afraid of bugs before then, but that made me worse. The only bug that really doesn't bother me is a ladybug. Most bugs make me break out into a cold sweat . . . my pulse races and my breathing becomes shallow.

During certain times of the year, there are so many caterpillars around my house that you can't get out the front door without one or two falling on you. I send somebody out of the house in front of me, then I go out with a hand in front of my face. If there's no one to help me, I don't leave home.

If I walk into a room and see a flight of stairs, I panic. Open stairs are the worst, especially if I'm wearing heels. By the time I'm ten feet away my legs start to shake. I've gone down quite a few staircases on my behind . . . by choice.

My husband used to think something was wrong with me. He would say, "Are you crazy? What's your problem?" But I think he's used to it by now. If there's any other way to get from floor to floor, I'll find it. I hate elevators, but nothing is as bad as stairs. I feel like I'm going to fall any minute. Sometimes I just wish someone would push me down and get it over with. I'll grip the banister, scrunch my feet into the cracks, and work my way down step by step while hugging the wall. By the time I get to the bottom, the last few steps look like paradise.

Going up steps isn't nearly as bad as going down. But I usually run up, like I'm in a race. I just don't want to be on the steps any longer than I have to be. And I can't go up or down stairs in the dark. I have to see the steps and my feet clearly. I feel like things are coming at me . . . I suppose I have a vivid imagination.

When Mary was pregnant with her second child, she experienced sudden and dramatic changes in her physical and mental health. She recalled:

When I was pregnant, I became terrified of heights. I also became extremely sensitive to motion. I couldn't go up and down elevators . . . I just didn't like the feeling. Then I started getting sick in airplanes. It took breathing exercises and all of my powers of concentration to make it through the flight. I also stopped driving. I would get nauseous in the car every time I turned my head. Although some of these problems got better, most of them have remained since my pregnancy. That's twelve years that I've been living like this.

Brian B.

Brian, a severe claustrophobic, described his condition as follows:

If I had only one wish, I'd wish I could fly. But there's just no way—planes give me severe claustrophobia. Elevators, tunnels, crowds . . . they all terrify me. But planes are the worst.

I've only been in a plane once. That was enough. As soon as the door closed, I freaked. I just had to get out and breathe some fresh air, not that recycled airplane air. I really lost it . . . I started screaming at the stewardess. I told her I was sick . . . that I needed to go to a hospital. I lied. I just had to get off that plane. They finally did let me off, and I've never even tried to fly since.

So many things make me claustrophobic—like driving. Traffic jams wipe me out, and I never drive at night or when it's raining. Not being able to see makes me feel trapped in the car. When I was young I couldn't sit inside the car and wait for my mother in a parking lot. I always had to sit outside on the hood. And I always got the window. I'm the same way in restaurants. I can't sit in a booth unless I'm on the outside. Even then I don't feel great. I also don't like bathing. I feel like I'm going to suffocate, so I take showers—no big deal.

My life has been far from wonderful, but I guess things could be worse. I have a few close friends who really understand me, and my parents have always been great. Actually, my mother has a little bit of the same problem, but she's not as bad as I am. She won't fly either, but she says she doesn't fly because it's not safe. I'm sure she's afraid for the same reason I am. She just won't admit it because it makes you sound like you're crazy.

Alan G.

Alan, who is thirty-eight, has suffered from severe, debilitating panic attacks and agoraphobia since he was twelve. During our first meeting, he related the following information:

One day when I was twelve years old, I was sitting in class and suddenly I experienced a panic attack. I felt extremely light-headed and off-balance—as though I was going to pass out. Simultaneously, it seemed as though the room was closing in on me. But that was only the beginning. Soon I was having these attacks constantly. They would occur without warning. I found myself constantly anticipating one. No doubt I initiated a few by my anticipation.

Following the onset of these panic attacks, my difficulties in school and my behavior worsened. I was more distractible and hyperactive than ever. I was also unable to concentrate, because I was always fearing the onset of another attack. But the more I feared these attacks, the more they seemed to occur.

Since I was only twelve years old, I was very frightened. I was sure I had a brain tumor. I felt that everything was closing in on me, and I was convinced I was going to die. I felt utterly confused, disoriented, and out of control. Being out of control was the greatest part of my fear.

These panic episodes, and the anticipation of them, have ruled every aspect of my life. A year ago I visited a panic-disorder clinic for conditioning therapy. I was, and still am, under psychotherapy. These have helped, but I have not had total relief.

CHAPTER 2

Is There a Physiological Basis for Your Phobias?: A Self-Test

Are your phobias the result of a *physio*logical problem? The following simple test will give you your first clue.

The questions in the test may appear to be totally unrelated to phobic behavior. But all of the symptoms and behavior patterns noted actually stem from the very same physiological problem that is responsible for most phobias: *a malfunction within the inner-ear system.*

Therefore, if your phobias are due to an inner-ear malfunction, one or more of these other, seemingly unrelated, symptoms and behavior patterns may also be present.

SELF-TEST

Balance and Coordination   Yes   No

1. When you were young, did you have difficulty with balance and co-ordination tasks such as skipping, hopping, jumping rope, roller-skating, gymnastics, tumbling, or riding a bike?   ___ ___
2. Is your handwriting messy, poorly angulated, infantile, or difficult to read?   ___ ___
3. Are you clumsy, klutzy, or accident-prone—always bumping into things, tripping, or falling?   ___ ___
4. When you were young, did you have difficulty mastering fine-coordination tasks such as tying your shoes, using utensils, buttoning buttons, and zippering zippers?   ___ ___
5. As a child, were you prone to bed-wetting or soiling?   ___ ___
6. Did you, or do you currently, have any of the following speech difficulties: stuttering, slurring, stammering, slips of the tongue, saying words in reverse, or rambling?   ___ ___

Vision and Hearing

7. Do you have poor depth perception or limited peripheral vision (i.e., tunnel vision)? —— ——
8. Do you tilt your head when you read, have to lie down, lose your place easily, or use your index finger to help you? —— ——
9. Do you scramble words and sentences when you read, or tend to confuse letters (such as *b* and *d*), numbers (such as *6* and *9*, *14*, and *41*, etc.), or words (such as *saw* and *was*)? —— ——
10. Do you experience any of the following while reading: headaches, nausea, dizziness, blurred vision, double vision, or vomiting? —— ——
11. Do things not "sink in" the first time you hear them, forcing you to ask people to repeat what they've just said (and making them accuse you of not listening)? —— ——

Sense of Direction

12. Do you have difficulty distinguishing left from right? —— ——
13. Do you easily get disoriented, lost, or confused? —— ——
14. Do you need directions every time you go somewhere, even if you've been there before? —— ——

Sense of Time

15. Do you have difficulty judging elapsed time or making time projections? —— ——
16. Did you have problems learning to tell time? —— ——
17. Are you always late or always early? —— ——

Motion Sensitivity

18. Were you prone to dizziness or motion sickness as a child? (Are you still?) —— ——
19. Do you dislike or avoid buses, trains, boats, amusement-park rides, and other motion-related activities? —— ——

Memory

20. Do you have difficulty remembering names, faces, dates, spelling, grammar, lists, directions, or proper sequences? —— ——
21. Do you find yourself endlessly making lists of things you need to do because you don't trust your memory? —— ——
22. Are you absentminded, forgetful, or prone to experiencing mental blanks or blocks? —— ——

23. Do you make the same mistakes over and over again, almost as though you had no recollection of the last time you made the mistake? ____ ____
24. Do you have difficulty remembering simple addition, subtraction, and multiplication facts and/or count on your fingers? ____ ____

Concentration and Distractibility

25. Do you have difficulty concentrating and find yourself distracted by the slightest noise or thought? ____ ____
26. Do people accuse you of being spacy or scatterbrained? ____ ____
27. Do you tire easily or get "foggy" quickly when you read, write, or study? ____ ____
28. Do you have difficulty reading a book from cover to cover, or find "dry" reading a torture? ____ ____
29. Can you listen to music and study at the same time? ____ ____
30. Do you tend to ignore, or have difficulty following, written instructions? ____ ____

Hyperactivity and Overactivity

31. Were you hyperactive or overactive as a child? ____ ____
32. Are you restless, fidgety, driven to rapidly shift from task to task, idea to idea, job to job, person to person? ____ ____
33. Do you have a low frustration tolerance? ____ ____
34. Are you prone to temper outbursts? ____ ____

Obsessions and Compulsions

35. Do irresistible, repetitive thoughts and actions (obsessions and compulsions) drive you crazy and render you unable to relax? ____ ____
36. When you leave your house, do you often find yourself going back repeatedly to make sure you locked the door, turned off the gas, etc.? ____ ____
37. Do you find yourself driven to check and recheck, touch and retouch, think and rethink? ____ ____

Academic Difficulties

38. Did you, or do you, have difficulty with reading, writing, spelling, math, or grammar? ____ ____
39. Do you make dumb mistakes all of the time, even though you feel that you're smart? ____ ____
40. Were you viewed as an underachiever, an overachiever, a late-bloomer, or an academic puzzlement? ____ ____
41. Did you hate or avoid school and/or school-related activities? ____ ____

42. Do you suspect you are, or were you ever diagnosed as, dyslexic or learning disabled?   — —

Related Mental Symptoms

43. Have headaches, migraines, stomachaches, nausea, or other psychosomatic symptoms sent you from doctor to doctor to no avail?   — —
44. Were you an anxious, nervous child?   — —
45. Are you prone to mood swings?   — —
46. Do you have hypochondriacal worries, or are you prone to worrying about nothing?   — —
47. Do you suffer from sleep disturbances such as insomnia, nightmares, or sleepwalking?   — —
48. Do you procrastinate and have difficulty making decisions?   — —
49. Are you self-conscious about your intelligence, speech, or appearance?   — —
50. Do you often feel inferior, stupid, ugly, or clumsy?   — —

The exact significance of each of these questions will be discussed in detail in Chapter 9.

PART II
FEAR AND THE INNER EAR

Three Types of Phobias

Claustrophobia. Agoraphobia. Triskaidekaphobia.* All of these names have one thing in common: they add mystery and confusion to what is already one of the most poorly understood aspects of human behavior.

Phobias have always been classified according to their obvious triggers—the objects or situations that provoke the fear. These triggers are customarily dressed in exotic Greek and Latin labels, giving each phobia a more scientific air.

Unfortunately, the traditional phobic classification system has shed little light on the real, but hidden mechanisms responsible for creating and shaping phobic behavior. In fact, this Greek and Latin name-calling may have done a great deal of harm. For instead of encouraging us to search for underlying common denominators capable of unlocking the many secrets of phobic behavior, it has led many to believe that these secrets are already known.

Even worse, this classification system has unintentionally led many of us to believe that each and every type of phobia (xenophobia, aerophobia, etc.) is a separate and distinct disorder with a unique cause having no relation to other phobias aside from the obvious similarity in symptoms.

WHAT'S IN A NAME?

The drawbacks of our traditional classification system are best illustrated with a few examples.

*Fear of the number 13.

Suppose that a woman is cynophobic and agoraphobic. What do these two labels tell us, apart from the fact that she is afraid of dogs and wide-open spaces? (Even this may not be accurate, as you will see later when agoraphobia is discussed in greater detail.)

According to our current classification system, this woman suffers from two separate phobic illnesses, each requiring individual treatment. But what if her fear of dogs stems from a realistic fear of being chased by a dog into a wide-open space, namely, the street (realistic, because it has happened to her). If so, her fear of dogs is clearly part and parcel of her fear of wide-open spaces. The two are *not* separate disorders.

The connection between this woman's agoraphobia and her cynophobia is vital if she is to receive proper treatment. But the traditional classification system does not encourage us to look for such interrelationships. Let's look at another example.

Fear of Flying

Four men suffer from aerophobia, the fear of flying. Although all four men are classified as having the same illness, a closer examination might reveal that each fears flying for a completely different reason.

One man, for example, may be afraid to fly because his neighbor recently died in a plane crash. Another may be afraid because planes fly over water and he can't swim (hence he does not fear all flying, just flying over water). The third may be afraid of small enclosed spaces, such as the cabin of an airplane. And the fourth man may be afraid of heights.

Each of these possibilities suggests something entirely different about the mechanisms responsible for the fear of flying. More important, these differences clearly demonstrate that each case may require a different treatment approach. But once we label all four men "aerophobic," we unwittingly make a tragic mistake. For our label implies that one common mechanism is responsible for the fears of all four men. This makes no more sense than assuming that four men with the same name have the same mother. Yet in essence, this is exactly what we are doing.

This kind of mistake can only encourage physicians and other therapists to search for answers in all the wrong directions. Worse, it encourages them to subject all four men to the same treatment regimen. At best, the results of this kind of treatment approach will be less than satisfactory for at least three of the four.

Two Flaws in the System

These examples clearly illustrate that two important characteristics of phobic behavior are masked by our traditional classification system:

- Phobias of different names may have one and the same underlying mechanism.
- Phobias of the same name may have distinctly different underlying mechanisms.

Superficial phobic triggers provide an important clue to understanding phobic behavior, but they are only one aspect of the highly complex phobic phenomenon. By focusing only on these triggers, we are ignoring the far more important underlying mechanisms that create and shape phobic behavior. This interferes with our ability to make an accurate diagnosis and prevents us from developing a successful treatment approach.

A NEW CLASSIFICATION SYSTEM

To gain real insight into the phobic puzzle, we must first discard our traditional classification system, with its confusing Greek and Latin nomenclature. What we need is a simple, scientifically determined system—one that classifies phobias according to their underlying mechanisms, not their obvious triggers.

If we can do this, we will no longer have hundreds of labels that lead us to a never-ending series of dead ends. Instead, we will have a system that classifies all phobias according to three key types. The first two types are as follows:

Type 1: Realistic Phobias

Type 1 phobias develop after the traumatic exposure to a real and present danger. For example, one night, while walking down the street, a woman is brutally mugged. This incident sticks in her mind and develops into an uncontrollable fear of walking the streets at night. Her phobia would be considered to have a realistic basis.

Here are a few more examples of realistic, Type 1 phobias: a man develops a fear of knives after being stabbed; a woman develops a fear of horses after being thrown from one; a child develops a fear of flying insects after being stung by a swarm of bees, etc. (Type 1 phobias are discussed in detail in Chapter 17.)

Type 2: Neurotic Phobias

Type 2 phobias develop "all in the mind," through a series of subconscious or unconscious Freudian processes.

These phobias are generally related to some repressed childhood trauma (usually sexual and/or aggressive in origin) and are triggered by some symbolic reminder of that trauma during a current emotional conflict. An example here would be helpful.

A young girl's parents discover that she is masturbating and scold her severely. They frighten her further by warning her that girls who masturbate become prostitutes. This warning, and the fear associated with it, sticks in the girl's subconscious mind, remaining active and alive for many years to come. As a result, she is now vulnerable to developing phobias.

When this girl grows up, any number of sexual triggers may cause her fear and anxiety to resurface during a period of emotional stress. She may, for example, become afraid of walking the streets alone, since subconsciously or unconsciously she symbolically associates this "street walking" with the behavior of prostitutes. Or she may develop a fear of trains and cars, because subconsciously or unconsciously she sees these objects as phallic or sexual symbols. All of these fears would be considered to have a neurotic, Type 2 basis. (Type 2 phobias are discussed in detail in Chapter 17.)

Two Mechanisms, One Label

Notice in the examples I have given how completely different underlying mechanisms can result in the development of agoraphobia. The traditional phobic classification system would have grouped the Type 1 agoraphobic and the Type 2 agoraphobic together because both women seem to fear the same thing. That system also would have implied that both women should receive similar treatment. But using our new classification system, it is clear that the phobias of these two women are related in name only. It is also clear that each woman requires a completely different treatment approach if she is to overcome her phobia, an approach dependent upon the specific underlying mechanisms determining that phobia.

Everything makes perfect sense so far? Good. But there is one last giant piece still missing from the phobic puzzle. You see, most clinicians would probably agree that all phobias can be classified as either Type 1, Type 2, or a combination of the two. They would also agree that Type 2, neurotic mechanisms probably account for the vast majority of all phobic behavior, with Type 1, realistic mechanisms accounting for just a small minority. But clinical evidence (see Chapter 22) suggests that Type 1 and Type 2 mechanisms *together* may account for less than 10 percent of all phobic behavior! What about the other 90 percent? They are Type *3* phobias.

TYPE 3 PHOBIAS: THE MISSING LINK

Neurotic and realistic factors may be entirely responsible for some phobias—and they may contribute to others. But twenty years of clinical research have proved to me that the vast majority of phobias can be traced to a *physio*logical problem: a malfunction within the inner-ear system.*

Throughout this book I intend to prove to you that:

1. More than 90 percent of all phobic behavior is the result of an underlying malfunction within the inner-ear system.
2. This physiological malfunction is partially, if not entirely, responsible for most phobias currently believed to have a purely neurotic basis.
3. This physiological malfunction predisposes an individual to develop a long-lasting phobia following exposure to a realistic trauma.
4. It is this common physiological malfunction that renders some 20 percent of the population vulnerable to phobic behavior.

Beginning here, I will refer to all the phobias of inner-ear origin as Type 3 phobias.**

---

*Once again, when I say the inner-ear system, I am really referring to the cerebellar-vestibular system. [See Chapter 11.]

**For the sake of accuracy, I must point out that other central nervous system disturbances are occasionally responsible for phobic symptoms. But my research to date suggests that these other physiological factors account for only a small minority of phobic cases and do not merit further discussion in this text.

Typical Responses to Treatment

There is no microscope that can take us inside the brain and prove beyond the shadow of a doubt that the inner-ear system is responsible for the development of most phobic behavior. Fortunately, this isn't necessary, for the role of the inner ear becomes extremely obvious when you attempt to treat phobics. In fact, my theory actually developed after I had observed a wide variety of improvements in phobic symptoms among patients being treated for a different inner-ear disorder. (This discovery is described in detail in Part IV.)

Had I not seen these improvements with my own eyes, I would probably never have discovered that the inner ear is responsible for phobic behavior. These truly remarkable, and totally unexpected, improvements actually highlighted the presence of hidden physiological mechanisms I had never suspected. But once these inner-ear mechanisms were revealed, an endless number of seemingly unconnected observations began to fit together:

- For the first time, patients' descriptions of their phobic symptoms made complete sense. In fact, these symptoms correlated perfectly with the findings of Nobel-prize winners and other scientists who had devoted much of their lives to studying the inner-ear system.
- For the first time, an explanation of the basis of phobic behavior made sense to phobic patients, many of whom had always suspected or insisted that they had a physiological problem.

- For the first time, the correlation between the sudden onset of phobic behavior and the presence of ear infections, sinus infections, mononucleosis, concussion states, and other illnesses that affect the inner-ear system was understandable.
- For the first time, it was possible to explain why phobic symptoms were sometimes triggered and sometimes alleviated by inner-ear surgery performed for other, nonphobic symptoms.
- For the first time, *all* the pieces of the phobic puzzle fell neatly into place.

SOLVING THE PUZZLE: NOW IT'S YOUR TURN

In this chapter, I would like to give you the opportunity to draw some of your own conclusions. For this reason, I have presented a variety of excerpts from the progress reports of my patients.

I firmly believe in a holistic approach to treatment (see Part V). But all of the improvements presented in this chapter came about after patients were treated solely with vestibular medications—medications known to specifically improve the functioning of the inner-ear system.* Therefore, the careful study of these treatment responses clearly highlights the inner-ear mechanisms responsible for their creation.

Responses to medications vary significantly from one patient to the next. These responses are sometimes dramatic and sometimes mild; more often, they are somewhere in between. Needless to say, every clinician wants to present his or her greatest successes. But if the progress reports in this chapter sound almost too good to be true, please note that these case reports are typical of hundreds if not thousands of similar ones—a number of which can be found throughout this book.

---

*These simple vestibular medications are not sedatives or tranquilizers, nor do they have any such effects when used appropriately and in proper dosages. You can read more about these vestibular medications in Part V.

Beth P.

Beth came to me after suffering from a debilitating fear of heights, a fear of driving, and numerous other phobias for almost twenty years. Diagnostic tests revealed the presence of an inner-ear dysfunction, and Beth was put on medication.

Four months after starting treatment, Beth sent me a progress report. She wrote:

> My fear of heights has all but ruled my life. A long flight of stairs provoked panic and seemed insurmountable. Now my ability to tackle any kind of height is amazing. And I no longer have panic attacks regarding this symptom—the fear that had been forever present before. If nothing else had improved during my treatment, I would have been thrilled that this crippling symptom had all but vanished.
>
> My sense of direction has improved as well. I used to get lost in my own town. All you had to do was turn me around, and I wouldn't know where I was or how to get back home. This would frequently result in panic. As a result of treatment, I can find my way almost anywhere. In fact, my mother was amazed last week when I drove by myself from White Plains to Staten Island without asking for help and rewritten directions, and that trip is a trial by fire for anyone.
>
> Speaking of driving, my ability to handle heavy traffic and thruways has undergone a revolutionary change. I am no longer frightened and overwhelmed . . . not even by the F.D.R. Drive at rush hour! Before treatment I could barely drive in downtown White Plains. And I no longer get carsick either.
>
> All in all, you cannot imagine how these medications have changed my life. My mother and I marvel at the change it has made in everyday living. It was almost as though a haze or screen was lifted from my eyes, enabling me to see and think clearly for the first time. It is a miracle! For years I wondered what was wrong with me, and you have solved the mystery. I can never thank you enough!

Sue S.

Sue S., whose story appears in Chapter 1, recently sent me a progress report with the following information:

> My fears of change and unknown places, my fear of drowning, and my nightmares and fantasies centered around high places have all become vague memories of the past.

I rarely have nightmares like I used to, and I never have difficulty bringing myself out of a deep sleep. In fact, my sleeping patterns are much more normal, and therefore I require less sleep. I used to require ten to twelve hours at night and a nap in the afternoon. Now I average six to eight hours, and a nap is unheard of.

Less energy seems to be needed in order to get through a day's routine. And my perception of reality is no longer confusing. These changes have helped me to discover who I am and have led me to view myself as a highly gifted individual who has a tremendous amount to offer.

Anita L.

Anita is a thirty-two-year-old married woman who came to me complaining of various fears, including a fear of bridges, heights, and driving. In addition, she was constantly anxious, prone to stress, and obsessed with feelings of jealousy.

Anita's examination revealed clear-cut signs of an inner-ear dysfunction, and medications were prescribed. Here are some excerpts from her progress report:

Driving is now enjoyable. Before I began taking medication I'd become severely dizzy and nauseated when I looked out of the window and saw oncoming traffic. As a result, I would become anxious and avoid driving. Now I look forward to it.

My fear of heights is gone. I can drive over a bridge or look out of a window or even down from a rooftop and feel comfortable. This was not possible before treatment.

I'm neither depressed nor anxious all the time, as before. As a result, I sleep better. I used to have severe anxiety dreams or nightmares due to the continuous state of stress I was in. And I was prone to constant headaches that aspirin did not relieve. Now bad dreams and headaches are a rarity.

My self-image has improved considerably. I just seem to feel good about myself. And I no longer feel ugly. I didn't realize how bad I felt about my appearance until I improved. As a result, I'm no longer driven or obsessed by jealousy. If my husband is late, he is just late. Before treatment, if my husband came home late or angry or tired, it always meant one thing: he was out, and in love, with someone else. This obsession is gone.

Joanna K.

When Joanna first came to my office, she was suffering from agoraphobia. She recalled:

I found myself avoiding going out unless someone accompanied me. It was easier to stay home. I had no perception of speed or distance, so I was afraid to even cross the street; I felt I was taking my life into my hands. I didn't know how close a car was to me, and I could not judge the speed.

Each time I boarded a bus or plane, or stepped into a car—altered my space—I was filled with a sense of anxiety and fear. Gradually, I preferred to remain at home where I was safe . . . I resented the fact that others didn't understand why I could not travel and why I was unable to engage in most social activities. More and more, my world became smaller.

In her first progress report, Joanna wrote:

I felt better almost immediately after taking the medication. I felt happier, more relaxed, and self-assured. Gradually, the feelings of anger, confusion, frustration, and inner turmoil left me. I am no longer afraid, clumsy, or stupid. I can now forgive myself for having a problem. I can accept myself! Do you know what that means?

Lisa B.

Lisa was fourteen years old when her mother brought her to my office for treatment. At the time, she was terrified of stairs, heights, and other settings that provoked fears of falling. After six weeks of treatment, Lisa's mother wrote:

For the first time in her life, Lisa doesn't have a constant fear of falling. She now runs up and down stairs. Before treatment, she used to hang on to the banisters with both hands for dear life. And at times she was forced to actually creep up and down the stairs. Her fears of walking, running, navigating up and down stairs . . . are actually gone.

Lisa's brothers and other adults have noticed a new thinking process in her. It appears that her mental equilibrium and coordination have improved along with her physical balance. Is it any wonder that she has infinitely more self-confidence?

Sister Elizabeth H.

Sister Elizabeth was referred to me by her physician because she was experiencing severe panic attacks, anxiety, and phobias. Her phobias included: fear of elevators, fear of bridges and tunnels, fear of crowds, stage fright, fear of dogs, and fear of cars (when she was not driving, hence not in control). Furthermore, the changes her church was undergoing frightened her and made her panicky. For example, she could not cope with the fact that some nuns were teaching and praying while wearing ordinary clothes rather than the traditional garb. In fact, she could neither face nor talk to her own sister, a nun who wore secular clothing.

After eight weeks of treatment, Sister Elizabeth sent me the following progress report:

> I feel so much better since I began taking the medications. I can now face certain people and converse with them. Two months ago, I ran away from them.
>
> Much of my anxiety and panic have disappeared. In church I always sat in the back. And being seen or conversing with people triggered tremendous anxiety and discomfort. Yesterday I actually led a procession carrying a large cross in church. There must have been about three hundred people present. For sure, I could not have done this two months ago.
>
> My greatest fear was facing and socializing with any sister who wore lay clothes. I could not talk to them . . . just seeing them made me panic. I feared losing control . . . losing my anchor to the past. As a result, I was forced to actually run the other way when I saw them—even when I saw my own sister. Now I can talk to them more easily. I have better relations with them. In fact, several people have told me what a tremendous change they see in me lately. Thank you, and thank God!

A year later, Sister Elizabeth wrote:

> As time goes on I am more and more encouraged by the progress I feel within me. I don't seem to get as upset as I used to. Large bridges had always petrified me. Recently, I even drove over a bridge at night—alone. I felt this to be a huge accomplishment.
>
> I seldom, if ever, rode in elevators. I was afraid the door wouldn't open once it closed and that I would be trapped. This past year I

have been able to ride some elevators, even alone. But I still fear the elevator in the convent I live in, maybe because it is very old and thus seems unreliable to me.

Last, but not least, is my ability to socialize. I feel this has been my biggest accomplishment. As you well know, last year this nearly drove me crazy. Overcoming this anxiety has made my year and my life so much better. Thank God again!

Edwina L.

Edwina has had a fear of swimming since childhood. She had to be able to touch the sides of the pool or the bottom—otherwise she would panic. Before treatment she also feared getting lost and would never drive far from home. Of these and a variety of other, related phobias, she wrote:

> Now I have no fear of being in eight feet of water—I enjoy it immensely. At times I would return home calm and yet exhilarated. I was also afraid of swimming alone. Now I belong to a club and swim alone all the time.
>
> I often go beyond my old twenty-mile perimeter. And my fears of heights, open spaces, and narrow passages have also lessened. I still have them, but I am now able to pull my energy together and overcome the fear.

Lauren D.

When Lauren first visited my office she had numerous phobias, including a fear of bridges, tunnels, crowds, airplanes, and noisy places. Vestibular medications were prescribed. Lauren recently wrote:

> I have almost total freedom from physical symptoms, and I now drive anywhere without panic—bridges, tunnels, etc. Most social activities are now attempted and achieved in relative comfort. Shopping in large stores has not given me any more panic attacks. And although some mild hangover effects of the phobias remain, basically I am feeling much better.

Donald W.

Donald, a bright fifteen-year-old, came to my office because he was suffering from severe learning disabilities. During his examination, I learned that he had numerous phobias, including a fear of heights, a fear of crowds, and a fear of being in small, enclosed spaces. A treatment program was started. Donald's mother recently wrote:

> Before treatment Donald was terrified of any height—even if he were inside a building looking down. Now he can even look down from exposed heights, such as the roof of a building or a ledge.
>
> As a family we have always camped a lot in a camper trailer. Donald couldn't stand the closed spaces. When we went on vacation he wouldn't sleep inside the truck unless it was raining—and even then he made us keep the window open. Now there is no problem at all.
>
> Donald has always been in the Boy Scouts, but he refused to sleep in a tent with the other boys. It seemed to be a combination of being closed in and being in a crowd. Recently he slept not only in a tent but in a pup tent.
>
> Prior to treatment Donald could not tolerate being in a large restaurant with lots of people. He always had to have someone to hang on to. This past year we went to Disneyland, and he had absolutely no problems. The crowds didn't bother him, the stores didn't bother him, the restaurants didn't bother him . . . nothing. He also used to be afraid of bugs. Now he has become interested in biology and has even taken up bug and butterfly collecting.
>
> Donald had terrible sleeping difficulties. He would wake up from his sleep in a terror. Often, he would sleepwalk right out of the house. When he woke up with night terror, he'd tear his bed to shreds. There is no longer any night walking, and his bed has been in good shape almost since treatment began.
>
> Donald is just a different child. He is more mature, confident, and much more aware of his surroundings. I can only thank my lucky stars.

Theresa B.

Theresa had a fear of heights that was literally almost paralyzing. Furthermore, turning her head while driving would bring on dizziness and panic. She had to rely entirely on her mirrors when backing up or passing. Though she was an accomplished pianist, recitals would make her dizzy, dyscoordinated, and panicky. As these symptoms intensified, she could not even play the piano for pleasure. After starting treatment, Theresa commented:

> All of my phobias have decreased a great deal. I feel more relaxed and in control. On the whole, I feel as though a weight has been lifted.
>
> I am able to play the piano for my own pleasure again. There is no dizziness, no coordination problems, and no more panic. I am even able to turn my head when I park my car! I truly feel reborn!

Margarita M.

For most of her life Margarita has been afraid of crossing big intersections, afraid of sports, afraid of going anywhere alone, and afraid of making decisions. As she got older, she also developed a fear of driving. Following treatment, Margarita wrote:

> I'm feeling no more anxiety or fear—it is all easier. I can drive a car with assurance, play tennis, and I have vacationed alone for the first time in twelve years! Everything looks and feels so crisp and fresh! I am calmer, more in control of myself, able to make judgments and arrive at decisions. No more procrastinating!
>
> Also, I'm unbelievably better organized! One week after being on medication I returned home and was shocked to see the disorganized, messy state of my house. I went through the house and garage, cleaning, discarding, and reorganizing like mad. Just as my chaotic, messy house reflected the old me, it now reflects the new me.

CHAPTER 5

Why Am I Afraid?

Perhaps more than anything else, phobics want to know *why* they are afraid. They ask: "Why am I terrified of things most people don't even think about?" . . . "Why can't I drive like everyone else?" . . . "Why can't I fly like everyone else?" . . . "Why can't I ride an elevator or escalator like everyone else?" . . . "Why do stairs frighten me?" . . . "Why do crowds frighten me?" . . . "Why am I different from other people?"

Type 3 phobic behavior is extremely complex and varied. Not surprisingly, so are the underlying physiological mechanisms. Yet all of these mechanisms share a common denominator: an inner-ear malfunction. This is easy to say. And it is easy to verify. But it is not that easy to explain. In fact, a detailed analysis of these Type 3 mechanisms could fill many books. Yet every phobic is entitled to an explanation.

To overcome this problem, I have decided to present the reader with two explanations of the physiological basis of phobic behavior: a simple one and a more complex, hence more accurate, one. This chapter contains the first, simplified explanation.

Part III of the book is devoted entirely to a more thorough, comprehensive explanation of phobic behavior. Some sections may be somewhat technical, complicated, and difficult for you to work your way through. But your patience and persistence will be rewarded with tremendous insight and understanding. Although this knowledge alone cannot cure phobic behavior, it is a tremendous psychological help, and it can ensure that you receive the proper treatment.

WHEN ANXIETY GETS OUT OF CONTROL

All phobics have one thing in common: they are afraid. But what is fear? Quite simply, fear is intense, overwhelming anxiety. Everyone experiences anxiety under certain circumstances. Non-phobics are usually able to control it. But phobics are often overwhelmed by it—their anxiety controls them.

Anxiety is a physiochemical reaction that is triggered when the brain is under stress. This can be any kind of stress: emotional, physical, chemical—all of which provoke the same anxiety response. All physiochemical reactions in the body are internally regulated and controlled. The anxiety response is no exception. Clinical evidence clearly indicates that an integral part of our anxiety-control network is located in the cerebellar-vestibular system (CVS). This CVS is the anatomical complex that I call the inner-ear system. (The CVS is discussed in detail in Part III.)

If the inner-ear system is impaired, the entire anxiety-control network may be affected. As a result, your body may be unable to properly dampen or regulate anxiety. In plain English, this means that a mild or moderate amount of anxiety can quickly mushroom into intense fear, or even total panic.

A racing heart, difficulty breathing, sweating, light-headedness, jelly legs, a sense of dread . . . these are all typical symptoms of an anxiety response that is out of control. These symptoms can make you think you are losing control, or going insane, passing out, having a heart attack . . . even dying. Or you may just be frightened out of your wits. The feelings vary, but the problem is the same.

WHAT PROVOKES ANXIETY?

So far I have only presented half of the story. I've told you that a malfunction within the inner-ear system can render you incapable of controlling your anxiety. Hopefully, this makes perfect sense. But what provokes that anxiety in the first place?

Sometimes the answer is obvious. Flying in a plane can be dangerous . . . that often provokes anxiety. Driving in a car can be dangerous . . . that often provokes anxiety. Speaking in front of a crowd can be embarrassing . . . that often provokes anxiety. If this anxiety is not properly dampened or controlled, it can mushroom into fear or panic, and phobic behavior may result.

But many phobias are not so easily explained. What, for example, is dangerous and anxiety-provoking about a restaurant . . . or a movie theater . . . or a small flight of stairs . . . or a shopping mall . . . or a bathtub . . . or a parking lot? Once again, the answer lies within the inner-ear system.

The Inner Ear and Its Many Jobs

The inner-ear system plays an important role in modulating and controlling anxiety. But this is not its only job. It also performs all of the following functions:

- It acts like a gyroscope, giving you your sense of balance.
- It acts like a compass, giving you your intuitive sense of direction.
- It acts like a sensory processor (or tuner), tuning in and fine tuning all of the sensory information entering the brain—including light, sound, motion, gravity, temperature, barometric pressure, chemicals, etc.
- It regulates your internal time clock, giving you a sense of time and rhythm.
- It acts like a guided-missile system, coordinating and sequencing movements (voluntary and involuntary) and thoughts in time and space.

If the inner-ear system is impaired, one, several, or all of these functions may be impaired. Under certain circumstances, these impaired functions may be further aggravated. This can provoke anxiety. If this anxiety is not adequately dampened or controlled, fear and panic may result. But what are these "certain circumstances"?

YOUR PHOBIC TRIGGERS

Many things can aggravate inner-ear problems and trigger anxiety. These vary from individual to individual and depend entirely on which inner-ear functions are impaired. Let me give you some examples of the more common Type 3 phobic triggers.

Balance-Related Phobias

If your balance system—your inner-ear gyroscope—is impaired, it can be further destabilized by heights, bridges, stairs, escalators, wide-open spaces, the dark, and many other phobic triggers (any or all). These triggers may provoke any or all of the following balance-related "broken gyroscope" symptoms:

Anxiety (and other related symptoms, including racing
 heart, sweating, hyperventilating, jelly legs, and so on)
Dizziness
Light-headedness
An off-balance or off-center feeling
Floating sensations
Spinning or whirling sensations
A magnetic "tug" from the ground below
Falling
Fainting
Tipping or swaying

When the triggered anxiety is severe or uncontrollable (due to a maladaptive anxiety response), phobic behavior may result.

Balance-Related Phobias: Some Examples

Deborah H. is afraid of bridges. Notice how her description of this fear clearly reveals an underlying balance problem:

I experience terrifying fear when I cross a long, high bridge. The flat, level ones don't present any problems, but the other kind do. I become extremely dizzy, light-headed, nauseous, shaky, and faint. I cling to my husband's arm and hang on for dear life. I also urge him to talk to me so that I will be distracted. Although my husband is a patient man, he does become angry with me sometimes.

Another patient, Cathy G., has a balance-related fear of heights. She describes her problem as follows:

Height terrifies me. In fact, I can't even look down from the window of a tall building without feeling terror within me. I know it sounds crazy, but I'm afraid of falling through the window . . . even if it's closed. When I was young I was always falling and hurting myself. I even had difficulty walking a simple balance beam on the ground. My gym teachers never believed I was frightened. In fact, I remember one saying I was just lazy and uncooperative. But that wasn't true. I was scared . . . really scared.

Rita D. developed agoraphobia after having a panic attack in a museum. Notice how her description of this attack reveals the presence of an underlying balance problem:

I was visiting a museum and looking at the paintings on exhibit. Suddenly the ground beneath me shifted and I started experiencing weird sensations. As I walked, these feelings intensified. I felt uneasy, unsteady . . . off-balance. Moving my head down or sideways intensified my imbalance and dizziness. I had to concentrate as hard as I could to stop myself from swaying, tipping, or falling.

Some people realize that their phobias are balance related. Most people don't. Even though you may know you have a poor sense of balance, it may never have occurred to you that this could be responsible for something as severe, and seemingly unrelated, as phobic behavior. Yet once you know that balance problems can be magnified by certain triggers, the connection becomes obvious.

Compass-Related Phobias

When the inner-ear compass is impaired it can be aggravated by tunnels, wide-open spaces, shopping malls, darkness, small enclosed spaces (such as elevators, airplane cabins) and other disorienting circumstances (any or all). These triggers may provoke any or all of the following "broken-compass" symptoms:

Anxiety (and other related symptoms)
Disorientation
Confusion
A floating sensation
Spaciness
Light-headedness
Feelings of unreality or disassociation
Dizziness

When the anxiety is severe or uncontrollable (due to a maladaptive anxiety response), phobic behavior may result.

Compass-Related Phobias: Some Examples

Connie M. has numerous compass-related phobias, including a fear of shopping malls, department stores, and supermarkets. She explains:

I would only shop in small stores or in department stores I knew well. Anything complicated seemed to overwhelm and consume me. It was as if I became overloaded, confused, and dizzy all at the same time. Panic would result. Once I even got lost and couldn't find my way out of my own school library. It was as if I had completely lost my orientation and sense of direction. I panicked. I don't think I've ever been so scared.

Cynthia N. has compass-related agoraphobia. Notice how her problem differs from Rita's balance-related agoraphobia:

My sense of direction is so poor I feel that if I go out, I won't be able to find my way back . . . even if I'm in a familiar setting. I can get totally disoriented . . . I feel like my head is going off into space. Then I panic. So I go out as little as possible . . . usually with my husband or daughter close at my side.

Notice how Diane R.'s description of her crowd phobia and department-store phobia indicates underlying compass *and* balance problems:

I feel dizzy and off-balance when I'm in a crowd. As I approach people I'm not sure of the distance or direction, and I almost have to put my hand out to make sure I don't bump into anybody. I get so disoriented and dizzy I'm almost afraid of dissolving into the crowd. When I used to go to department stores, I felt as though I was on another planet. I suppose you can understand why I order most of my clothes by catalog.

This combination of underlying inner-ear mechanisms is quite common in Type 3 phobic behavior.

In a humorous piece entitled "My Favorite Phobias," Roberta B. describes her compass-related fear of driving:

> My special phobias have to do with my vehicle—like the dream that I'm going to die in my car. My husband would enjoy being buried in his (only because it's a Cadillac Seville), and I fear being buried alive in mine.
>
> What caused my complex? The sights and sounds of furious traffic? No, I can handle the hoots and hollers and all the fingers of defiance raised against me. I believe most of my fear of driving has to do, not with such a curse, but with the fact that I have absolutely no sense of direction. No wonder I fear the highways and byways. At any moment I could lose track of whether I'm coming or going. That's why when I travel to a new address I take the long route. That is, I get out of the car and walk. Is that what's known as getting a feel for a neighborhood?

Roberta knows her phobias are related to her poor sense of direction. Yet not all phobics realize that something as simple as a poor sense of direction can result in something as complex as phobic behavior. This association becomes obvious only after you have learned that disorientation problems can be magnified by certain triggers.

Motion-Related Phobias

The inner-ear processes all motion-related information. If it is impaired, you may be hypersensitive to horizontal motion, vertical motion, clockwise motion, counterclockwise motion, or any combination of the above. Depending on what *types* of motion you are sensitive to, and your *degree* of sensitivity to each, the movement of a boat, plane, car, elevator, escalator, or even a rocking chair can provoke any or all of the following symptoms:

Anxiety (and related symptoms)
Dizziness
Light-headedness
Nausea
Vomiting
Retching

If your anxiety is severe or uncontrollable, phobias may result.

Motion-Related Phobias: Some Examples

Vanessa L.'s fears of elevators and escalators are both motion related. The first time we discussed these phobias, she told me the following:

> The speed of the elevator definitely has something to do with it. Those fast elevators that take off like a rocket and suddenly stop . . . when they stop I feel myself shortening or condensing like a squashed accordion. At the same time, I feel my stomach coming right up to my mouth. Just the anticipation is enough to make me panic.
>
> Escalators make me feel weird. It's like I'm being pulled in two different directions at the same time—forward and backward. If I have to go on an escalator, I run up the steps two at a time to get it over with as fast as I can.

Chris B. has a motion-related fear of flying. Notice how his fear is specifically related to horizontal motion sensitivity:

> I've only been on an airplane once. That was enough. It was during takeoff. The plane started picking up speed, and suddenly I was pinned to the back of my seat. I couldn't move. I could barely breathe. My stomach was inside out. It was as if I had lost control of my body . . . like I was having some kind of seizure. As soon as the plane stabilized I felt a little better, so I started drinking. I don't remember much after that.

William J.'s phobias stem from a combination of underlying motion sensitivity, balance, and compass problems. He explains:

> Motion terrifies me—any kind of motion. It overloads my senses. I become disoriented and uneasy. Often I experience this whirling, rolling, floating, speed sensation. In order to stop this and prevent

myself from falling or being drawn into its center, I close my eyes and focus on some object close to me. The exertion leaves me spent.

An inner-ear dysfunction can also result in motion *in*sensitivity. Individuals with this problem *need* to be in motion and become anxious when they are stuck, trapped, tied down, or unable to move (literally or symbolically). This motion-related claustrophobic anxiety can result in a wide variety of phobias. (Claustrophobic anxiety can also be compass related, balance related, vision related, etc. This will be discussed in greater detail in Part III.)

Some individuals have the worst of both worlds. They are *hyper*sensitive to some forms of motion and *hypo*sensitive to others. These individuals often suffer from numerous motion-related phobias.

Visual Phobias

The inner-ear system processes all visual information. If this system is impaired, you may be hypersensitive to bright lights, fluorescent lights . . . even certain colors. Any or all of these may provoke anxiety.

A wide variety of visual distractions can also provoke anxiety, including: flickering lights, blurred images, the dark, and various hypnotic patterns (tiled floors, moving cars, oncoming headlights, crowds, wallpaper patterns, food displays, etc.). If visually triggered anxiety is severe or uncontrollable, various phobias may develop, including: fear of the dark, fear of bright lights, fear of crowds, fear of supermarkets, fear of driving, etc.

A Visual Tracking Problem

Sensitivity to visual distractions is often the result of a tracking problem. The inner-ear system guides the movement of our eyes, enabling us to track the movement of visual information in our environment. If this tracking process is impaired, the eyes may be incapable of keeping pace with this visual information and anxiety may surface.

Gloria H.'s fear of driving stems from a visual tracking problem. Note how she describes her fear:

Driving has always terrified me. Even if I'm being driven somewhere, I can't look at the road all of the time—I get overloaded.

I thought that if I could learn to drive I wouldn't be so frightened, so I signed up for a driver's education course. I quit as soon as we started driving on big streets. I just couldn't handle it. There were too many things to watch for—cars in front, cars behind, cars on your sides, lights, signs. And everything seemed to be coming at me so fast. I had no time to react. I froze—total panic. The instructor started to scream at me. Then the car behind us hit us. That was the end of my driving career.

A Combination Effect

Many visual phobias are partially determined by underlying balance and/or compass and/or motion-related problems.

When our senses of balance, direction, and/or motion stability are impaired, we often become more dependent on visual information to compensate (think of how getting a visual fix on land suppresses motion sickness). If the brain is not receiving this necessary visual information, balance, compass, and motion-related problems are aggravated. This triggers anxiety. Although the anxiety is provoked by visual distractions, it really stems from other, inner-ear problems.

The interaction of visual and balance problems can be clearly seen in Charlotte W.'s description of a frightening panic attack:

We had gone to see a Broadway show—*The Rink*—and my husband didn't tell me that he had gotten balcony seats. There was a mirrored ball that hung in the middle of the ceiling. Flickering lights would bounce off the ball and spin around the theater while the skaters skated in a circle. I was looking down from the balcony, and the place suddenly started to spin. I panicked. I literally had to crawl out, pretty much on my hands and knees, to get out of the balcony seat. I got so dizzy . . . just from watching the skaters going in a circle and the lights and the ball spinning.

Some phobias result from poor depth perception, another visual coordination problem. These phobias will be discussed later in this chapter.

Auditory Phobias

All auditory (sound) information is filtered, sequenced and fine tuned by the inner-ear system. If this system is impaired, you may be hypersensitive to certain loud or piercing noises, such as: a clap of thunder, a fire alarm, a police siren, screeching brakes, a ringing telephone, a tire blowout. If any of these sounds provoke severe or uncontrollable anxiety, phobias may develop.

Notice how this mechanism is highlighted in Evan T.'s description of his auditory phobias:

> There are certain sounds that I have always been very sensitive to and therefore avoid: high-pitched or shrill female voices on the radio, running water, dishes banging together, dogs barking, and normally pitched voices in small, confined areas. The sound of speeding trucks on the turnpike drives me crazy. And music—even classical music—must be kept at a low volume. If not, I feel jangled and upset.

When auditory information is not being properly processed you may be hypersensitive to *all* loud noise or even to garbled noise, such as the noise of a crowd. Thus, for example, Robert S. has panic attacks that are triggered by various noisy environments. He explains:

> I can't go to a restaurant unless I know it's a really quiet place. If I'm stuck in a noisy restaurant I start to sweat. I just want to jump up and scream, "Shut up . . . please . . . before I go crazy!" Obviously I don't. I just run out of the room. I know this isn't normal, but I can't help it. The noise just freaks me out.

Loud or garbled noise makes some phobics dizzy or disoriented. This indicates that several faulty inner-ear mechanisms (e.g., auditory, balance, and compass) can jointly contribute to the development of phobic behavior.

Coordination-Related Phobias

The inner ear acts like a guided-missile system, coordinating and fine tuning your movements (voluntary and involuntary) and thoughts. When this system is impaired, coordination problems may trigger anxiety—especially when these problems subject you to embarrassment, frustration, or danger. If this anxiety is severe or uncontrollable, phobic behavior may develop.

Coordination-Related Phobias: Some Examples

Sylvia R. has a coordination-related fear of driving. When questioned, she told me:

> I'm embarrassed to admit it, but I can't drive. I panic at the wheel. I can't steer the car. I can't keep it on a straight line. This is terrifying. I could never understand why it was so easy for most people. It's hard to believe that only you can't drive. Even now, as I think about this, I could cry.

Liza M. also has a fear of driving. But her fear is related to poor depth perception, a typical symptom of visual dyscoordination. She explains:

> I can drive if I'm in a twenty-five mile an hour area where I intellectually know that if I stay in my lane I'll be all right. But if I go fifty or fifty-five miles an hour I can't make rational judgments. I can't judge distances . . . it's overwhelming. I get sweaty and stiff. And I'm sure a car or truck is coming at me head-on . . . or at least halfway head-on. I can't drive in that situation. It's the speed that bothers me. The faster I go, the less concept I have of the distance.

Scott S. has numerous coordination-related phobias, including a fear of sports, a fear of dancing, a fear of sex, and a fear of eating in public. He comments:

> Anything that involves movement frightens me, especially if other people are watching. When I'm with people I don't feel totally comfortable with, even something as simple as eating an ice-cream cone can provoke sheer terror.

Scott's poor motor coordination also makes it difficult for him to speak. As a result, he is shy, withdrawn, and terrified of speaking in public.

Stairs, Escalators, and Elevators

The fear of escalators, stairs, and elevators frequently stems from coordination problems. Recall how Susan S. (Chapter 1) described her fear of escalators and elevators:

> . . . I would go up the escalator, but never down. I was terrified of falling. Actually, I feared that my foot might become caught on the step. I couldn't figure out which foot to step on with first.
>
> I was afraid of riding in an elevator unless someone was with me. I was afraid the door would crush me. It just didn't seem that there was enough time to get safely inside before the door closed.

A number of other interesting and unusual coordination-related phobias are discussed in Part III.

Other Typical Type 3 Phobias

The phobias discussed in this chapter are only a small sampling of the hundreds of physiologically determined phobias I have observed during the many years I have been in practice.

In Part III I will discuss Type 3 phobias and their mechanisms in greater detail. There you will learn how the fear of bugs, knives, snakes, telephones, water, school, traveling, and public speaking, as well as many other common, and not so common phobias, can be traced to an underlying malfunction within the inner-ear system.

ANTICIPATING THE WORST

When a phobic trigger provokes anxiety, fear, or panic, that response is imprinted in the memory banks of your brain. Once this happens, your brain has actually *learned* to panic in the same way it once learned to tie a shoelace or ride a bicycle.

As a result, the majority of phobics don't have to look down from the top of a twenty-story building to know they are afraid of heights . . . they don't have to hear thunder to know they're afraid of loud noises . . . they don't have to stand alone in an empty parking lot to know they're afraid of wide-open spaces . . . they don't have to get stuck in an elevator to know they're afraid of small, enclosed spaces . . . *they feel it in their very souls*. In fact, the mere anticipation of such a confrontation is often enough to trigger anxiety, fear, or total panic. The many ramifications of phobic "imprinting" will be discussed in detail in Parts III and V.

CHAPTER 6

How Did I Become Phobic?

Many of my patients want to know more about the physiological roots of their phobic behavior. If you think your phobias are the product of an inner-ear dysfunction, you may have the same concerns. How did you get this dysfunction in the first place? Can it get worse? Can it get better? In this chapter I will try to answer these questions.

INNER-EAR DYSFUNCTION: THE CAUSE

As might be expected, many people are born with an inner-ear dysfunction. But this problem can also be acquired in any number of ways throughout the various stages of your life. Let's examine some of these possibilities.

Genetically Acquired

Inner-ear dysfunction is frequently in the genes, passed down from generation to generation in a faulty genetic blueprint. If you inherited your inner-ear problems, chances are that other members of your family (parents, grandparents, siblings) have similar problems.

Some of your family members may have phobias—maybe even the same ones you have. Some may have different inner-ear-related symptoms (see Chapter 9). Others may have phobias and other related symptoms. And some fortunate members of your family may have no visible signs of inner-ear dysfunction.

It all depends on the luck of the draw. But if your inner-ear dysfunction was inherited, chances are you will find ample evidence of some inner-ear problems in your family tree (once you know what to look for).

Acquired During Fetal Development

Many factors affect the physiological development of an unborn child. If any of these specifically affect the development of the inner-ear system you may be born with an inner-ear dysfunction, even though it's not part of your genetic blueprint. These factors, which the pregnant mother may or may not have been aware of, include:

Toxemia
Disease states during pregnancy (such as diabetes and
　　various glandular disorders)
Infections during pregnancy
Drug use or abuse during pregnancy
Falling or other accidents during pregnancy
Anoxia during pregnancy (oxygen deprivation from a
　　twisted or wrapped umbilical cord)
Malnutrition

Acquired at Birth

Various complications during delivery can damage a previously healthy inner-ear system, including:

Premature birth
Oxygen deprivation (from umbilical cord strangulation
　　during delivery)
Fetal "concussions" caused by:
　　improper use of forceps
　　tight birth canal
　　forced labor
　　precipitated birth

Acquired During Childhood or Adolescence

Even if you are born with a perfectly healthy inner-ear system, many factors can interfere with its normal development, including:

Severe or repeated ear infections
Mononucleosis
Sinus infections and other illnesses known to affect the
    inner-ear system
Concussion states (from a fall or other accident)
Whiplash
Malnutrition
Allergic or toxic disturbances
Drug use or abuse
Various degenerative disorders
Unusual or prolonged emotional stress
Endocrine disorders (hypothyroidism, etc.)
Surgery or anesthesia

Acquired During Adult Life

Regardless of your age, and regardless of how healthy your inner-ear system is, a variety of factors can damage that system at any time. Every item on the preceding list is capable of inflicting this damage. In addition, a healthy inner-ear system can be disrupted by the chemical changes brought on by menopause and by the degenerative effects of old age.

SETTING THE STAGE

As you can see, there are innumerable ways to acquire an inner-ear dysfunction. No wonder this physiological problem is present, to some degree, in more than 20 percent of the population. But regardless of whether you were born with this dysfunction or acquired it at some point in your life, the stage has been set. For once the inner ear is impaired, you are vulnerable to the onset of a vast array of phobias and related symptoms.

CHAPTER 7

Born Phobic

If you were born with an inner-ear dysfunction, you may have a long history of fears and phobias. Some of my patients tell me they feel as though they were born phobic. Eleanor, Allison, Edward, Amy, and Gina are five such patients. Perhaps their stories sound something like yours.

Eleanor C.

The first time I met Eleanor she told me she couldn't remember a time in her life when she wasn't afraid of something. She vividly recalled how as a child she was afraid of heights, afraid of the dark, afraid of getting lost, afraid of snow-sledding, and afraid of most amusement-park rides. Eleanor has also suffered from terrible motion sickness since she was an infant, making her prone to numerous motion-related fears.

To say the least, Eleanor did not have the typical "fun" childhood many children have. As she got older she became worse, especially after puberty. By the time she was eighteen she was deathly afraid of driving (though she had never been behind the wheel), flying (though she had never flown), elevators, escalators, heights, bridges, and tunnels. Interestingly, but not surprisingly, Eleanor's mother had some of the same phobias.

For many years Eleanor held a good job doing layout and design work for a large New York publishing firm; she proved to be extremely gifted in her field. But one day, when her company decided to move their offices from the third floor of the building to the twenty-seventh floor, Eleanor quit her job. She explained: "I could handle walking up and down three flights of stairs several times a day. But the thought of riding in an elevator to the twenty-seventh floor just once was enough to make me break out into a sweat . . . I had to quit." And she did, before ever taking a single elevator ride to the twenty-seventh floor.

Embarrassed to tell her boss why she was really leaving, Eleanor told him that she had been unhappy with her job for some time and had decided to accept another job offer. She explained:

> I just couldn't tell him the truth. I knew he wouldn't understand. Later, I heard that another woman left the company for the very same reason I did, but she tried to explain it to her boss. He told her that all she really needed was a good shrink and that it was probably better she was leaving anyway. She must have been humiliated. Besides, it turns out that this woman already had a shrink. For that matter so did I, but that didn't seem to be enough to get either of us to the twenty-seventh floor.

Eleanor added, "I've floated from job to job ever since. But I never let my work take precedence over my phobias."

Her diagnostic evaluation confirmed the presence of an inner-ear dysfunction, and treatment was started. One month later, she wrote:

> I can get on an escalator without even thinking about it! I've also started taking short elevator trips. So far, so good . . . I'm trying to work my way up to a big one. The other day I was in an elevator and it got stuck for a second between floors—the one thing I've always dreaded. But I didn't panic!

Although Eleanor still has a long way to go on the road to recovery, she recently wrote:

> I feel free for the first time in my life. Looking back, it's hard to believe how bad I actually was; it's like it was some kind of a horrible dream, but I know the worst part is over.

Allison A.

When Allison first came to my office she related the following information:

I was probably phobic since the day I was born. I've been claustrophobic since I was two years old. That's why I don't wear glasses.
I can't be encumbered. I wear very little jewelry. If I can get away
without wearing underwear, I do. I don't lock doors if I don't know
whether or not the lock works . . . I'm that claustrophobic. Friends
used to have to stand guard outside the bathroom waiting for me
because I couldn't lock the door. Now I do . . . I've made some
inroads.

When I was in kindergarten and elementary school I was afraid
of throwing up in class. If someone threw up in school I thought it
was terribly humiliating. I was afraid it would happen to me. You
see, the terror of making a fool of myself is a big deal for me.

In high school I had terrible problems. In grammar school I just
feared throwing up, but in high school, when I should have been
concentrating on my studies, I was thinking, "How do I get out of
this room before I go crazy?"

I never went to assembly. I was phobic about screaming out in
a small room. I had to sit next to the door. Thank God I was the
smallest. And besides, my last name began with "A," so I was
always first. I would even lie if by some strange chance I got to the
back of the room and the door was in the front. I would go up to
the teacher and say I couldn't hear or I couldn't see, just to get to
the front of the room. Luckily, I was nearsighted. But I exaggerated
it so I could sit in front next to the door. This way, if I felt I was
going crazy I could run out.

Allison's fears got worse as she grew older. She suffered
through a particularly bad period just before she graduated from
college. She recalled:

It was a hot, humid day, and I was feeling very anxious. I was
dreading graduating from college and going to New York City to
seek my fortune. But I couldn't express my fear to anyone.

Anyway, I started feeling terribly anxious . . . worse than usual.
My father, who was my fearless savior, was away. Not far away . . .
maybe six blocks. And I was waiting for him to come home. Suddenly I couldn't stand waiting another second. I ran to my mother
and said, "Take me to the doctor . . . I'm dying . . . I think I'm
having a nervous breakdown." My mother is phobic too, even though
she denies it, so she understood what I meant. The doctor gave me
an injection and drove me home.

Then I started seeing this maniac shrink. Every shrink I've seen
since has told me I should have sued this guy. Not only wasn't he
of any help, he was dangerous. I think if it wasn't for him I wouldn't

have gotten so bad. He wanted to give me shock therapy. And he wouldn't talk to me. He'd let fifteen minutes go by in silence . . . that was perfectly okay. Then he'd do crazy things: he'd put on sunglasses, do tricks . . . crazy stuff. I thought I was crazy anyway. But this thing is sitting there with sunglasses on, making faces at me. And I would say, "I'm very uncomfortable . . . I don't want to lie here. Can I sit up and talk?" And he would say, "No. Stay on the couch and free associate." So my free association was, "Why am I lying here in this room?"

Discussing her agoraphobic condition, Allison continued:

There's an area around my apartment where I'll go. Sometimes it grows in size, sometimes it shrinks. I'm trying really hard to get out more often and go farther, but it's so hard. Recently I had to meet a client at the other end of town. It was next to impossible. I had to take Valium, vodka . . . and I called three friends who lived near my route and made them stay near their phones until I got to my meeting. Sometimes I think it's a miracle I'm able to function. But look at me. I have a successful business in spite of everything. Still, this is no way to live.

Edward D.

Edward, twenty-eight, has suffered from numerous phobias for most of his life. Many of these fears are compass and balance related. Heights, for example, make him feel off-balance and disoriented. So do crowds. He even gets disoriented when he puts his face underwater. Explaining his fear of crowds, Edward told me, "I lose my grasp of reality in a crowd . . . even if it's a family gathering. I feel like I'm going crazy."

Terrified of school, Edward quit when he was in the ninth grade. He remembers being chronically nauseated, especially when he had to go to gym. According to him, coordination problems and the disturbing effect of the wide-open gymnasium both contributed to his discomfort. He also suffers from severe compulsions, another typical symptom of inner-ear dysfunction (see Chapter 9). He explains:

If I can't organize things in a certain way, I can't function. I have to organize everything at my desk in exactly the same spot. If I don't, I am completely lost and I'll never find something again except by accident—even if it's in front of my face. Sometimes I confuse directions and put things on the wrong side. I have to tell myself that it's all right, otherwise my anxiety quickly builds up.

Amy C.

Amy, who is six years old, has suffered from numerous fears all of her short life. Her mother recalls:

It's normal for newborns to have a fear of falling when they are not being held close and protected. But for Amy it was excessive, and it didn't disappear after a couple of weeks.

At four months of age I noticed that she wouldn't maintain eye contact or look at you intently like other babies. Her eyes moved constantly, even when she was sleeping. When Amy first started to sit or crawl, she would hide her face when anyone talked to her or noticed her—she couldn't stand to look at anyone or make eye contact. Other people just noticed how shy Amy was and thought it was cute for such a little baby to be so shy. But I knew that there was something wrong.

Even as a toddler Amy feared heights. She was unable to walk across docks or anything with slats or holes. The bathtub scared her—she would be terrified when the drain was released to let out the water. Toilet training was difficult because of her fear of a flushing toilet. Police cars, fire engines and balloons scare her and leave her shaking in fear because of the noise they make—even when there isn't any. She is usually more afraid of what is going to happen than of what has happened. These fears were noticeable when she was four months old.

Gina P.

Gina had suffered from intense, chronic anxiety and numerous other phobias since she was a child. What little sleep she had was plagued by nightmares: falling off cliffs, falling off buildings, getting hit by speeding cars, etc. Often in the middle of the night she would be seized by severe vertigo, anxiety, and sudden blindness. Every morning she woke up with a racing pulse, shortness of breath, and severe anxiety. For many years she thought this was the way everyone felt in the morning. Even as a very young girl, Gina's anxiety frequently escalated into total panic. She recalled:

> Anytime my coordination was being tested, I panicked. I couldn't do anything . . . I couldn't ride a bike, roller skate, play sports. I was also terribly sensitive to motion. Just stepping on the ground near an amusement park and feeling the vibrations would make me panic.

Gina's list of fears and phobias increased with age. She became frightened of crowds, traffic, shopping malls (and other mazelike structures), escalators, traveling, public speaking, class participation, sports, dancing, and other coordination-related activities. Her inability to neutralize anxiety and other emotions often resulted in long-lasting, paralyzing panic episodes. She recalled:

> I feared getting up every day. School, especially college, was a terrifying ordeal. Professors caused me great anguish. I let my appearance suffer terribly; I stopped coloring my hair, thus paving the way for black roots with blond ends. And I dressed and spoke in a little-girlish and sloppy manner.
>
> An acquaintance got me involved in meditation, TM, hypnosis, self-hypnosis, etc. The fog thickened. I walked around in a daze, zombielike, my hair undone and unkempt, my clothes resembling a little girl's. Then this acquaintance introduced me to other people who were involved in these "leisure activities." I soon found out that these were temporary measures that could help me to relax. I was so anxious and depressed, I desperately sought out anything and everything that might help.
>
> Eventually I developed a secret ritual that consisted of locking myself in my especially darkened room for hours at a stretch, putting on earplugs and turning on my cassette recorder and listening to tapes on self-hypnosis, autosuggestion, and altered states of consciousness.
>
> My bizarre behavior mushroomed like a weed out of control. I became more and more fatigued. Insomnia set in. I became more and more sheltered. The friendships I had were weakening. I looked like a zombie almost all of the time. Dizzy spells, late-night crying jags, and panic-type attacks became increasingly frequent.
>
> My phobias and fears continued. They became worse after I fell on the sidewalk and suffered a mild concussion. I began to fear driving, especially at night. No doubt this was due to my severe disorientation, my lack of direction, and my propensity for getting

lost (often fifty or more miles from my intended destination). I couldn't drive over a bridge or in New York City. And subways gave me an eerie feeling.

Diagnostic testing confirmed the presence of an inner-ear dysfunction, and Gina was placed on medication. Her improvement was most dramatic. Her social fears, coordination fears, and balance-related fears disappeared almost immediately. "I go on escalators without even holding the rail," she told me, "and I'm going to be giving a lecture at a local college next month."

Gina's disorientation fears have also decreased significantly, and her chronic anxiety has practically dissolved. But perhaps the best outcome of Gina's treatment is her new understanding of herself. She recently wrote:

> The day I began treatment stands as a monumental symbol of rebirth for me. The fears, anxieties, phobias, and mood disturbances were all caused by a simple inner-ear disorder—not my mind! What relief. The fog and stormy emotional weather have receded into the past. Images have cleared. Problems have faded away. I have begun to reconstruct out of ashes and cinders . . . out of destruction. This will be my new beginning, my new lease on life!

CHAPTER 8

Suddenly Phobic

One of the most frightening aspects of phobic behavior is the way it sometimes appears so suddenly and unexpectedly. One day you're perfectly healthy, happy, and normal. The next day you're phobic. The sudden onset of phobic symptoms is often more frightening than the phobias themselves. Patients wonder: Am I sick? Am I dying? Am I going crazy? Do I have a brain tumor? What is happening to me?

IT'S ALL IN YOUR EARS

More than 20 percent of the population have some form of inner-ear dysfunction. Some of these individuals are phobic all of their lives. Others never suffer from a single phobia. And some live phobia-free lives for twenty, fifty, or even eighty years before problems suddenly surface. Yet all of these observations can be easily explained and understood once the culprit—the inner-ear system—has been identified. Let me explain.

Even though an impaired inner-ear system is a necessary prerequisite for the development of most phobias, the presence of such a problem does not necessarily lead to phobic behavior. Basically, there are two factors that determine whether or not phobias ever surface:

- *The nature and extent of the dysfunction.* The inner-ear system has millions of cells and circuits. The presence or absence of phobic behavior depends to a large extent on *how many* of these cells or circuits are malfunctioning and *which* are malfunctioning.

■ *Your ability to compensate.* The brain is often capable of compensating for an impaired inner-ear system—adjusting to it, in a sense, by developing and strengthening mechanisms that counter or neutralize phobic symptoms. If your brain is successfully compensating, you may never be more than vaguely aware that anything is wrong. In fact, more than three-quarters of my phobic patients never realized they had any inner-ear problem until they learned about the many symptoms that characterize inner-ear dysfunction (see Chapter 9).

But an impaired inner-ear system is a vulnerable system. If your inner-ear dysfunction is aggravated or your ability to compensate for it is reduced, phobic symptoms may suddenly surface. A wide variety of factors are capable of destabilizing your inner-ear system and bringing on phobic behavior. These factors include:

Severe or repeated ear infections
Mononucleosis
Sinus infections and various other infections known to affect
   the inner-ear system
Concussions and/or whiplash
Degenerative disorders
Old age
Tumors or blood clots (or other lesions that put pressure on
   the inner-ear system)
Prolonged or turbulent air travel
Surgical procedures
Temporomandibular joint syndrome
Chemical changes* in the brain due to:

drug use or abuse	menopause
allergies	birth control pills
changes in diet	emotional stress
pregnancy	fluctuating hormone levels
menstruation	anesthesia

---

*The effect of chemicals on the inner-ear system explains why the chemical lactate can trigger panic only in panic-predisposed individuals.

Now You Feel It, Now You Don't

When phobias suddenly surface, one or more of the afore-mentioned destabilizing factors are usually responsible. In addition, these factors can make preexisting phobias worse. But some patients have noticed that the reverse is also possible: phobias may improve or disappear when destabilizing factors lessen or disappear. Unfortunately, this does not always happen. Once your fears have been imprinted within the memory banks of your brain, they often take on a psychological life of their own that has little or nothing to do with their inner-ear origins (see Chapter 12). But this seemingly spontaneous improvement is possible and is clearly related to inner-ear functioning.

Although the sudden appearance, disappearance, and intensification of phobic symptoms has always been noticed by phobics and clinicians, no one has ever offered an acceptable explanation—and for one very good reason. All previous phobic theories have overlooked the vital importance of the inner-ear system. As a result, they have necessarily overlooked the importance of various factors that can destabilize that system.

WHY ARE MORE WOMEN PHOBIC?

The reported incidence of phobic behavior is at least four times greater for women than it is for men. Some estimates suggest there are ten times as many phobic women as phobic men. Yet no one has ever been able to offer a satisfactory explanation for this.

Of course many people—both professional and nonprofessional—have tried to explain these puzzling statistics. Some suggest that "women are more emotional than men," that "women think too much," or that "women have nothing better to do all day than worry." Others suggest that men are less willing to admit they have a problem and that these "closet phobics" are biasing the statistics.

Some of these explanations could have more than a grain of truth in them. Others are quite ludicrous. But none of them satisfactorily accounts for the significantly higher incidence of phobic behavior reported among the female population. However, once you have established that phobias are the result of an underlying inner-ear disorder and you are aware of the many factors that can destabilize the inner-ear system, it suddenly becomes very obvious why there are more phobic women than phobic men. *Women are more susceptible because their internal chemistry is less stable.*

In other words, the physiochemical changes brought on by the menstrual cycle, pregnancy, menopause, and so on, are all capable of aggravating the inner-ear system and triggering phobic symptoms. Therefore, though the incidence of inner-ear dysfunction may be the same in both sexes, this dysfunction is less likely to be aggravated if you are a man. Hence, fewer men are phobic.

WHAT ABOUT EMOTIONAL STRESS?

Many clinicians and nonprofessionals have tried to attribute the sudden onset of phobic behavior to one factor: emotional stress. They tell phobics: ''You're just under a lot of pressure. Take a vacation; take it easy. Rest and you'll feel better.'' But this kind of advice rarely helps.

There is no question that stress can precipitate phobic behavior (as in the case of Deborah H. in Chapter 1). Stress causes anxiety, anxiety is a physiochemical reaction, and physiochemical reactions can destabilize an impaired inner-ear system.* But once you have established that the underlying source of phobic behavior is the inner-ear system, it immediately becomes obvious that emotional stress is only one factor capable of provoking phobic behavior. There are *dozens* of others that are equally capable.

Attributing the sudden appearance of all phobias to emotional stress is amazingly shortsighted. It can even be dangerous. By

---

*In certain cases the severe, prolonged stress of such situations as war trauma or torture can bring on phobic symptoms in the absence of inner-ear dysfunction. But this is clearly the exception, not the rule.

ignoring the influence of other destabilizing factors, and by ignoring the role of the inner-ear system in predisposing individuals
to phobic symptoms, patients are often prevented from obtaining
valuable insight into their condition. Furthermore, they are deprived of proper treatment. This typically leads to the perpetuation
or worsening of phobic symptoms.

THE "SUDDENLY PHOBIC"

In the following cases you will notice the undeniable correlation
between various destabilizing factors and the sudden onset of
phobic symptoms. If you were "suddenly phobic," some of these
stories may sound eerily familiar. Hopefully the experiences of
these patients will help to clarify why your phobias suddenly
surfaced.

Marcie T.

When Marcie was sixteen years old she developed mononucleosis. This left her with a severe labyrinthitis, an inflammation
of the inner ear. For the next four years she suffered from balance
disturbances, difficulties with perception, and a variety of fears
and phobias. The first time she came to my office she told me:

> Since the mono I've had a terrible fear of heights. Even getting up
> on a step stool to change a light bulb throws me off-balance. And
> right after the mono there were times I was fearful of leaving my
> house. I felt like an animal with no feeling of time and space—no
> protection. I wasn't paranoid. I just felt incapable of protecting my-
> self from things that were happening to me or coming at me—like
> cars, people . . . even stepping off a curb. There was no barrier or
> filter to protect me from life. I felt defenseless . . . unbalanced. I
> had no sense of a physical center.

Disturbed by her worsening condition, Marcie started psychotherapy. Her fears and phobias were the main theme of her sessions. When asked if her symptoms had improved, she laughingly
replied, "No, I just live with them better. Sometimes I can focus
on them and control them. At other times I feel out of control."

Like many a desperate phobic, Marcie went to several physicians in hopes of finding a better answer. One after another, they examined her and left her with the same diagnosis: "Nothing is wrong—it's all in your head." After testing Marcie, it was clear to me that she had an inner-ear disturbance. This was one examination that didn't send her home with the diagnosis "it's all in your head."

Blanche R.

Blanche R. visited my office shortly after ending a four-year battle against agoraphobia. She recalled:

> One day as I was about to leave my home to run a few errands, I suddenly became rooted to the floor, just as I was about to open the front door. I was physically unable to walk through that door.
>
> From that day until four weeks ago, I was unable to leave my home unless my daughter accompanied me and I had a cane to help support me. In order to move around in the house I had to hold on to furniture. I felt dizzy, dyscoordinated, and off-balance. Although I tried several drugs, my agoraphobia and an acute fear of falling persisted. I became totally dependent upon my children to help me whenever I needed to go to the store or the doctor. Then, as suddenly as they had appeared, my phobias disappeared.

Alan S.

Alan, a twenty-nine-year-old businessman from Washington, D.C., came to my office following the sudden, seemingly unexplainable onset of two phobias: a fear of small, enclosed spaces, and a fear of death.

It all began when Alan, who had never suffered from any phobias or panic attacks, went into the hospital for a minor hernia operation. After receiving two pre-op injections to anesthetize him and make him drowsy, Alan was moved from his hospital bed to a stretcher. A hospital attendant then pulled up the metal bars on the sides of the stretcher and proceeded to wheel Alan out of his room and down the hall to an elevator bank. Only able to look up at the ceiling, Alan began to find the perspective from the stretcher mildly disorienting. The elevator took him down to the basement of the hospital, and as he was being wheeled toward the pre-op room, the perspective from the stretcher, and the bars on either side of him, made Alan feel increasingly uncomfortable. He was beginning to feel trapped.

Once inside the small, windowless pre-op room, things got much worse. The room took on a surreal quality, and Alan began to feel seriously disoriented and dizzy. Within moments, he was panic stricken. He recalled:

> It was like something out of *Night Gallery*. Everything was so unreal. I felt like I wasn't really there . . . like I was witnessing everything in the third person. Suddenly I wanted to get up and run out of the room. I needed to get to a window or door . . . get some fresh air . . . see some sunlight. But I was stuck on the stretcher with an intravenous in my arm, trapped inside those bars, thinking that any minute I was going to start screaming like a madman . . . it was like I was going crazy or something.

Shortly thereafter the injections must have taken full effect, for Alan barely remembers the surgery. Once he was fully conscious again in the post-op ward, his fears returned. But this time he was no longer scared of being trapped in a stretcher . . . he was thinking what it would be like to be trapped in a coffin, six feet underground, for all eternity. For Alan, a coffin represented the ultimate claustrophobic nightmare—the smallest enclosed space in which a human being could fit.

Alan was released from the hospital within a few days. But for a full week he could think of little else but dying and being put into "the box." He thought about being cremated, but that seemed worse. He tried to watch TV to distract his mind, but every program seemed to have someone being killed or someone dying of a disease. All this did was make him think of "the box." Clearly, Alan's phobia was beginning to take on a life of its own.

Soon Alan's small studio apartment had taken on a boxlike quality—especially at night when he couldn't see anything outside his windows. Furthermore, the thought of having hundreds of people living on top of him in his building (he lived on the second floor) was becoming unbearable. He panicked several times and ran to the window for air. But in his condition leaving the apartment was impossible, especially since the last thing he wanted was to wind up back in the hospital.

As soon as Alan was well enough to go out, his girlfriend convinced him to "lighten up" and go with her to the movies. Once inside the theater, he immediately felt uncomfortable. As soon as someone sat near him he would get up and change his seat. Ultimately, he found he could only be comfortable sitting in an aisle seat near the exit.

Sensing that Alan had become "a different person" since the surgery, his girlfriend suggested he see a psychiatrist. Instead, Alan called his regular physician and told him everything that had happened since he received the two injections in the hospital. His doctor told him, "You don't need a psychiatrist, you need a priest." Needless to say, this made Alan much worse. He began to be suspicious of everybody, including his girlfriend and his doctor. He felt like a victim in a crazy conspiracy, that he "really didn't know any of these people at all." It was at this point that Alan came to my office for help.

Diagnostic evaluation revealed clear signs of inner-ear dysfunction. Although Alan had no phobias prior to this episode, his history revealed numerous other inner-ear-related symptoms. This suggested to me that his dysfunction had been severely aggravated by one or both of the drugs he received in the hospital, setting the stage for the onset of his phobic nightmare.

Alan's acute claustrophobia dissolved almost immediately when he started treatment. He wrote:

> It's been almost six months since I've had any serious attacks. I know the medication has helped, but knowing why this happened to me has also helped. I still think about death a lot—not as much as I used to, but more than I should. I've decided to see a therapist here, as you suggested.

James N.

James came to my office several months after receiving a concussion and whiplash in an automobile accident. He was still suffering from directional confusion, anxiety, nervousness, and headaches (all brought on by the accident). But he was most upset because he had developed several intense phobias since the accident.

Understandably, the accident had made James extremely fearful of driving. But he had also developed a fear of heights and was now unable to look out the window of the office where he worked without being overwhelmed with panic. In addition, he found himself getting terribly anxious and uncomfortable whenever he was surrounded by more than a few people at any one time. Listening to two people talk at the same time brought on outright panic.

James's many symptoms had made it impossible for him to go back to work. Now he was beginning to think he might never work again. And to make things worse, an insurance company was insisting that he was making up these symptoms so he could collect more money.

Listening to James describe his symptoms, I immediately sensed that he was telling the absolute truth. Not surprisingly, all of the diagnostic tests confirmed my suspicions. James was indeed suffering from an acquired inner-ear dysfunction.

Risa A.

Until she was twenty-five, Risa led a perfectly normal, healthy life, with just one small exception: once every few years she would have a fainting spell. Most of the times Risa fainted she had been very hot and tired. One Sunday morning, for example, after a night of little sleep, she passed out while standing inside a hot, poorly ventilated church.

Whenever Risa fainted she would go to a doctor for a thorough examination. But this never yielded any insights or help. Meanwhile, her mother always reassured her that there was nothing to worry about. "When I was your age," she would say, "I was fainting all the time."

One day, just after her birthday, Risa blacked out while walking on the beach with her husband. But this time she hit her head hard when she fell. Unlike previous fainting episodes, she recalled that "This one was harder to come out of." Her arms felt tingly, and she couldn't focus her eyes. She had suffered a minor concussion.

The next day Risa felt much better and went to work. But standing on the subway platform waiting for the train to come, she was suddenly and unexpectedly gripped by panic. Her heart was racing, her hands were sweating, she was having trouble breathing—sensations that were all totally unfamiliar to her. She ran up the steps of the subway station and out into the street. Within moments, she was feeling better. Frightened but determined to get to work, she hailed a taxi.

Risa tried to start working as soon as she reached her office, but her subway scare was making it difficult for her to concentrate. No more than fifteen minutes after she sat down to work she felt a second panic attack coming on. She ran out of her office and into the hallway where she could "get some air." This time, it took a little longer for her panic to subside, and this scared her more. Clearly, what had happened in the subway was not just an isolated incident. Too upset to continue working, Risa had a friend drive her home.

She went to work again the next day, but her fear and anxiety had escalated considerably. She refused to go into the subway, so her husband drove her to work. But she even felt panicky in the car, especially when they drove over the Fifty-ninth Street bridge to enter Manhattan. Then she panicked in the elevator on the way to her office.

Afraid to work at her own desk, Risa temporarily switched desks with her secretary. But she was unable to concentrate on her work. All she could do was think about what was happening to her. She left work early and requested the rest of the week off.

That evening, while dining out with her husband, Risa had another panic attack. Standing in the restaurant parking lot, she cried for half an hour. Then she vowed to go to every doctor in New York until she found out what was wrong. Fortunately, a good friend of hers was one of my patients. When she heard Risa's story she called my office immediately and set up an appointment, assuring Risa that there was a very rational basis for her seemingly irrational problem.

My first conversation with Risa revealed many interesting details related to her inner-ear problem. Although she said she didn't have any phobias prior to this incident, many situations made her uncomfortable. She was, for example, not fond of flying; she also hated driving through tunnels because she feared "there might be a leak." Not surprisingly, Risa's mother and sister had similar problems.

Risa also told me she had difficulty looking out into the ocean or staring up at the night sky for a prolonged period of time. If she stared too long, she would suddenly find it difficult to breathe and become panicky. Although these mild fears didn't appear to have any relationship to her current phobic condition, I suspected the origins of both problems were the same.

During her examination, Risa asked if it was possible that her concussion and the subsequent onset of her phobic symptoms could have been coincidental. After all, she had been under a lot of pressure at work and her husband was about to go away for several weeks; a lot of bad things seemed to be happening at the same time. I told her this was a possibility, but that I suspected her current symptoms were the result of an inner-ear malfunction that had been aggravated by her mild concussion.

Risa's tests for inner-ear dysfunction were all positive, and medication was started. Her improvement was virtually immediate. Several months later, she wrote:

> Within one day my anxiety had subsided considerably. I felt more grounded. Although my husband and I were both skeptical, I am now totally convinced that you have discovered the root of my problem. In less than a month I was feeling so much better that I started forgetting to take my medication. Then one afternoon I started feeling panicky again. Although I was upset at first, I realized that I hadn't taken my medication in four days. I've been taking it religiously ever since, and have had no further problems. I'm back at work, back in elevators, and even back on the subway.

Brenda K.

Brenda's story clearly illustrates that a sinus infection can aggravate the inner-ear system and bring on phobic behavior. She recalled:

In December I developed a sinus infection that left me with burning, heavy eyes and no energy. It was during this time that I had my first panic attack.

I was driving on a highway, when all of a sudden it seemed like a dark curtain had been dropped over my head. I sort of "blanked" (not blacked) out, pulled off the road, and waited until I could focus again. Then I turned around and drove home. This incident really added to my already punk feeling. So I made an appointment with an internist. He examined me and found nothing wrong, but suggested that I see a psychiatrist. Otherwise, he said, there would be nothing but a small piece of the original me left.

After the panic attack, and because it happened on a highway, I began to avoid all highways. I would go places where I could turn right to get to wherever I was going, or choose a place where there was a traffic light and practically no traffic. And I had decided that I did not need a psychiatrist (I was too cheap to pay the hourly fee) and that bit by bit I would learn to cope with this problem. My husband was (and is) always understanding, but he was not totally convinced that I was not making up this avoidance act. For several years I managed to get to wherever I had to go by using the "right turn only and back roads" route.

Meanwhile, I started reading anything I could on the problems other people had that seemed similar to mine. I finally stumbled on the term "agoraphobia" and realized that my symptoms fell nicely under that category. About five years ago, I read a newspaper article about a self-help group for agoraphobics. I called the number and began to attend the meetings. I felt a little like a fish out of water, because my driving problem did not seem as serious as the problems affecting the others. Then I joined a group of five other women, each of whom had a different type of phobia. On the fifth session, we were to go to a shopping mall (the others in the group had crowd problems) and I was to drive! As soon as the evening's session was over, I ran to the car and told my husband what I would have to do for the next session. We made a practice run immediately, and I did beautifully. I even drove home, about thirty miles on highways. I felt okay as long as I had another driver in the car who could take over in case I had another "blank out."

My doctor said I should get into the car and drive, drive, drive. The panic attack I experienced initially, he said, was probably the worst it would ever be and I was to repeat the phrases he had given us to help us cope (I forget them now). Well, being a master at avoidance, I rationalized that it was easy for people who were afraid of supermarkets to face their phobias, etc. But the fact that I could unintentionally kill several people on the highway forced me to revert to my old habits.

CHAPTER 9

Are My Phobias Physiological?

By now you are probably wondering whether or not your phobias are due in part, if not entirely, to an inner-ear problem. But how do you know for sure?

There are several highly sophisticated diagnostic tests your doctor can use to confirm the presence of an inner-ear dysfunction (see Chapter 22). However, even before taking these tests, you can begin to make your own preliminary diagnosis (bearing in mind that only a qualified physician can make a confirmed diagnosis). But first, of course, you have to know what to look for. In Chapter 5 we established that the inner-ear system has many functions, including the following:

- It acts like a gyroscope, giving you your sense of balance.
- It acts like a compass, giving you your intuitive sense of direction.
- It acts like a guided-missile system, coordinating your movements (voluntary and involuntary) and thoughts in time and space.
- It regulates your internal alarm clock, giving you a sense of time and rhythm.
- It acts like a sensory processor (or tuner), tuning in and fine tuning all of the sensory information entering the brain—including light, sound, motion, gravity, temperature, pressure, chemicals, and so on.
- It regulates and dampens anxiety.

If the inner-ear system is impaired, one, several, or all of these functions may be impaired. As you have seen, this can lead to phobic behavior. But that's not all. When the inner-ear system isn't working properly, its poor job performance can give rise to a number of additional symptoms and behavior patterns. In other words, phobic symptoms are not the only indication of inner-ear dysfunction—there are *dozens* of other symptoms and behavior patterns that may stem from this malfunction.

These other symptoms and behavior patterns may appear to be unrelated to phobic symptoms, but their presence is no coincidence. On the contrary, these problems are so common among Type 3 phobics that their presence helps to confirm a Type 3 diagnosis.

The various manifestations of inner-ear dysfunction may be evident in any or all of the following areas:

1. Balance and coordination
2. Vision and hearing
3. Sense of direction
4. Sense of time
5. Motion sensitivity
6. Memory
7. Concentration and distractibility
8. Hyperactivity and overactivity
9. Obsessions and compulsions
10. Academic performance
11. Anxiety level

INNER-EAR DYSFUNCTION: RELATED SYMPTOMS AND BEHAVIOR PATTERNS

Before examining these symptoms and behavior patterns in greater detail, it is important for you to know the following:

- All were painstakingly recorded and studied for years before their true meaning and significance were recognized.
- All were analyzed to determine the underlying inner-ear mechanisms responsible for their creation.

- All were statistically analyzed in large samples.
- A particular individual may have some, many, or most of these problems, depending upon the nature and extent of his or her inner-ear dysfunction.
- All vary in intensity from individual to individual, depending upon the extent of the inner-ear dysfunction.
- Many can be partially or entirely masked by compensation and therefore may not appear to be present.
- If your inner-ear malfunction was recently acquired (through a concussion, acute infection, etc.), you may have little or no past history of these problems.

Note: An absence of symptoms is not sufficient grounds to rule out the possibility of inner-ear dysfunction. The only accurate tests for this dysfunction are those performed by a qualified physician.

BALANCE AND COORDINATION

The inner-ear system regulates and controls our balance and coordination. Not surprisingly, the majority of inner-ear-impaired individuals exhibit some degree of difficulty with these two functions.

Although some people experience only mild problems, many are clumsy, klutzy, or accident-prone in childhood and/or adult life (accident-prone children are often bruised and thus mistakenly diagnosed as abused). A small percentage have even experienced bed-wetting or soiling during childhood due to poor bladder and rectal sphincter coordination.

Many individuals with inner-ear dysfunction have difficulty performing more than one task at a time. For example, they may have problems learning to drive a car or learning to play a complex instrument, such as the piano or the drums, since these tasks require the simultaneous coordination of hands and feet. Some individuals can only perform a task properly when they are able to give it their full attention. Hence, they may not be able to drive a car and listen to the radio at the same time (especially if they're driving over a bridge or through a tunnel). Many may not even be able to walk and effectively carry on a conversation at the same time (or walk and chew gum, as the saying goes).

Inner-ear-related coordination problems can make it difficult for an individual to guide a pen across a piece of paper, resulting in discombobulated, illegible, uneven, or infantile handwriting. For the same reason, artistic skills, such as drawing and painting, also tend to be poor or nonexistent (although there are exceptions). Even copying skills can be poor—especially in children (adults often learn to compensate). In fact, the diagnosis of inner-ear dysfunction in children frequently includes an evaluation of these skills (see Chapter 22).

Gross-coordination and fine-coordination problems in children may also result in an inability to perform relatively simple motor tasks such as tying shoelaces, buttoning buttons, zippering zippers, and using utensils. Difficulties learning how to skip, hop, and jump rope are also common.

If movements of the mouth and tongue are poorly coordinated, a wide variety of speech problems may result, including: slurring, stuttering, stammering, lisping, tongue tying, slips of the tongue, and even delayed speaking as an infant. If you had any of these problems as a child, you may have required speech therapy. It is also quite possible that you still have speech difficulties.

Other signs of inner-ear-related balance and coordination difficulties include dizziness, fainting spells, delayed walking as an infant, spastic movements, poor aptitude for athletics, a tendency to fall (or an obsession with falling), an aversion to activities that require good balance and coordination (such as gymnastics, tumbling, rope climbing, and fence climbing), difficulty swallowing pills (or swallowing everything), difficulty learning how to blow your nose, head tilting, postural reading preferences, and a host of visual and time-related disturbances that will be discussed separately.

In addition, poor muscle tone can cause or intensify such symptoms as flat feet, toeing-in or toeing-out, knock-knee, strabismus ("lazy eye"), double-jointedness, and even scoliosis. Intermittent muscle-tone disturbances—especially when triggered by anxiety—may also result in "jelly legs."

Note that the balance and coordination problems discussed above, like all other symptoms of inner-ear dysfunction, can be compensated for, or even overcompensated for. Therefore they are not always noticeable. For example, increased concentration can enable you to partially overcome poor hand-eye coordination. It is only when your concentration is disrupted that you suddenly appear to be uncoordinated. Determination and other methods of compensation may even lead an individual with coordination difficulties to become an athlete, an artist, or a musician.

VISION AND HEARING

Individuals with inner-ear dysfunction frequently complain of various unpleasant vision-related symptoms especially noticeable when reading. These symptoms include: headaches, dizziness, nausea, double vision, blurred vision, word and sentence movement, change in word size, background streaking, etc. Most of these symptoms can be traced to dyscoordinated eye movements.

The inner ear guides and coordinates your eyes in much the same way that it guides and coordinates your hands and feet. If your eyes do not track properly when you read, the result can be omission or insertion of letters, words, or entire sentences. Sometimes these jerky eye movements cause words to blur, jump, or move on the page. At other times they cause the eyes to retarget the same word or phrase over and over again, a phenomenon known as ocular perseveration. These various ocular problems can lead to poor comprehension and confusion.

Frequently, these problems can be compensated for. Slow reading, for example, is one method of compensating for tracking difficulties (and even slow reading can be compensated for by learning how to scan or speed read). Pointing with a finger while reading is another common compensatory device. Finger pointing slows down the eye's movements while simultaneously providing a zigzagging eye with a reference point. This improves reading accuracy and also stops you from constantly losing your place. Some individuals develop a "mental" finger that guides the eyes from letter to letter or word to word. This single-targeting narrows the field of view, blocking out adjacent and peripheral distractions, and resulting in a type of tunnel vision. People who single-target typically read sentences word by word instead of phrase by phrase.

Blinking, squinting, and moving your head (or whatever you are reading) back and forth are other common methods of compensating for visual problems. All of these compensatory devices may work to some extent, but they are difficult, stressful, and tiring, and therefore tend to evoke any or all of the unpleasant visual symptoms listed on the preceding page. In addition, dyscoordinated eye movements can result in poor depth perception. This can make simple tasks such as catching a ball or driving a car extremely difficult and even dangerous.

The inner ear processes all sensory information entering the brain, including visual information. If it is malfunctioning, visual input may drift or become scrambled. If the drift is 180 degrees, reversals may occur. You may, for example, transpose letters, numbers, words, or even entire sentences, or you may confuse numbers such as *1441* and *1414*, words such as *saw* and *was*, letters such as *b* and *d*, etc. Reversals, slips, sequence errors, and directional errors can wreak havoc upon your ability to read, spell, write, think, speak, add, subtract, multiply, divide . . . even tell time. Problems with any or all of these can, in turn, seriously affect your level of comprehension.

Auditory (sound) input can also drift or be scrambled, resulting in misunderstanding, confusion, delayed comprehension, hearing things that weren't said, blending of foreground and background noises, oversensitivity or undersensitivity to sounds (all sound or specific noises), and a variety of other hearing-related symptoms.

People who suffer from auditory drift tend to respond slowly to questions. Typical responses are "What?" or "Could you repeat that?" These are compensatory stalling devices that provide you with more time to process drifting audio signals. Auditory processing problems can be compensated for by concentrating harder, "cupping" your ear, turning your head toward the noise source, or reading lips.

SENSE OF DIRECTION

The inner ear is your internal compass. It enables you to intuitively tell left from right, up from down, and front from back.
If this compass is impaired, it can cause any or all of the following: disorientation, confusion, spaciness, light-headedness, and
dizziness. A broken compass can lead to a host of other problems:
difficulty distinguishing left from right, a poor sense of direction
(no intuitive feel for north, south, east or west), a tendency to
get lost, and a tendency to stray or wander (especially when
young).

Many individuals with an impaired inner-ear compass are easily confused as to where they are going and how to get there,
even if they have driven or walked there many times before.
Some even get lost in their own neighborhoods. They tend to
rely on written or memorized directions rather than on intuitive
"feel," although even this is not always enough to keep them
from getting lost. Many of these individuals tend to be nervous
about traveling, especially traveling alone. Some are even resistant to discovering new routes to and from home.

There are individuals with an impaired compass who feel truly
comfortable only at home—even if they're not phobic. The pros-
pect of moving to a new home or a new job is an unpleasant one
(or, perhaps, one that is not considered), because it means having
to learn new routes and directions. In fact, any type of change
can be disorienting.

Compass disturbances can also foster an aversion to tumbling,
gymnastics, monkey bars, spinning, and other disorienting physical activities. In fact, many people with inner-ear problems get
hurt while performing these activities because they become disoriented and fall (while others are overly cautious to avoid anticipated difficulties).

Fortunately, many individuals with these compass-related
problems can compensate or overcompensate. People who lack
an intuitive sense of direction typically use other devices to compensate. For example, a woman with no intuitive sense of left

and right might wear her watch on her right arm to clue her in (she reasons, "I wear my watch on my right arm, so this must be right"). Similarly, a man with a poor intuitive sense of north, south, east, and west may be a great navigator because he has learned to pay close attention to street signs and landmarks, or to read the various positions of the sun. It is only when these compensatory devices are taken away (the watch is lost; an overcast sky blocks out the sun) that the problems surface.

SENSE OF TIME

The inner ear also helps to modulate, regulate, and coordinate the body's internal time clock. This internal clock gives you an intuitive sense of time and imparts timing and rhythm to various motor tasks. If your inner ear is impaired, you may experience difficulty judging how much time has passed and/or estimating how much time you will need to complete a certain task (time projections). As a result, you may be compulsively late or early, or lost without your favorite compensatory device: a watch.

Timing or rhythmic disturbances can lead to a variety of other problems. If, for example, speech timing is off, the result may be stuttering or other dysrhythmic speech patterns. This fact is supported by a number of observations:

- Stuttering frequently disappears when you sing.
- Stuttering problems often improve when a metronome is placed next to the ear (the metronome acts as a rhythmic pacemaker).

Poor speech timing can also result in rapid speech or unusually slow, monotonous speech that lacks modulation or inflection.

Lack of rhythm tends to manifest itself in sports and on the dance floor (among other places). It also makes it extremely difficult to learn rhythmic tasks, such as playing an instrument. In fact, many individuals cannot learn to play an instrument without the assistance of foot tapping or a metronome (two compensatory mechanisms).

MOTION SENSITIVITY

Many individuals with inner-ear dysfunction have a history of motion-related problems, including motion sensitivity, motion sickness, and headaches. Although these individuals may or may not have motion-related phobias, they may exhibit a variety of behavior patterns that are related to motion sensitivity.

As an infant, for example, you may have cried or vomited whenever you were lifted into the air. As a child you may have disliked, hated, or avoided playground activities (especially the swings, seesaw, and sliding pond), many or all amusement-park rides, riding in buses, cars, planes, trains, boats, etc., and other motion-related activities. As an adult, you may still feel the same way (although due to compensation, motion sensitivity often dampens with age).

At the other end of the spectrum are individuals with motion *in*sensitivity. These individuals may need to be in motion all of the time and may seek out the very motion-related activities that scare others away. In fact, the more motion, the better.

Motion sickness and motion *in*sensitivity represent two different ends of the motion-processing spectrum. Yet neither of these need be present for phobic behavior to develop. In looking for signs of inner-ear dysfunction, it is important to remember that symptoms do not have to be extreme to indicate a dysfunction. Understanding this will help you and your physician to make a far more accurate evaluation of the nature of your phobic disorder.

MEMORY

If the inner ear, your sensory processor, is impaired, you may experience difficulties in processing and/or retrieving information you have seen, read, or heard. This can result in a wide variety of memory problems. The following specific memory functions are commonly impaired or delayed by an inner-ear dysfunction:

- The ability to learn or retain people's names and/or faces, important dates, important phone numbers and addresses, the names of shapes and colors (in children), the multiplication tables, basic addition and subtraction skills, etc., or all of the above. (Individuals with no memory for basic mathematical facts are unable to perform even the most simple calculations in their heads and thus resort to counting on their fingers, using scrap paper, or using a calculator.)
- The ability to learn or retain sequential information such as the steps in a series of directions, the order of the letters of the alphabet, the order of the months of the year, directions, etc., or all of the above.
- The ability to appropriately erase information from your memory. Individuals with this problem cannot forget something, even if it is wrong. Often they continue to make the same errors throughout their lives. The learning of new and correct information does not lead to the erasing or correcting of the old. Instead, this new information and old, incorrect information remain equally strong in your memory, resulting in conflict, doubt, and uncertainty. An individual with this trait might be able to spell new, highly complex words without difficulty but continue to misspell simple words mislearned in childhood.

The failure to erase or correct undesirable memory impressions bears a striking similarity to the perseveration exhibited by the eyes when they fix on something and return to it like a needle on a scratched record. This broken-record effect appears in a wide variety of behavior patterns related to inner-ear dysfunction. It is a fascinating yet frustrating problem, because the strongest need or desire to overcome perseveration may not be enough to do so with any degree of success.

Severe memory-storage problems may make it difficult or impossible for you to remember what you've just read, heard, or thought, no matter how hard you try. Everything seems to go in one ear and out the other. When you were a student, you may have forgotten everything you studied the moment after you were tested or you may not have been that lucky, forgetting it all just before the test. This memory instability often predisposes students to test anxiety and phobias. Test anxiety further weakens pre-existing memory instability, and failure is ensured by this vicious cycle.

If you have severe retrieval problems, you may find yourself constantly drawing a blank, losing thoughts in mid-conversation or mid-sentence, or having words on the tip of your tongue. In these instances the information has been stored in your brain, you just can't bring it back into conscious memory. Difficulties with word and thought recall can also cause loose, disjointed, or rambling speech patterns. (These styles are often present in aphasic and psychotic patients as well, and must be clinically differentiated by a doctor.)

Typical methods of compensating for memory dysfunction include overstudying, the use of mnemonic devices, and compulsive list making. Because many inner-ear-related memory problems increase with age, affected individuals frequently fear they are developing Alzheimer's disease or brain tumors. Clearly, careful professional diagnosis is essential.

CONCENTRATION AND DISTRACTIBILITY

When an inner-ear dysfunction results in sensory scrambling or impaired coordination, extra concentration is required to compensate. Individuals with these problems must often devote all their energy and effort to task performance, especially since numerous errors occur when they don't. In other words, the brain is always in a controlled state of high alert—always on guard. But the body pays a price. The need to constantly overconcentrate quickly brings on fatigue and burnout. Many children and adults with this problem burn out by midday or late afternoon and require extraordinary amounts of rest and sleep to recover. Some recover only partially and feel fatigued all of the time.

Overconcentration can also result in a variety of other symptoms, including headaches, anxiety, fogginess, fatigue, and blocking. Because of this need to overconcentrate, many people with inner-ear dysfunction appear to have a short attention span.

In reality, these individuals are expending far more energy and effort on task performance than do nonimpaired individuals. As a result, they run out of juice faster.

A malfunction in the inner-ear system can also disrupt your concentration mechanisms, resulting in an actual short attention span, daydreaming, spaciness, poor or delayed comprehension, and distractibility. Distractibility can also be the result of a sensory processing problem. If the inner-ear system, your sensory processor, is malfunctioning, you may be unable to shut out irrelevant sensory information while focusing on important information. Individuals with this problem may find that they are unable to do something as simple as read or write while listening to music. Extraneous background noise (even that of a pin dropping) may drive them crazy. They may also find it extremely difficult to sleep through the night, because they are constantly awakened and disturbed by every little noise. Distractibility and other concentration problems are often associated with three other common signs of inner-ear dysfunction: disorganization, procrastination, and overactivity.

Some people do compensate for their difficulties by developing super concentration skills that are resistant to fatigue and distractions. But for the most part, individuals with these problems are constantly struggling to keep up their level of concentration and are forever plagued by feelings of tiredness, fuzziness, and other symptoms discussed previously. As a result, some are driven to such stimulants as caffeine, nicotine, and amphetamines. Others unwittingly provoke anger to get their adrenaline pumping, because they need this adrenaline in order to function normally.

HYPERACTIVITY AND OVERACTIVITY

Although severe hyperactivity is generally not a sign of inner-ear dysfunction, mild hyperactivity, restlessness, and fidgety behavior often are. I prefer to refer to this behavior as overactivity. This may stem from (or contribute to) concentration and/or coordination problems that make even the simplest task difficult or impossible. The resulting inability to stick to a task for any period of time predisposes individuals to rapid boredom, drifting, day-dreaming, and wandering.

If you have this problem, you may be capable of concentrating only on something that fascinates you or something that you really love. If you're not interested, forget it. Overactivity may make it difficult for you to do something as simple as read a book, article, or set of directions from beginning to end. If, and when, you do read, you may find yourself constantly checking to see how many pages are left until the end. Such a pronounced inability to focus the mind for any length of time can result in disorganization and inconsistency in both habits and speech, and affected individuals are often looked upon as scatterbrained, stupid, or even crazy.

Concentration and coordination problems generate tremendous frustration. The need to discharge this frustration may lead to the development of destructive defense mechanisms such as drug abuse and alcoholism, and a variety of avoidance mechanisms such as procrastination, last-minute work habits, job neglect, playing hooky, and dropping out. Overactivity is also frequently associated with low frustration tolerance. This may lead to impulsive verbal discharges and behavior patterns, including temper outbursts and cursing.

OBSESSIONS AND COMPULSIONS

Many individuals with inner-ear dysfunction are victimized by obsessions and compulsions. Obsessive thoughts and compulsive behavior patterns often stem from a malfunction in the inner-ear system as it processes and coordinates thoughts and actions.

In a sense, thoughts are perseverated in much the same way a word on a page is perseverated. When the mind gets stuck on a thought (an obsession), the result is a "broken-needle" behavior pattern (a compulsion), such as the need to touch something, move something, or do something over and over again. In other words, the physiologically based inability to suppress a recurring thouht results in a need to act on that thought repeatedly.

A typical obsessive-compulsive person may never be able to leave the house without returning several times to make sure the door is locked, the gas is off, the dog is inside, etc. Many obsessive-compulsives must constantly organize their desks, closets, or even their lives in a particular way. If they can't, they may feel lost or threatened. Although memory instability and disorientation, and the resulting need to check and recheck often contribute to obsessive-compulsive patterns, perseveration is frequently at the core of the behavior.

Many of my phobic patients are very superstitious. This often reflects the presence of perseverating superstitious thoughts that cannot be controlled or suppressed. Typically, the appearance of these thoughts, and the resulting behavior patterns, can be traced to a malfunctioning inner-ear system. In a sense, the inner ear fails to inhibit background thoughts, which results in "thought flooding." Certain phobias develop in the same fashion and are actually little more than obsessive, perseverating worries. Since the mind is unable to suppress these worries, the individual feels compelled to act on them.

Perhaps the worst by-product of obsessive thinking is the way it often complicates the phobic disorder. Thought perseveration makes it extremely difficult for phobic individuals to suppress concerns over their fears. During the day, during the night, at work, at home . . . nothing else seems to matter. This repetition of fearful thoughts only heightens anticipatory anxiety, making the phobic's condition progressively worse. In fact, it is this obsessiveness that often gives phobias a "life of their own," creating strong psychological barriers to successful treatment.

ACADEMIC PERFORMANCE

Many phobics had, or continue to have, a wide variety of problems with reading, writing, spelling, math, grammar, and other academic skills. These problems stem from concentration difficulties, distractibility, memory dysfunction, visual and auditory scrambling or dyscoordination, visual and auditory drifting or reversals, and various other inner-ear-related symptoms.

Academic problems typically get worse as grade level advances because the volume of information to be learned or recalled increases substantially, while the amount of time allotted to do so decreases. Both factors put additional strain on an already strained system. If you had any of these difficulties, you may have hated or feared school as a child and been accused of being pampered, spoiled, or indulged. You may have been called a brilliant overachiever or a disappointing underachiever, or you may have been diagnosed as learning disabled or dyslexic. As you will learn in Part IV of this book, the association between these labels and an accompanying phobic disorder is no coincidence. In fact, it provided me with my first clue to solving the phobic puzzle.

When you were a teen-ager you may have avoided school by cutting classes, dropping out, or getting yourself expelled. Or you may have been a workaholic, spending countless hours on academic assignments that classmates completed in a fraction of the time. As an adult, you may have learned to compensate for whatever academic problems you had when you were younger and been called a late bloomer. On the other hand, you may still have any or all of the following problems, all of which can be traced to an inner-ear dysfunction:

- You may be vexed by difficult brainwork, such as structured writing and dry reading.
- You may still be unable to do simple mathematical calculations without using a piece of paper, a calculator, or counting on your fingers.
- You may read slowly (unless you took a speed-reading course) and still have difficulty reading a book from cover to cover.
- Your grammar may still contain elementary flaws.
- Your spelling may be poor.
- Your writing, even if it is brilliant, may not come easily, and you may frequently experience writer's block.
- Your ability to memorize facts and figures may still be poor unless you can visualize or hear this information in your head.
- You may have to double- and triple-check your math, spelling, writing, etc., since you are so prone to making errors.

- You may have to look up the same word in the dictionary over and over again.
- Your speech and writing may still be characterized by reversals and slips.
- You may have difficulty sitting at a desk and working for long periods of time on difficult cerebral tasks.
- Your handwriting may still be infantile or illegible, or you may have to print everything in block letters.

ANXIETY LEVEL

When the inner ear is malfunctioning, your brain is under stress almost all of the time—even when you are sleeping. Whereas some individuals can compensate quite well, others may constantly feel anxious, nervous, worried and ill at ease.

Many phobics suffer from sleeping disorders, including insomnia and nightmares, because of their inner-ear problems. Furthermore, various other signs of chronic anxiety, such as "psychosomatic" headaches or migraines, stomachaches, dizziness, nausea and vomiting are also common. I qualify the word "psychosomatic" because these symptoms are not psychological in origin but are *physiologically* triggered by an impaired inner-ear system. Although these symptoms appear to have little in common with the frightening symptoms of phobic behavior, they are part of the same syndrome and are evoked by the same physiological problem.

Over the years I have observed that many inner-ear-impaired children and adults have as much difficulty controlling their anger and frustration as they do neutralizing and regulating their anxiety. As a result, these individuals may suffer from all of the following: temper outbursts, "short fuses," mood swings, high anxiety, and a tendency to panic. This has suggested to me that all of these problems are linked to the same common denominator: inner-ear dysfunction. Not surprisingly, these symptoms often improve dramatically when a patient is treated for this dysfunction.

Once again, let me remind you that an individual with an

impaired inner-ear system may experience varying degrees of any or all of the symptoms presented here, especially since most of these symptoms can be masked by compensation. Furthermore, the appearance, intensification, or disappearance of symptoms, as well as the many possible variations and combinations of symptoms, may be affected by fatigue, allergies, dyes, toxins, metabolic and chemical disorders, mononucleosis, ear infections, concussions, or any other factor that can destabilize the inner-ear system. With this in mind, review your answers to the self-test in Chapter 2. How many questions did you answer with a "yes"?

CASE HISTORIES: EVIDENCE OF RELATED SYMPTOMS AND BEHAVIOR PATTERNS

Let's return to some of the case histories I have presented thus far and review them for additional signs of inner-ear dysfunction. As you read about the various combinations and intensities of symptoms present in each case, you will develop a much better understanding of the complexity and enormity of this physiologically based disorder.

These cases have been selected because they clearly illustrate the many possible ramifications of inner-ear dysfunction. Please note that your symptoms may not be nearly as severe as those of some of these patients.

Brenda K. (Story in Chapter 8)

Brenda summarized her various inner-ear-related problems as follows:

1. Nausea: I can't ride as a passenger in a backseat, I also get nauseous in boat cabins, elevators, crowded places, etc.
2. Difficulty verbalizing: When I talk to myself I am a brilliant orator with an immense vocabulary. But as soon as I open my mouth, my speech becomes fragmented and disjointed, and I find that my vocabulary has shrunk. I shy away from public speaking. I worry that I will say something dumb. I also stumble and bumble on the telephone, especially when someone important is listening.

3. Poor math skills
4. Poor spatial skills
5. Poor sense of direction: I cannot give directions unless I position myself in the direction of the person who is asking me.
6. Clumsiness (sometimes)

and so on. . . .

Sue S. (Story in Chapter 1)

During her examination, Sue S. recalled:

I was unable to master the skills or the phonetics required to read. It wasn't until the sixth grade that I finally learned to read—to satisfy school requirements, not for pleasure!

I recall I was always a poor speller and would become upset and embarrassed if I had to spell aloud. The other activity I absolutely disliked was gym because I was so uncoordinated. I remember falling off the balance beam and feeling so humiliated. I was always the last one selected as a partner in my gym classes.

I also had an auditory problem as a child, which compounded my problems.

Sue added that as a child she was frequently upset and did not understand why she felt that way. As she grew older, she began to realize that she had a severe, frustrating problem because reading was much harder for her than it was for her friends, especially when she had a great deal of material to read.

Sue continued to find certain academic courses, such as literature and history, difficult because of the quantity of material to be read. She said she relied mainly on the lectures because she was never able to complete all of the reading for her college courses. She experienced blurring of letters and words, and focusing difficulties when she read, which resulted in headaches and eye fatigue.

Sometimes I felt as though I were in a fog, especially in the mornings. I would find myself shaking my head, as though to clear it. The problem of concentration and being "out of it" was more pronounced if I had a respiratory infection or an allergy attack.

Most of Sue's inner-ear-related problems improved or disappeared when she began taking medication.

Susan S. (Story in Chapter 1)

Susan has had numerous severe inner-ear-related problems all her life. She recalls:

> I've always been klutzy, and people have always laughed at me. I learned to make fun of myself. That way, I developed a good sense of humor and had lots of friends.
>
> As a child I had a lot of trouble staying upright. I was falling constantly. I tried roller skating and ended up on my backside most of the time. I was falling, tripping, and bumping into things and people; it was terribly humiliating.
>
> I've always had a problem with time. I'm always late because I'm very slow . . . I never seem to allow enough time; my judgment is off. If I have company, I invite them at a certain time but I'm never ready. I don't mean to be late. I just have no conception of time. I don't know if it's months or years since a particular event. I can't remember. I don't know how long ago my mother died. I latch on to a number, say six years. Now I know it's been over six years, but I don't know how long it's been unless I ask somebody. I also can't remember when my daughter was born or how old she is. I don't remember the hospital she was born in either. I always have to figure it out.
>
> I could never tell my left hand from my right hand. I thought people really had to think about it. Then I asked my husband and he said that he just knows. I asked him which arm was his right arm, and he just knew. I always mix up the two.

Cathy G. (Story in Chapter 5)

Cathy's experiences as a young student typify those of many inner-ear-impaired individuals. She recalls:

> I truly remember hating school when I entered junior high. I was unable to listen and absorb anything the teacher said. And I had to study very, very hard in order to get a mere 65% in subjects. I was also having great difficulty with algebra. I just couldn't understand any of the math concepts. My teacher didn't believe I was really trying to learn. Instead, she claimed I wasn't paying attention in class and was just lazy or defiant.
>
> I remember not being able to draw. As a result, art embarrassed me something awful. And the other children would laugh at my attempts. My schoolwork became increasingly difficult to understand. And although my father tried to help me, he became frustrated and soon began yelling. All I could do was cry.

I remember doing very poorly in history. I couldn't read a map. Obviously all the other kids laughed at me. I couldn't read a paragraph out loud and explain the meaning of what I had read. And when I could read out loud, I'd forget what I had read shortly afterward. I couldn't even hold a pencil or pen the right way. To this day I can't hold a fork properly. Can you imagine how self-conscious this makes me feel?

I also had a lot of trouble with vocabulary, spelling, and grammar. But no one did anything about it. My English teacher would ask me to write two essays in order to make up for every test I failed. But I couldn't! I truly felt school was a waste of my time and energy. I always thought I was on the dumb side and didn't belong. We had a saying in school that I felt really applied to me: "When God gave out brains, you must have been at the end of the line." I thought I was last on line!

William J. (Story in Chapter 5)

During his initial visit, William discussed his various inner-ear-related symptoms in detail:

Reading and concentrating are major problems for me. My eyes seem to jump around involuntarily all the time, and my mind races around continuously, as though it were on a merry-go-round.

When I'm with others, I periodically lose the drift of the conversation. My mind is always darting here, there, and everywhere. And when my mind returns to the conversation, I must piece it together. This kind of thing happens when I'm watching TV, too. Thus, any kind of reading, TV watching, or concentration is very difficult and exhausting.

Going through life like this presents me with a constant struggle to sort the pieces and prevent them from jumping around. I only see a tunnel view of life. This reduces whole concepts to their component parts, and much is lost in the process. To illustrate, when I look at a word, I see the letters individually. I then piece it together, and in the process I usually lose its various shades of meaning. Because of this fragmentation everything I do is an overwhelming task.

Robert B. (Story in Chapter 1)

Robert's poor self-image can be traced to numerous inner-ear-related problems. He commented:

For as long as I can remember my memory has been poor, my ability to concentrate and learn have been poor, and my attention span has been short. As a youngster, I can remember having difficulty with academics. I was forced to leave night school because the pressures were more than I could handle.

I have always been somewhat slow, unable to function at a fast pace. As a result, I've always felt compelled to explain my slowness to other people. Part of the reason for my slowness is my inability to concentrate and do two things simultaneously. And part is due to my fear of making a mistake. I dread having my colleagues discover that I'm not as smart or as competent as they think I am.

Part of my job involves writing reports. Despite the fact that I have a stenographer at my disposal, I do not use her because I can't dictate material off the top of my head. Instead, I must carefully review my notes and records many times and write and rewrite reports several times before I'm sure they're correct.

In spite of poor coordination and directional abilities, I am an excellent dancer, and I love to dance. However, I have difficulty understanding and remembering new dance steps. Yet I often find I'm able to execute intricate dance steps without really learning why or what I'm doing. I can't logically explain the gap between learning and performing. This is true of many things I know—I have no conscious knowledge of how I learned them.

Marcie T. (Story in Chapter 8)

Marcie became severely phobic after contracting mononucleosis at the age of sixteen. But even before then, she had numerous other inner-ear-related problems (as do most "suddenly phobics"). She recalls:

> I've always been very bright . . . but most people think I'm really spacy. I have a lot of memory problems. I grasp abstracts—concepts, principles, etc.—very, very quickly, and understand them completely. But I don't remember simple facts . . . things that I really need. Being this way makes me feel really stupid.

Memory problems like this are quite common among inner-ear-impaired individuals. Their memory instability allows for more complex concept understanding but fails them when it comes to concrete details or simple tasks. This conflict leaves the person feeling confused, dumb, and inferior.

During her bout with mononucleosis, Marcie's memory problems grew worse. Her balance and coordination were also severely affected by the illness. She explains:

My balance jumped in and out. It was episodic. It would bother me most in winter. My head would feel very cloudy, as if I had a bad cold. I could not orient myself in space. Knowing where I was, what time it was, and moving from one space to another became a struggle.

This sudden appearance or magnification of related inner-ear symptoms is also quite common among "suddenly phobics."

Deborah H. (Story in Chapter 1)

Commenting on her various inner-ear-related symptoms, Deborah writes:

As a child I had difficulty telling time, organizing my words and thoughts, and learning and memorizing factual material. I had difficulty using forks and knives, and was accident-prone. I was often sick, suffering from numerous allergies, and I was always carsick —dizzy, nauseous, and light-headed.

As an adult I've always had a poor self-image, despite the fact that I'm a college graduate and taught second grade for five years. My memory has been generally poor, too. I can recall walking to the back of the classroom and then forgetting why I went there. At the time, I rationalized. After all, I reasoned, teaching a lively class of second graders can be very distracting and demanding.

Driving, too, has always been very difficult and nerve-racking for me. I become easily disoriented and confused, especially when I must follow a map or directions. I am never sure which is right and which is left. Frequently, in the process of deciding, I become lost.

As you consider the wide variety of symptoms presented in this section, I hope you are beginning to see that the phobic symptoms you are most familiar with, and most frightened of, are probably just the tip of the inner-ear iceberg. *Indeed, inner-ear dysfunction may shape and define not only your phobias, fears, and anxieties, but your likes, dislikes, moods, attitudes, behavior patterns, and much more.*

The possible ramifications are startling, mind-boggling, and endless. Let us hope they are no longer ignored or repressed.

CHAPTER 10

Why Wasn't This Discovered Sooner?

If an inner-ear malfunction is indeed responsible for the development of most phobias, it is only natural to wonder why this wasn't discovered sooner. There are, of course, many reasons.

The greatest obstacle to discovering the true basis of phobic behavior has been our inability to consider the possible existence of a *physio*logical problem. Conventional theory has always assumed there is an underlying *psycho*logical explanation for all phobic behavior. As a result, clinicians have always looked for strictly psychological solutions to the phobic puzzle. Unfortunately, the fruits of their labors have been less than modest.

To make matters worse, the phobic arena has been divided for some time into two camps: the Freudians and the behaviorists. The conflicts between these two schools of thought have often gotten in the way of progress.

THE FREUDIAN APPROACH

The Freudians believe in a strictly psychoanalytic approach to phobic analysis and treatment. Most Freudians are thoroughly convinced that phobic behavior occurs when displaced anxiety surfaces. This anxiety, they claim, stems from unresolved, repressed, emotional conflicts left over from childhood—conflicts generally of a sexual and/or aggressive nature.

Freudians also believe that if these conflicts are uncovered and resolved, the phobias will disappear. And if psychoanalysis does not succeed? Then the analyst simply digs further into the patient's unconscious, looking for buried or repressed sexual traumas and conflicts that occurred during the first few years of life.

For the phobic, this could mean years and years of psychotherapy with no guarantee of results.

THE BEHAVIORIST APPROACH

Behavior therapists believe that finding, and attempting to resolve, deeply embedded emotional conflicts will not necessarily, if ever, lead to the improvements predicted by Freud's followers. They therefore suggest that the best way to treat phobic behavior is by treating the symptoms, not the alleged source of those symptoms. In fact, some behaviorists recommend that we ignore the assumed emotional causes and conflicts underlying phobias. Instead, they believe in treating phobias solely by desensitizing patients to the various triggers.

Although behaviorists claim their approach is usually far more successful than strict psychoanalysis, the improvement rate is still less than satisfactory. Needless to say, the Freudians refute the claims of the behaviorists, insisting that just the opposite is true.

Although both the behaviorist and the Freudian approach have some merit, neither has sufficiently explained the facts of phobic life. Even when the two approaches are combined there remains a significant void. Clearly, something important is missing from both of these explanations.

A "NEW" APPROACH

Only very recently and, I might add, reluctantly, has a third school of thought emerged. Noting the seemingly unexplainable improvements some phobics have made on antidepression and so-called antipanic medications, a growing number of clinicians have suggested that there may be a physiological component, perhaps even a physiological basis, for certain phobic behavior. Yet until now, no one has been able to do anything more than speculate about the exact nature of this physiological component.

The notion that there is a physiological component to phobic behavior may sound "way out" and perhaps even heretical to many psychiatrists and psychologists. Yet any good student of psychology should realize that this notion is not entirely new. In fact, it was the great Sigmund Freud himself, the founding father of psychoanalysis, who predicted that a somatic link—a physiological connection—to psychological symptoms such as phobias would one day be discovered. Freud called this link between mind and body *somatic compliance*.

DID FREUD KNOW?

What, one might ask, prompted Freud to make such a prediction? Was it his disappointment with the limitations of strictly psychological models and theories? Was it the hard-to-ignore fact that many, if not most, phobics appear to be as mentally and emotionally strong as nonphobics? Or was it, perhaps, a gut feeling that certain "psychological" symptoms, such as those associated with phobias and other neuroses, were far too severe and complex to have only a psychological basis?

Reading through Freud's work, it becomes clear that it was his research, not his intuition, that indicated that psychological conflicts often centered around a weak somatic link. In fact, Freud tried to construct a comprehensive neurophysiological theory of phobias and other neuroses many times. But the limitations of medical insight into human neurophysiology at the time prevented him from developing a successful theory. Still, Freud knew that a strictly psychological model of neuroses was incomplete. He knew that some other factor or factors must set the stage for such neuroses to occur. His understanding and insight must not be dismissed or forgotten.

It is interesting to note that Otto Fenichel, one of Freud's most brilliant disciples, observed a correlation between phobias, anxiety states, and two symptoms known to be of inner-ear origin: dizziness and motion sickness. This correlation suggested to Fenichel that sexual conflicts in childhood stimulated the inner-ear system, resulting in the appearance of these symptoms. Had Fenichel been able to stand back and take a more objective look at his findings, he might have recognized his error, and this book could have been written a long time ago.

PART III

PHOBIAS AND THEIR MECHANISMS

CHAPTER 11

The Inner-Ear System: The Seat of Phobic Behavior

A proper analysis of phobic mechanisms begins with an analysis of the anatomical complex responsible for those mechanisms: the cerebellar-vestibular system (CVS). The CVS, our inner-ear system, is comprised of the cerebellum and the vestibular system. Let's take a close look at each of these two components.

THE CEREBELLUM: OUR "OLD" BRAIN

The cerebellum is the primary brain in many less advanced species. Accordingly, it is called the "old brain." The fact that these species have managed to survive and reproduce for thousands of years with little or no cerebral cortex should be enough to make the scientific community extraordinarily curious about the role of the cerebellum in human behavior. Yet until very recently, the vast majority of research has focused on the cerebrum, our "new," *thinking* brain. This has relegated the cerebellum to the backseat.

Perhaps the lack of interest in the cerebellum has been a subconscious effort on our part to deny our animalistic origins. Or perhaps the larger, seemingly more complex cerebrum, being the seat of our intelligent behavior and the organ that has distinguished us from thousands of other, less physiologically advanced species, stimulates more genuine curiosity and interest. Whatever the reason, we have until very recently been left more or less in the dark regarding the workings of our cerebellum.

A Supercomputer

Today, thanks to a tremendous amount of clinical research, the complex role of the human cerebellum is beginning to unfold. Already, one fact has been established: it is no longer acceptable to view the cerebellum as an organ whose only responsibility is the management of voluntary and involuntary muscle activity. On the contrary, it has now been clearly documented that the cerebellum:

- Administers all *motor* responses dictated by the thinking, speaking brain.
- Integrates and processes virtually all of the *sensory* information transmitted to the brain from the millions of sensory receptors located throughout the human body (while communicating constantly with these receptors via a series of feedback loops).

The cerebellum is not unlike a supercomputer, handling millions upon millions of pieces of information at any moment. The outer layer of the tiny cerebellum alone has 75 percent as much surface area as the cerebral cortex, and an estimated 10^{11} cells (100,000,000,000). If each of these cells is responsible for just one task, imagine how complex the cerebellum really is.

It is interesting to note that it was once estimated that the entire brain had only 10^{10} cells—less cells than are now known to be in the outer layer of the cerebellum alone. Citing this erroneous scientific fact, Sanford Palay of the Harvard Medical School once humorously commented, "Of the 10^{10} cells in the brain, 10^{11} are in the granular layer of the cerebellar cortex." In a magnificent article entitled "The Cerebellum" (*Scientific American*, 1958), R. S. Snider discusses the cerebellum's role in modulating sensory motor information:

> In the back of our skulls, perched upon the brain stem under the overarching mantle of the great hemispheres of the cerebrum, is a baseball-sized bean-shaped lump of gray and white brain tissue. This is the cerebellum, the "lesser brain." In contrast to the cerebrum, where men have sought and found the centers of so many vital mental

activities, the cerebellum remains a region of subtle and tantalizing mystery, its function hidden from investigators. . . . Its elusive signals have begun to tell us that, while the cerebellum itself directs no body functions, it operates as monitor and coordinator of the brain's other centers and as mediator between them and the body. . . . One is tempted to see the cerebellum as the great "modulator" of nervous function . . . in the meantime we have to contend with the possibility that the cerebellum is involved in still more diverse aspects of the nervous system. It becomes increasingly evident that if "integration" is a major function of this organ, trips into the realm of mental disease may cross its boundaries more frequently than the guards in sanitariums suspect.

THE VESTIBULAR SYSTEM: A PRIMITIVE BRAIN?

It is difficult for me to discuss the cerebellum any further without simultaneously discussing its close associate: the vestibular system.

The vestibular system, our so-called inner ear (see Figure 1 in Appendix B), has long been recognized for the vital role it plays in maintaining our equilibrium and balance. Many scientists have even recognized the role it plays in establishing our intuitive sense of direction (see Chapter 13). What is often not recognized, however, is that this intricate system, with its tiny semicircular canals, cochleas, and vestibules, shares an intimate relationship with the cerebellum. This relationship is so intimate that it is often hard to determine where the work of the cerebellum ends and that of the vestibular system begins. In fact, without the assistance of the vestibular system, the cerebellum would be unable to properly perform most, if not all, of its functions.

The relationship between the inner ear and the cerebellum has a fascinating evolutionary history. In some very primitive species lacking both a cerebrum and a cerebellum, the inner ear *is* the brain, performing many of the same functions performed by the cerebellum in higher species. This has led some scientists to hypothesize that the cerebellum developed as an extension and elaboration of the inner-ear system, just as the cerebrum later developed as an extension and elaboration of the cerebellum.

Because of the high degree of integration between the cerebellum and the inner ear, it is unwise and counterproductive to treat them as two separate and independently functioning systems. For this reason, I refer to these two systems as one larger system: the cerebellar-vestibular system (CVS) (or, more simply, the inner-ear system).

THE CVS: OUR INFORMATION PROCESSOR

Clinical evidence has now made it very clear that the cerebellar-vestibular system is the sensory-motor processing center of the brain: the area where an endless flow of vital sensory information heading for the brain as well as vital motor information leaving the brain is filtered, integrated, coordinated, and controlled.

Let me explain this further. The human body is constantly being bombarded by a vast array of sensory information, including light and sound in all existing wavelengths, motion (internal and external), gravitational (electromagnetic) energy, air pressure, chemicals (external and internal), odors, tastes, textures, and so on. The CVS acts as an intermediary between our sensory receptors and the brain as a whole, filtering and organizing this sensory information, then transmitting it to the rest of the brain in a usable form and at a usable rate.

To say the very least, the CVS plays a vital role in processing and modulating light, sound, motion, taste, touch, smell, gravity, temperature, barometric pressure, chemicals, direction, balance, time—even our position in space. But this is just half of the job constantly performed by the inner-ear system. For while it is processing all of the sensory information being sent to the brain, the CVS is also filtering, integrating, coordinating, and controlling all of the instructions the brain wishes to send to the various parts of the body—the so-called motor information. Hence, the CVS also plays a crucial role in all motor functions—including our ability to walk, cry, breathe, make love, and play tennis.

CIRCUIT SPECIFICITY AND THE INNER-EAR SYSTEM

What is particularly interesting about the CVS (and, as you will see later, highly relevant in regard to the development and manifestation of phobic behavior) is that it appears to process information in a highly compartmentalized, area-specific fashion. Certain aspects of this behavior have been noted for some time. As R. S. Snider wrote in *Scientific American* in 1958:

> As in the cerebrum, the various functions of the cerebellum are localized in distinctly defined areas of its cortex. Detection and plotting of the electrical activity of the cortex has made it possible to map these areas.

But it has recently become apparent that information processing in the CVS is even more highly compartmentalized than was initially suspected. In fact, each highly specific area in the CVS appears to be further subdivided, resulting in not just area-specific but circuit-specific processing of all sensory and motor information. This means that a separate circuit—a unique mechanism—is responsible for the processing of each and every different type of sensory and motor information.

To illustrate this, let's take a look at our sense of motion. Not only is there a specific area (or areas) in the CVS that is responsible for processing all motion-related information entering the brain, but within that area there are a multitude of individual circuits—representative of separate and distinct mechanisms— each of which is responsible for processing a different type of motion. In other words, one circuit may be processing counterclockwise motion while another processes clockwise motion, and still another processes vertical motion, and so on. In addition, the quality of each and every motion is processed by a unique combination of circuits—one group of circuits processes the motion of a car, another group processes the motion of a boat, and so on.

To a great extent, the highly specific circuits of the inner-ear system function independently of one another. As a result, a disturbance or dysfunction in one circuit may have little or no effect on the performance of another circuit, regardless of the similarity in information they are processing. This explains why, for example, some individuals may get motion sick from vertical motion (such as the motion experienced when a roller coaster drops) and not from clockwise motion (such as the motion of the amusement ride the whip). It also explains why an individual may get carsick but not airsick.

But no circuit of the CVS is entirely independent. There are innumerable additional circuits responsible for interconnecting all of these highly specialized circuits so that the inner-ear system can function as an integrated whole. This integration accounts for the "spillover" effect sometimes observed when, for example, an individual conditioned to tolerate horizontal motion (such as the side-to-side rocking of a boat) becomes resistant to the disturbing effects of vertical motion with no further conditioning. Integration also accounts for the linkage observed when, for example, an individual is oversensitive to most forms of motion rather than just one particular form.

A Telephone Switchboard

To understand the concept of CVS integration it might be useful to think of the integration in a telephone switchboard. Because everything on a switchboard is interconnected, damage to the system can take many forms. Sometimes only one number may be malfunctioning (one cerebellar-vestibular circuit, such as the circuit that processes horizontal motion). Sometimes two adjacent numbers may be malfunctioning (the circuits processing horizontal *and* vertical motion). Sometimes two nonadjacent numbers may be malfunctioning (the circuits processing horizontal motion and ultraviolet light). Sometimes an entire section of the switchboard may be malfunctioning (all motion-processing circuits). And sometimes the entire switchboard may be malfunctioning (all sensory-processing circuits).

Furthermore, repairing one section of the switchboard may affect only that section or it may affect other sections as well . . . or even the entire switchboard (damage or repairs to one section of the CVS may affect just that section, other sections, or the entire CVS). It all depends upon the nature and extent of the dysfunction. We will see many examples of linkage, spillover, and circuit-specific dysfunction as we examine the many facets of phobic behavior in greater detail.

THE INNER-EAR SYSTEM AND ITS MANY ROLES

To summarize, the cerebellar-vestibular system (CVS)—our inner-ear system—is the processing center of the brain. More specifically, it constantly performs the following functions:

■ The CVS is our sensory processor. It filters and fine tunes all *sensory information* entering the brain—light, sound, motion, gravitational (electromagnetic) energy, chemical information, air pressure, etc. Therefore it is responsible for coordinating, controlling, and fine tuning our vision, hearing, balance, sense of direction, sense of motion, sense of altitude and depth, sense of smell, anxiety level, etc.
■ The CVS is our motor processor. It coordinates, controls, and fine tunes all *motor information* leaving the brain. Therefore it is responsible for guiding and coordinating our eyes, head, hands, feet, limbs, etc., as well as our various mental and physical functions (voluntary and involuntary) in time and space.

In the rest of Part III we'll examine how a breakdown in any of these processes can independently, or collectively, account for the development of phobic behavior.

Sensory Phobias:
An Overview

Balance-related phobias, motion-related phobias, compass-related phobias, visual and auditory phobias—all of these are *sensory* phobias. The origin of these sensory phobias can be traced to a breakdown in our sensory-processing center: the inner-ear system (CVS).

The role of the inner-ear system in the development of sensory phobias isn't difficult to understand if you think of the brain as a giant TV set with millions of different channels. The cerebrum, the thinking brain, would be the screen. This is where you actually see and understand the composite picture of all sensory information being sent to the brain—information being transmitted through various sensory channels. The CVS, on the other hand, would consist of the antenna, the channel selector, and the various knobs that help you to tune in and fine tune your picture.

In other words, it is the CVS's responsibility to selectively filter and regulate the flow of all sensory input through the different channels—to tune in and fine tune all vital sensory foreground information while simultaneously tuning out unimportant or distracting background information.

A BROKEN ANTENNA

Everyone knows what happens when the tuning mechanism on a television set is broken: you see drifting, double-imaging, blurring, static, volume fluctuations, horizontal or vertical scrambling, color loss, etc. Sometimes the screen even goes blank. In essence, the same thing happens in the brain when your sensory tuner—the inner-ear system—malfunctions: sensory input is over-filtered, underfiltered, scrambled, or even lost entirely.

As a result, your brain may suddenly be *starved* of vital sensory information, *confused* by scrambled (thus, useless) information, or *flooded* with far more sensory information than it can handle. You may not consciously realize that this is happening. But unconsciously your brain is under considerable, if not severe, stress.

Let's look at an example: the processing of motion input. It's a beautiful, sunny day and you are invited out on a friend's boat. As you leave the bay and enter the open ocean, you start to feel "different." Soon your stomach is doing flip-flops . . . you start to sweat . . . your heart starts to race. The boat continues to rock up and down. Suddenly you find yourself begging your host to turn back—though you're trying as hard as you can to control yourself, you know you are going to be sick any minute. Your host is fine. And so are the other people on the boat. Only you are getting motion sick. Why? Because your CVS is not processing motion properly. While everyone else feels fine, your brain is being flooded with motion input. Ultimately the brain cries out for help by triggering the motion-sickness response.

It is common knowledge that motion sickness is a by-product of a defective inner-ear system, not a defective stomach. In fact, all medications for motion sickness target the CVS, not the stomach. But motion is only one sensory input that is regulated by the inner-ear system. What about all of the others? What about light, gravity, sound, etc.? What happens when this sensory input is improperly processed?

THE FIGHT OR FLIGHT RESPONSE

When any type of sensory flooding, deprivation, or scrambling occurs, your brain has a very specific way of warning you that something is wrong. This reflex response—your automatic, unconscious, built-in alarm system—is known as the "fight or flight" response. The symptoms of this response are typically several, or all, of the following:

Waves of anxiety
A sense of dread
A skipping or racing heart
Tightness in the chest
Hyperventilating and/or difficulty breathing
Sweating
Shaking and/or trembling
Hot flushes and/or cold chills
Light-headedness
Stomach distress
Jelly legs*

If you have ever studied biology, you probably learned that this fight or flight response is your body's reaction to a known danger, such as a man with a gun, a house on fire, or extreme emotional stress. What you did not learn is that these symptoms are also the body's response to dangers we may not be conscious of—such as sensory flooding, sensory deprivation, or sensory scrambling.

All three of these sensory effects put severe physiological stress on the brain. Not surprisingly, the brain reacts: it trips the fight or flight alarm. In other words, whether the danger is known or unknown, the response is the same: an internal state of alarm.

AN INTERNAL ALARM

Thanks to the research pioneered by Walter Cannon and Hans Selye, we know that the fight or flight alarm is not an all or nothing response. On the contrary, the intensity of these symptoms can vary considerably.

A *one-alarm* fight or flight response, for example, may be nothing more than a slightly elevated breathing rate, increased perspiration, and a modest release of anxiety. Subjectively, this entire one-alarm response may simply feel like everyday anxiety.

A *two-* or *three-alarm* response might be characterized by

---

*Jelly legs is not a normal fight or flight symptom, but it is often present in Type 3 phobic behavior. The nature of this symptom is discussed in detail in Chapter 14.

substantial but seemingly manageable anxiety, further elevation in heartbeat and respiratory rate, stomach distress, light-headedness, and tension. These symptoms probably make you feel uncomfortable in your surroundings. They may even provoke mild fear, panicky feelings, and a desire to get away from or avoid whatever seems to be making you so anxious (be it a party, a dark room, your car, your job, your spouse, or whatever).

The symptoms of a *four-alarm* response are quite strong. They are collectively experienced as the emotion of *fear*, and they will make you want to escape from or avoid whatever is provoking them.

Finally, there is the full-blown *five-alarm* response. In a five-alarm response you are flooded with anxiety and overwhelmed by various other magnified fight or flight symptoms. This provokes more than just fear; it provokes *terror*. Suddenly you find yourself in the grip of severe, uncontrollable panic. You may think you are going insane, losing control, passing out, having a heart attack, or dying. The sensations vary from one individual to the next, but the terror is the same.

WHAT DETERMINES THE STRENGTH OF THE ALARM?

What determines whether the brain triggers a one-alarm response, a five-alarm response, or something in between? One important factor is the severity of the threat. In the case of sensory phobias, the threat is the physiological stress being placed on the brain by a malfunctioning sensory processor. The stronger the sensory flooding, scrambling, or deprivation effect, the greater will be the stress. The greater the stress, the greater will be the anxiety response. Hence, a small amount of sensory stress may trigger a one- or two-alarm response, while severe sensory stress may trigger a four- or five-alarm response.

In other words, different amounts of sensory stress produce different intensities of fight or flight symptoms. Therefore the difference between being ill at ease, anxious, frightened, or terrified to the point of outright panic merely reflects a difference in the amount of stress being placed on the brain by your malfunctioning inner-ear system. Although the milder anxiety states appear to have little similarity to the terrifying, full-blown, five-alarm response, they are all part of the same syndrome and are indicative of the same underlying *physiological* problem.

But this is only half of the story. The degree of the anxiety response also depends to a great extent on the proper functioning of the alarm itself. . . .

A BROKEN ALARM

The inner-ear system filters and regulates anxiety in much the same way it filters and regulates all other types of sensory information. As I have said before, anxiety is a physiochemical reaction, and all changes in body chemistry are monitored, at least in part, by the CVS.

When the anxiety-processing mechanism is malfunctioning—when our anxiety filter has "holes" in it—the brain may be unable to control and dampen anxiety buildup. As a result, the anxiety generated by a slight or moderate amount of sensory stress can snowball into a flood. In other words, when the anxiety-processing mechanism in the CVS is impaired, a one- or two-alarm response can escalate into a four- or five-alarm anxiety response.*

But what does any of this have to do with the fear of elevators, crowds, or telephones?

WHAT'S SO SCARY ABOUT PHOBIC TRIGGERS?

What is it about elevators, tall buildings, windowless rooms, bridges, tunnels, and noisy restaurants that scares some people

*An impaired CVS anxiety filter can also *over*filter anxiety signals. Hence, even the most severe stress on the brain may elicit a minimal anxiety response or *no* anxiety response. This overfiltering can result in antiphobic behavior—a fearlessness that is abnormal and often dangerous. This CVS-induced fearlessness (as well as a CVS-related failure to imprint anxiety or guilt) may even be at the root of various sociopathic and psychopathic disorders.

to death? Why are fight or flight symptoms triggered every time they confront or even think about these seemingly innocuous objects and situations? Are these things really threatening you? Are they symbolically threatening because they trigger repressed sexual and/or aggressive conflicts? Or is their presence merely a coincidence?

The association between these so-called triggers and the onset of fight or flight symptoms is no coincidence. These triggers are responsible for bringing on symptoms of phobic behavior. They really *are* threatening you. Not because the bridge is going to collapse. Not because the tunnel has a leak. Not because you are going to jump out of a high window. These sensory triggers are threatening you because they are overloading the brain with sensory information, depriving the brain of sensory information, or confusing the brain with scrambled information. Let's examine each possibility.

Sensory Overload

The inner-ear system—your sensory tuner—is like a collection of filters that control the flow of sensory information entering the brain. When this system is impaired there may be holes in one, several, or all of these sensory filters. If the spillage of information through these holes is severe, the brain may be overwhelmed by a flood of sensory information. When the brain is under "sensory siege," it cries out for help: it trips the fight or flight alarm. This results in anxiety, fear, or even total panic (depending upon the severity of the flood and the condition of the alarm).

Severe sensory spillage is most likely to occur in an environment in which there is an abundance of sensory information. Typical overloading environments include: a rocking boat (an abundance of motion), a busy intersection (an abundance of noise, visual distractions, etc.), a noisy restaurant, a floodlit stage, a strong sun, a crowded party, a noisy classroom, a dance club, a busy highway, an accelerating airplane (excessive motion), a moving escalator, or a crowded supermarket.

From now on I will refer to these overloading environments

as *flooding environments*, because they literally flood the brain with sensory information. Although these flooding environments may not overwhelm an individual with a normal, healthy CVS, they often prove to be too much for the individual with an impaired CVS.

When sensory flooding triggers anxiety, fear, or panic, you will feel compelled to escape from these flooding environments. This is no accident—it is your body's way of keeping you out of danger (or perhaps, more accurately, what your brain perceives as danger). As an individual, you may be sensitive to one, several, or all flooding environments . . . or even none. Furthermore, your degree of sensitivity to each environment may vary considerably. The reasons for this will be discussed later in this chapter.

Sensory Deprivation

When the inner-ear system is impaired, sensory filters may be too "thick." These thick filters stop important information from reaching the brain, creating a sensory shortage. Sometimes this shortage is so severe that the brain is literally starved of vital sensory information. This can trip the fight or flight alarm, bringing on anxiety, fear, or even total panic (depending upon the severity of the shortage and the condition of the alarm).

When is the fight or flight alarm most likely to be tripped? When you are in a sensory-deprivation environment. Typical deprivation environments include: elevators, deserted streets, empty highways, small windowless rooms, the dark, underwater, the enclosed cabin of an airplane, empty buildings, tunnels (especially a long tunnel where there is no end in sight), closets, underground subway stations, or empty parking lots.

From now on I will refer to these environments as *shielding environments*, because they physically shield, or block out, vital sensory information. Although the deprivation effects of these shielding environments may not upset an individual with a normal, healthy CVS, they often prove to be far more than an individual with an impaired CVS can handle. It is no coincidence that these very shielding environments are typically referred to

as claustrophobic environments. Shielding effects provoke claustrophobic feelings. In other words, claustrophobic anxiety is often
the fight or flight anxiety triggered by a shielding environment.
It has a *physiological* basis.

When sensory deprivation triggers anxiety, fear, or panic, you
will feel compelled to avoid or escape from these claustrophobic
shielding environments. As I said before, this is your body's way
of protecting you, even though you may not realize it at the time.
Again, note that as an individual you may be affected by one,
several, or all shielding environments. Furthermore, your degree
of sensitivity to each environment may vary considerably.

Sensory Scrambling

Sometimes an impaired inner-ear system scrambles incoming
sensory information in the same way a broken TV antenna scrambles incoming TV signals. But the brain can't use this scrambled
information. Therefore even though sensory information is available, there is a shortage of viable information.

In a shielding environment this shortage is even more pronounced, and the brain may be starved of vital sensory input. In
a flooding environment scrambling effects are magnified, resulting in severe sensory confusion. In either case, the brain may
cry out for help by tripping the fight or flight alarm. When sensory
scrambling brings on anxiety, fear, or panic, you will feel compelled to avoid or escape from the flooding and shielding environments that appear to have triggered these feelings.

TRIPPING YOUR ALARM

Every sensory trigger—every flooding and shielding environment
—is somewhat different. Each therefore has a slightly different
effect on the brain. There are three principal factors that determine
whether or not a particular sensory trigger will actually trip your
fight or flight alarm:

The Intensity of the Trigger

The greater the intensity of a particular trigger, the greater is the flooding or shielding effect. The stronger the flooding or shielding effect, the greater is the stress. And the greater the stress, the greater is the likelihood that your fight or flight alarm will be tripped. In other words, one hundred strobe lights have a much stronger flooding effect than one strobe light, and are therefore far more likely to trip your alarm. Similarly, a long underground tunnel has a much stronger shielding effect than a short aboveground tunnel, and is therefore more likely to trip your alarm. And so on.

The Nature and Extent of Your Inner-Ear Dysfunction

Since the nature and extent of CVS dysfunctions differ, however slightly, from individual to individual, so does the sensitivity to sensory flooding, scrambling, and deprivation. The greater the sensitivity of a particular individual, the easier it is for his or her fight or flight alarm to be tripped. Therefore while one person's alarm may be tripped by a 1000-watt floodlight, another's may be tripped by a 100-watt bulb . . . while one person's alarm may be tripped by a pitch-black room, another's may be tripped by a dimly lit restaurant . . . while one person's alarm may be tripped by a blaring siren, another's may be tripped by a noisy party . . . etc.

Furthermore, since an inner-ear dysfunction can affect one, several, or all sensory-processing circuits, each sensory filter in a given individual (visual, auditory, gravitational, etc.) may have a different sensitivity to flooding, scrambling, or deprivation. Hence you may have a high tolerance for bright lights and loud noises but a low tolerance for tunnels and heights . . . or you may have a low tolerance for loud noises but a high tolerance for bright lights, tunnels, and heights . . . etc. It all depends on the nature and extent of your CVS dysfunction.

Your Ability to Compensate

Your brain is often capable of compensating for many of the disturbing effects of sensory flooding, scrambling, and deprivation—adapting, in a sense, to the inner-ear dysfunction. If, for example, electromagnetic-compass information is in short supply, your brain may compensate by using your eyes to help you orient yourself. If motion input is underfiltered, resulting in an oversensitivity to motion, your brain may automatically compensate by making you focus on nonmoving objects, such as the horizon (many motion-sick individuals are quite familiar with this process).

If these compensatory mechanisms are adequate, they can prevent the tripping of the fight or flight alarm. But if they are inadequate, weakened, or disrupted, an alarm may be tripped. Just as CVS dysfunction varies from one individual to the next, so does the ability to compensate for this dysfunction.

It is the interaction of the three factors detailed above that determines whether you as an individual will be affected by one, several, or all types of flooding and shielding environments. It also determines whether you will be affected by one, several, or all variations of a particular type of environment.

A SUDDEN TERROR

Flooding and shielding environments create so much sensory stress that the brain perceives them as being no less dangerous than other, more obvious threats. In other words, to a brain with a damaged CVS, an elevator can be every bit as threatening as a snarling Doberman . . . a crowded room can be every bit as threatening as an armed assailant . . . and all will elicit the same fight or flight response. In essence, it doesn't matter whether or not you truly are in danger. If your malfunctioning inner-ear system is making your brain "feel" as though you are, it will react accordingly.

There is only one problem. When you see a Doberman, you know why you're afraid . . . you know why you're experiencing these fight or flight symptoms. In fact, you are grateful for the rush of adrenaline that brings on these symptoms because it helps you to either fight the danger or take flight. But when your body has the same reaction to an elevator, a tunnel, or a staircase, the onset of these symptoms makes no sense. You don't know there is a malfunction in your inner-ear system. You don't know that these triggers are aggravating that malfunction. All you know is that the sight of an elevator, a tunnel, or a staircase is throwing your body into a state of alarm.

Total Panic

When the onset of fight or flight symptoms is sudden and severe, you may be overcome with terror. You may actually feel that you are going to lose control and start screaming at any minute, or that you are about to pass out; you may think you are having a heart attack . . . or a nervous breakdown . . . or that you are dying. Usually you don't know what to think. All you know is that you are scared to death.

You panic. Suddenly you have to take flight. You *have* to get out of the elevator, pull your car off the road, or run out of that crowded room or supermarket . . . you *have* to get out of the tunnel or off the bridge . . . you *have* to get to an open window or door. *You have no choice*. You must get away from those terrifying triggers.

For purposes of clarification, I will refer to this trigger-induced five-alarm panic response as a *panic episode*. This is to temporarily distinguish it from a panic attack, which has been defined as the spontaneous appearance of panic in the absence of any obvious trigger. (This is discussed in detail later in this chapter.)

Taking Flight

Panic physically forces you to escape from or avoid the triggers that aggravate your malfunctioning inner-ear system. This is no accident. The fight or flight response is a primitive adaptive mechanism designed to get you out of trouble. Since you cannot fight a bridge or a tunnel (at least, not in the conventional sense), you are literally forced to take flight. Furthermore, you don't take flight in just any random direction; you head for help. Help, in this case, is anything that will stabilize you: an open window, perhaps, where the brain can get more sensory information, or a protected environment, such as your home, where the brain isn't overloaded with sensory information. Under the circumstances, panic is really very useful. Not only does it drive you away from danger (or, perhaps more accurately, what your brain perceives as danger) but it encourages you to find help.

A Variety of Responses

Obviously not all phobics suffer from acute panic episodes. Many phobics merely experience fear, tremendous anxiety, or panicky feelings when they confront or think about certain triggers. These varying responses to an identical threat reflect individual differences in the nature and extent of the inner-ear dysfunction (and the ability or inability to compensate). Because of these differences some individuals may feel extremely uncomfortable in elevators, some may feel terribly anxious, some may be frightened, and some may panic—but all suffer for the same reason.

FROM FEAR TO PHOBIA

When a trigger provokes anxiety, fear, or panic, you will probably do anything to avoid confronting it. If the trigger is an elevator, you will take the stairs; if the trigger is a supermarket, you'll have your groceries delivered; if the trigger is a car, you'll stop driving. This is, of course, typical phobic behavior.

Sometimes, for reasons of necessity, disbelief, frustration, or whatever, you may try to confront your triggers and defy the development of phobic behavior. Some individuals are indeed able to overcome their fears by confronting them. In fact, some overcompensate by developing fearless or counterphobic behavior. But many who try to look fear in the mouth quickly discover that anxiety and other fight or flight symptoms set in faster and stronger each time. Sooner or later (usually sooner), most of these individuals are forced to retreat, even if it means changing their entire life-style . . . which it often does.

WHY DO PHOBIAS USUALLY GET WORSE?

This question can be answered with one word: *imprinting*. When panic and/or anxiety strike, the frightening details of the experience are imprinted in the memory banks of your brain. This memory reinforcement, or learning process, only makes it easier for your brain to panic the next time.

Not surprisingly, the process of imprinting has always been noticed in relation to motion sickness. Many motion-sensitive individuals who get sick on boats can actually become sick just by smelling a sea breeze or thinking about the motion of a boat. If this motion-related response can be imprinted, it only makes sense that other sensory fight or flight responses can also be imprinted.

If your brain has learned its lesson well, the anticipation of confronting a trigger can actually flood the body with anxiety. This anticipatory anxiety is psychologically triggered. It is provoked by memories of frightening experiences—memories that have been imprinted in the brain. But *psycho*logically triggered anticipatory anxiety feels just like *physio*logically triggered anxiety. Put the two together, and your fear is much stronger. In fact, some phobics can have a full-fledged panic episode from the flood of anticipatory anxiety alone. Not surprisingly, this makes you feel as though your phobias are getting worse.

When anxiety is physiologically triggered by a malfunction in the inner-ear system, I call it *primary* anxiety. When it is psychologically triggered, I call it *secondary* anxiety. I will use these two terms periodically throughout the rest of the book.

"I've Always Been Afraid"

When phobias develop in childhood, patients frequently feel as though they've always known what scares them. This instinct is a result of early imprinting. If you were sensitized to some trigger(s) when you were very young, you might not remember that, at the time, this trigger made you anxious, frightened, or panicky. But it did—just ask your mother. Once your fears have been imprinted, regardless of how young you might have been, you have learned your phobia. After that, you instinctively know the triggers you are afraid of without having to confront them directly.

WHEN PHOBIAS MULTIPLY

Perhaps the most frightening aspect of phobic behavior is the way phobias often multiply. No sooner do you have your first panic episode in an elevator than you find yourself having a second, similar episode in a tunnel . . . then in a movie theater . . . then in a dark room . . . etc. Before long, you feel as though no place is really safe.

This multiplication does not occur in a random fashion. It follows a pattern determined by your first panic episode, which in itself was predetermined by the nature of your inner-ear dysfunction. Once you have had your first panic episode, anything that reminds you of that episode can trigger a flood of anticipatory anxiety. If, for example, you panicked in a candlelit restaurant, anticipatory anxiety could subsequently be triggered by another dark restaurant, darkness, candles, food, an odor, a waitress, etc.

But many of these "reminders" (conditioned triggers) also have flooding or shielding effects. Although they may never have troubled you in the past (at least, not significantly), these mild flooding or shielding effects, compounded by your anticipatory anxiety, may now trigger a five-alarm panic response. Anticipatory anxiety has dramatically heightened your susceptibility.

In fact, if the flood of anticipatory anxiety is strong enough, all reminders of your previous panic episode—regardless of whether or not they have flooding and/or shielding effects—can trigger severe panic. As a result, you may develop any number of new phobias, all of which are associated with your original panic episode. Clearly, your phobias have taken on a life of their own.

A Sixth Sense

It may not be long before you develop a sixth sense: an ability to predict whether or not a particular situation will make you panic. This sixth sense is really just another by-product of imprinting. The memories of your previous experiences have made you exceedingly sensitive to any reminder of those experiences. You feel that you intuitively know ahead of time what will make you panic, even if you have no direct, conscious experience from which to judge. These premonitions are easily verified. For if you think you are going to panic, your anticipatory anxiety will increase and you probably will panic. You have created a self-fulfilling prophecy.

Agoraphobia: The End of the Line

As your phobias multiply, the memories of your frightening panic episodes, and the fear of future episodes, are sometimes enough to fill you with chronic anticipatory anxiety. In essence, your brain is constantly afraid of being afraid. In this hypersensitive condition, virtually any flooding or shielding environment, however mild, can trigger another panic episode—the combination of anticipatory anxiety and sensory flooding and/or shielding is just too great. The result: more and more phobias.

If this snowball continues to roll out of control, it may not be long before the only place you feel safe in is your own home. And even this, at times, is uncertain. This chronic fear that makes so many phobics prisoners in their own homes is commonly referred to as agoraphobia. Although many people think that agoraphobia is a fear of wide-open spaces, it is far more than that. It is a hypersensitivity to fear . . . an obsession with fear . . . a fear of fear itself that is a horrible, convoluted consequence of a physiologically based problem.

A TENUOUS BALANCE

Even the worst phobic does not suffer from crippling panic twenty-four hours a day. On the contrary, phobics are often capable of suppressing anxiety and other phobic symptoms, and keeping their phobic behavior under control. For some, this compensatory process requires little effort. But for others it is exhausting. These individuals feel as though their lives—especially their sanity—is in a state of tenuous balance.

Many of my patients tell me, "Everything gets worse when I'm tired." These patients are compulsive about their sleep and terrified of losing sleep. For them, fatigue is the enemy. There is, of course, an explanation for this. One of the primary methods of compensating for an inner-ear dysfunction is through increased concentration. Concentration can help you to overcome visual problems, balance problems, compass problems, etc. But as you grow increasingly tired, you become less and less capable of maintaining a high level of concentration. If you get too tired, your weakened powers of concentration may be incapable of adequately compensating for your CVS dysfunction. This *de*-compensation can give rise to phobic symptoms.

DECOMPENSATION

Concentration is only one form of compensation. The brain has many ways of overcoming an inner-ear dysfunction—both consciously* and unconsciously. But a variety of factors can interfere with this compensation process and bring on phobic symptoms. Once you have become phobic, you are usually even more vulnerable to these various destabilizing factors. Furthermore, there are a number of additional factors that can interfere with your ability to compensate for and suppress preexisting phobic symptoms. Any of these factors can precipitate or intensify your phobic symptoms. These decompensatory factors include:

Fatigue
Alcohol (including hangover effects)

---

*Some people consciously overcompensate. A man who takes up sky diving to overcome his fear of heights is overcompensating, as is a woman who takes flying lessons to overcome her fear of flying. Though overcompensation does help some people to overcome their phobias, attempts to overcompensate often aggravate inner-ear problems.

Illness
Physical stress (prolonged strenuous exercise)
Temperature changes
Barometric pressure changes

PANIC ATTACKS VS. PANIC EPISODES

Certain individuals appear to panic in the absence of any visible trigger. Clinicians have labeled this seemingly spontaneous phenomenon a *panic attack*, thereby distinguishing it diagnostically and therapeutically from panic episodes provoked by an obvious trigger.

Some clinicians suggest that this spontaneous panic is due to a chemical imbalance in the brain, though they are uncertain exactly what the chemical(s) is or how it acts. Furthermore, they suggest that phobias develop when an individual in the grip of spontaneous, chemically induced panic associates this panic with the situation he or she happens to be in at the time. In other words, if you spontaneously panic in a restaurant, you will develop a fear of that restaurant and perhaps of all restaurants. This association, according to these clinicians, is merely coincidental and has no realistic basis.

Although this view of panic and phobias is interesting, clinical evidence suggests that it is somewhat incomplete and somewhat in error. For one thing, many of these seemingly spontaneous panic attacks have proved to be nothing more than regular panic episodes with subtle, easily overlooked external triggers, such as odors, noise, or fluorescent lights. While the rest of these panic attacks may in a sense be internally triggered by a chemical imbalance, it is crucial to recognize that the CVS is the underlying culprit. In other words, a sharp fluctuation in hormone levels, or some other shift in the chemical balance of the brain, is destabilizing an impaired inner-ear system.

Once the inner-ear system is destabilized, the fight or flight alarm can be tripped by any flooding or shielding environment. Since virtually all environments have some sensory flooding or shielding effects, all are capable of affecting this highly sensitized, destabilized CVS (depending upon just how vulnerable it has become). Consequently, you may spontaneously panic anywhere—even in your own home. Furthermore, once this problem is compounded by anticipatory anxiety you become even more susceptible to panic.

Now that you are familiar with the many factors that can destabilize an impaired inner-ear system, this explanation probably sounds quite reasonable, if not obvious. But even more important, clinical evidence clearly supports this theory. Virtually all of my patients who have suffered from these spontaneous panic attacks have tested positive for CVS dysfunction. In fact, these test results contributed to the development of this theory—not vice versa. No doubt, the careful diagnosis of other panic-attack victims will yield similar results and hopefully put an end to the existing scientific misunderstanding.

A LIFE OF THEIR OWN

When anticipatory anxiety and other psychological factors become a part of the physiologically based phobic disorder, phobias quickly take on a life of their own—a life that is only as limited as the imagination of the individual.

Because phobic problems are constantly reinforced, both physiologically and psychologically, they are far more likely to get worse with time than to get better. This is clearly illustrated in the cases presented thus far. To minimize the psychological complications surrounding this physiologically based disorder, it is extremely important that all phobics receive proper medical treatment as quickly as possible.

The Type 3 mechanisms I have discussed thus far, though somewhat complicated, are still not complete. In the following chapter, I will expand and elaborate upon these mechanisms until they are capable of accounting for virtually every manifestation of sensory phobias.

CHAPTER 13

Sensory Phobias:
A Closer Look

To refine our understanding of sensory phobias, we need to take a closer look at sensory processing in the inner-ear system.

Any sensory processing malfunction can influence the development of phobic behavior. But the majority of sensory phobias can be linked to the improper filtering and/or fine tuning of gravity (electromagnetic energy), motion, light, sound, proprioceptive information,* and, of course, anxiety. As you examine the various types of sensory phobias in detail, the role of this sensory misprocessing will hopefully become obvious.

COMPASS-RELATED PHOBIAS

In 1957, Jakob von Uexkull, the famous biologist, described the vestibular system of a fish in the following words:

> It is apparently destined to act as a compass—not as a compass that always points to the North, but as a compass for the fish's own "front door." If all the movements of the whole body are analyzed and marked according to three directions in the canals, then the animal must be back at its starting point whenever it has reduced the nervous markings to zero as it moves about.
>
> There is no doubt that a compass for the front door is a necessary spawning ground. Determination of the front door by visual cues in visual space is insufficient in most cases, since the entrance must be found even if its aspect has changed.

---

* Proprioceptors are the sensory receptors located throughout the body that constantly keep the brain apprised of the location of various body parts.

As I have said before, the human vestibular system also acts like a compass. This internal compass uses gravitational information (electromagnetic energy) to help you orient yourself in space. As a result, you can intuitively determine left from right, up from down, and front from back. But if the inner-ear system is impaired, gravitational input may not be properly filtered and fine tuned. As a result, your brain may not be receiving proper compass readings.

This "gravitational deprivation" or "gravitational scrambling" can trip your fight or flight alarm, bringing on anxiety and various related symptoms. In addition, you may experience any or all broken-compass symptoms, including: disorientation, confusion, a floating sensation, spaciness, light-headedness, feelings of unreality or disassociation, and dizziness.

Compensating for a Broken Compass

A broken inner-ear compass does not always trip the fight or flight alarm (if it did, you would be frightened all of the time). It can often be compensated for.

If there is a shortage of viable gravitational information, the brain will try to compensate by using visual information (the landscape, the horizon, etc.), auditory information, proprioceptive information and/or memory cues to help you get your bearings. If this enables you to orient yourself, you may never be more than vaguely aware of any problem. But if your ability to compensate is for some reason reduced, or if the damage to your inner-ear compass is further aggravated, frightening broken-compass and fight or flight symptoms may suddenly surface.

Two Reasons to Panic

Basically, there are two types of environments that can destabilize your orientation mechanisms and bring on phobic symptoms:

Shielding Environments

In an elevator, tunnel, underground subway station, window-less room, or similar environment, your brain is being physically deprived of many of the visual and auditory cues it may have been using to compensate for your damaged compass. This sudden shortage of compensatory information can aggravate your preexisting compass problem considerably.

If the brain can't make up for this additional loss of sensory information, both the generalized fight or flight symptoms and the more specific, broken-compass symptoms may surface. Suddenly, you feel as though you *have* to get out of the elevator, get out of the tunnel, get out of the subway station, or get to a window or door.

Flooding Environments

In a sensory flooding environment, such as a noisy, crowded room, a busy highway, or a floodlit stage, your eyes and ears are overwhelmed with information. If the brain was depending on visual or auditory cues to compensate for a faulty compass, a flooding environment could seriously disrupt this process.

How, for example, can you use your eyes to help you orient yourself when they are practically being blinded by stage lights, or bombarded by cars, signs, lines, and other highway distractions? Therefore, even though you are in a flooding environment, your brain is being deprived of the information necessary to compensate for your faulty inner-ear compass. Once again, a shortage of viable gravitational information, compounded by a shortage of necessary compensatory input, triggers the onset of compass-related and fight or flight symptoms. Suddenly you feel as though you *have* to leave the party or stage, stop the car, etc.

The Woman in the Elevator

Let me give a specific example to help clarify these points. A woman with an impaired inner-ear compass gets into an elevator. When the doors close, vital sensory input (visual, auditory, and possibly electromagnetic) is cut off. The sudden shortage of information makes it far more difficult for this woman's brain to adequately compensate for her faulty inner-ear compass. This aggravates her problem.

Suddenly she feels disoriented, light-headed, disassociated, frightened, and perhaps even panic-stricken. Her brain, being starved of sensory information, has tripped the alarm. These feelings may not subside until she gets out of the elevator and into an environment where more sensory information is available.

With this in mind, consider the compass-related phobias of the following patients:

Anna R.

Anna has a compass-related fear of elevators. She explains:

My main fear of elevators is that I will get lost when I get out. I feel misplaced . . . disoriented . . . especially when I am unfamiliar with where I am going. If I have been there before, then I visualize some point—like a water fountain—and feel better about the whole experience. I am also afraid that I won't get out at the right stop. That means I have to keep going up and down until I find it again. This scares me even more.

Andrew S.

Andrew came to my office after experiencing the following compass-related panic episode:

One Sunday afternoon I decided to catch a movie. Usually I go to the movies at night, and when you walk out of the dark theater you expect it to be dark outside. But it wasn't . . . it was a bright, sunny afternoon. For some reason, this made me feel disoriented. All of a sudden I couldn't remember where I had parked my car. As I walked up and down the street looking for it, I began to panic. I thought I'd never find it. I became frantic. The town was so quiet . . . like a ghost town. Nothing seemed to be real. My pulse was racing . . . my hands were clammy. I felt like I was stuck in this surreal ghost town and couldn't get out. Then I spotted my car. I ran to it, jammed the key into the door, opened it up, and practically collapsed onto the front seat. Then I raced out of that town like there was no tomorrow.

Robert B.

Although Robert loves to scuba dive, he has given up the sport. It seems that he once became severely disoriented during a deep dive, panicked, and almost drowned. He recalled: "When I started panicking, I tried to swim up to the surface, but I was so frightened and disoriented that I started swimming further down." Fortunately, the buildup of pressure on Robert's ears ultimately made him realize that he was swimming in the wrong direction. "I'm lucky to be alive," he told me.

Many CVS-impaired individuals become disoriented when swimming underwater, even when their eyes are wide open. This is no doubt due to the pronounced shielding effects of an under-water environment. CVS-related disorientation is often at the root of swimming phobias, drowning phobias, and other water-related phobias.

Getting Specific

Due to the highly circuit-specific functioning of the CVS (see Chapter 11), each different type of shielding or flooding environment can have a different effect on the brain. Therefore, depending upon the nature and extent of your particular dysfunction (and your ability or inability to compensate), you may be sensitive to one, several, or all environments known to affect the internal compass.

In addition, every type of shielding and flooding environment has many variations within that type. There are small elevators, large elevators, fast elevators, slow elevators, glass elevators, metal elevators, empty elevators, crowded elevators, or any combination thereof; there are 200-watt strobes, 1000-watt strobes, red strobes, blue strobes, alternating strobes, sequential strobes, or any combination thereof.

Because the inner-ear system is so highly circuit-specific, each variation can also have a different effect on the brain. The nature and extent of your particular dysfunction (as well as your ability or inability to compensate) will determine whether or not you are affected by one, several, or all variations.

Circuit specificity explains why one man may be sensitive to all bridges, tunnels and elevators, another sensitive to all bridges and tunnels, but only *glass* elevators, another sensitive to dark tunnels, slow elevators, and all bridges, and yet another only sensitive to long, brightly lit tunnels. The number and combination of mechanisms is infinite and therefore the possible manifestations of phobic behavior are infinite.

BALANCE-RELATED PHOBIAS

It has been clearly established that the inner-ear system acts like an internal gyroscope. This gyroscope uses proprioceptive information and gravitational (electromagnetic) information detected in the inner ear to provide you with your intuitive sense of balance. But if any part of the CVS is impaired, gravitational and/or proprioceptive input may not be properly filtered and fine tuned. As a result, your internal gyroscope may be thrown off kilter.

A broken internal gyroscope can trip the fight or flight alarm and also bring on any or all of the following symptoms: dizziness, light-headedness, fainting, floating sensations, an "off-balance" or "off-center" feeling, a magnetic tug from below, spinning or whirling sensations, a feeling that you are about to fall, tipping, swaying, or falling.

Compensating for a Broken Gyroscope

A malfunction in the inner-ear gyroscope does not always trip the fight or flight alarm. Often the brain is able to compensate by using visual and auditory information to establish and maintain your sense of balance. For example, your brain may stabilize you by fixing your eyes on the horizon, or on various upright objects such as a telephone pole, a house, or the person beside you.

This visual compensation is usually a reflexive response; you are not consciously aware that your brain is using visual information to maintain a sense of balance (though if you closed your eyes, you might find out). In fact, if compensation is adequate, you may never be more than vaguely aware that you have an imbalance problem. But a broken gyroscope leaves you vulnerable, and your sense of balance can be destabilized:

- When a *shielding* environment (such as an elevator or an empty street) deprives you of vital compensatory information and/or vital gravitational information that is already in short supply.
- When a *flooding* environment (such as a noisy, strobe-lit dance floor) overwhelms your visual or auditory filter with extraneous, irrelevant, or distracting information, rendering you unable to compensate for your malfunctioning gyroscope.

In either case, destabilization of your balance mechanism will bring on various broken-gyroscope symptoms and trip the fight or flight alarm.

Analyzing the Fear of Heights

Think about what would happen to you on the rooftop of a tall building if your internal gyroscope was malfunctioning. If you looked beside or behind you, there might be another person or object on the roof to fix your eyes on and use to maintain your sense of balance. If you looked straight ahead, there might be other rooftops nearby to provide your eyes with the compensatory visual information required to keep you stabilized. But if you looked down, there is only a vast empty space, with the ground far, far below.

Although you might not think of a rooftop as a deprivation environment, in this case it is: your eyes are being deprived of the visual information your brain needs to compensate for a faulty gyroscope. Without this necessary information to stabilize you, you feel off-balance . . . magnetically drawn to the ground below . . . capable of falling to your knees, or off the roof at any moment. You may even feel that you want to jump. Suddenly you're terrified.

Many people don't have to look down from a rooftop in order to be frightened. They need only be on a rooftop or think about being on one. It all depends upon the nature and extent of the dysfunction in your internal gyroscope and your ability or inability to compensate for it.

Analyzing the Fear of Wide-Open Spaces

A similar reaction can occur when you are standing in a wide-open field, a vacant parking lot, or a big, empty street. As you look around, there is nothing but empty space—no compensatory information in the immediate vicinity for your eyes to focus on and use to maintain a sense of balance. As you search frantically for any helpful visual cues, fight or flight symptoms and balance-related symptoms set in. Suddenly you're terrified. You may feel that you're going to fall down at any moment and never be able to get up, or pass out, or even go crazy. If you are standing in an empty street, you may run into a store; if you're standing in a parking lot, you may cling to a wall or a fence and inch your way to your car; if you're in an open field, you may get on your hands and knees and crawl out. Whatever the situation, it's a nightmare.

Vicky J. has a fear of empty parking lots, open fields, and other wide-open spaces that is codetermined by imbalance and disorientation problems. She recalled an episode from her childhood that frightens her to this day:

I was around five years old. I was playing on the lawn of a neighbor about six houses from my house. When I decided to leave, I looked around for the direction of my home. But all I could see on both sides were more big lawns going endlessly in a long row. I suddenly became overwhelmed and didn't know where I was or where to go. Panic set in, and I became so gripped with fear that my legs fell from under me. I couldn't move them, which frightened me even more. Then I lost my voice and couldn't scream for help. I felt as though I was in a terrible nightmare and couldn't wake up.

In an effort to control my terror I thrashed my arms about so I could turn the upper part of my body around. After I managed to turn over on my stomach, I saw someone off in the distance who appeared to be my little sister. In a desperate attempt to reach her I crawled on my elbows, dragging my legs behind inch by inch across several neighbors' lawns. I kept focusing on her, determined with every ounce of my being that I would reach her. When I finally got close enough to see that it was really her, my fear melted away.

Analyzing the Fear of Stairs

Consider one more environment that can destabilize your balance mechanism: a long flight of stairs, such as the giant staircases that lead to underground subway stations. For many phobics, walking up a long flight of stairs is not nearly as threatening as walking down. Why? For one thing, when you go up steps you're going against gravity, but when you go down, you're going with gravity. This makes you feel as though you're more capable of falling. But this isn't the only reason.

When you walk up steps, there are other steps directly in front of you to fix your eyes on and use to stabilize your malfunctioning gyroscope. But when you go down a long flight of steps, your eyes are forced to look either at the large, wide-open space between you and the ground—a deprivation effect—or at the hypnotic pattern formed by the endless flight of stairs—a flooding effect. Either way, your eyes are deprived of the information necessary to compensate for a malfunctioning gyroscope. Soon fight or flight as well as balance-related symptoms set in, and you find yourself holding on to the banister for dear life. You may even have to sit on the stairs and work your way down step by step.

Gail M.

Gail suffers from a common balance-related fear of heights. She told me the following:

Several years ago my husband and I took the family to Chicago. My little girl begged me to go with her to the top of the Sears Tower. I hadn't been up high in a building for years. But for some dumb reason I agreed to go with her. What a mistake! Just one look through those giant glass windows and I was finished. I wanted to get down on my hands and knees and crawl around. There just wasn't anywhere to look that didn't make me dizzy. After about a minute I pleaded with my daughter to go back down. She must have sensed my terror, because it was one of the few times she didn't give me an argument.

I used to love to ski, but as soon as I got good enough to go on the better slopes, I gave it up. I'll never forget the time I was on a giant chair lift. I felt as if I would fall off into oblivion. By the time I got to the top of the mountain I was totally drained. Actually, once I got to the top I wasn't scared . . . it was just getting there, and having to look at the ground so far below.

Carla R.

Carla has numerous balance-related fears, including a fear of horses, steps, bridges, and gangplanks. She told me:

I can climb up a tree without difficulty because there are lots of branches to hold onto. But when I look down from a horse, it's like there is somebody there saying, "Come on down . . . fall right away and get it over with." I also have difficulty with bridges and gangplanks, like you find on a boat. I feel as if they're moving, not me. I just know I'm going to fall. I don't even like standing in a room when there is no wall to lean on.

Matt S.

Analysis of Matt's fear of bridges and heights revealed an underlying gyroscope malfunction. He commented:

When I'm being driven over a bridge I have to get down on the floor of the car. You can't imagine how humiliating that is for a grown man. And heights? Forget it. I can't look out of a window without feeling that I'm going to fall. I know I'm not going to, but I feel like I am. It's almost as though there's a voice in my head telling me to jump. It's so frightening it gives me nightmares.

Suzanne K.

Suzanne has a balance-related fear of bridges. She related the following story to me during her examination:

> I was driving my little sister to the train station, and I hadn't been there in so long I'd forgotten that you had to drive over this bridge to get there. About halfway to the station, I remembered. I immediately started to stiffen. My mind raced to figure out some other way to get there but I knew there wasn't any. By the time I reached the bridge I was frozen stiff . . . my heart was pounding like mad . . . I was soaked with perspiration. I didn't know where to look. If I looked ahead, there was this vast, open space . . . this void. If I looked down, I could see houses and cars far below. Everything made me dizzy. I was sure that I was going to drive over the edge at any minute. It was as if I was being pulled over. I almost felt like I was falling. By the time I got off that bridge I was so shaken up I thought I would collapse. I had to call a friend to meet me at the station and drive me home.

Because sensory processing is so highly circuit-specific, an individual with a malfunctioning inner-ear gyroscope may be affected by one, several, or all types and variations of shielding and flooding environments known to affect our sense of balance. It all depends upon the nature and extent of the CVS malfunction and your ability or inability to compensate.

VISUAL PHOBIAS

The inner-ear system filters and fine tunes all visual information. If this system is impaired, you may be hypersensitive to any or all types of visual flooding and deprivation. This hypersensitivity can lead to the triggering of fight or flight symptoms. Any or all of the following can have visual flooding effects: the intense light of the sun, bright lights, fluorescent lights, certain colors, and any flickering, blurring, or hypnotic visual patterns (strobe lights, candlelight, a passing train, moving cars on a highway, oncoming headlights, lines and signs on a highway, cables on a bridge, lights in a tunnel, wallpaper patterns, floor patterns, food displays, and so on). Typical visual-deprivation environments include: the dark, an empty street, a deserted parking lot, a great height, a room without windows, etc. Depending upon the nature and extent of your dysfunction, you may be affected by one, several, or all types of visual flooding and deprivation.

Two Vision-Related Problems

It is important to recognize that the improper processing of visual information plays two roles in the development of phobic behavior:

- It accounts for the development of "pure" visual phobias, such as the fear of bright lights,* the fear of fluorescent lights, and the fear of certain colors.
- It accounts for the appearance of compass, balance, and other sensory problems normally kept in check by visual compensation.

In other words, visual flooding or deprivation effects often trigger anxiety because they are destabilizing other inner-ear problems usually compensated for with visual information. Although the visual effect is provoking the fear, the real problem can be traced to one or several faulty inner-ear mechanisms.

Visual Tracking

As I mentioned in Chapter 5, sensitivity to flickering, blurring, or hypnotic visual effects can often be traced to an underlying visual tracking problem. The inner-ear system guides and coor-

* Photophobia, the oversensitivity to light, is a common vision-related phobia that has long been recognized as an inner-ear disorder. While many clinicians accept this premise, most ignore or overlook the obvious possibility that other phobias may also be sensory related and linked to CVS dysfunction.

dinates the movement of our eyes, enabling us to reflexively track visual information as it moves around us in our environment (or as we move around it). This visual reflex is called the optokinetic tracking reflex. When the CVS is impaired, this tracking reflex is usually impaired. (In fact, an evaluation of this tracking reflex is an important part of diagnostic testing for inner-ear dysfunction [see Chapter 22].) This makes it difficult for our eyes to keep pace with the movement of visual information in the environment.

As the speed and/or frequency of visual movements increases, this reflex becomes increasingly strained. Ultimately the eyes are incapable of tracking visual information properly, and flooding occurs. This flooding effect can also be a purely processing problem. If your visual-processing mechanism is malfunctioning, the more the visual information being fed into the CVS, the greater is the strain.

Visual Flooding and Driving Phobias

The phenomenon of visual flooding clearly explains why many phobics can drive a car at low speeds but not at high speeds. The faster the speed of the car, the greater is the likelihood that your eyes will be overloaded.

Visual flooding also accounts for many night-driving phobias provoked by oncoming headlights, street lights, reflecting highway markers, etc. It even explains why many people who are afraid to drive are not afraid of being driven. As long as you don't have to constantly concentrate on the road, your eyes are not likely to be overtaxed. And if they are, you can close them or look away since you're not driving.

Dean L. has a fear of driving that is codetermined by visual and compass dysfunctions. He describes his problems as follows:

> I'm fine on local roads, except at night when I can't see clearly, or when it's raining. I need to be able to see the road clearly; if I can't, I start feeling strange: floating . . . like it's not really me and I'm not really driving. It's almost like a dream . . . it's as though I'm witnessing everything in the third person. That scares the hell out of me . . . I feel like I don't have control of my car. If I can't pull the car off the road right away, I freak out.

Highway driving is worse. If there's a lot of traffic and I'm doing thirty-five or forty miles per hour, I'm okay. But as soon as I drive any faster, my eyes get mesmerized. It's as though I've been hypnotized by the lines on the road. Looking at oncoming cars or headlights does it, too. I try to look away and stare at my dashboard or at my rearview mirror . . . but that can be dangerous. I turn the radio up really loud to snap me out of it, but it doesn't always work. Before I know it, I'm floating again. Then it's total panic. I grab the steering wheel so tight my knuckles turn white, but I still don't feel I'm really driving my car. I feel like I'm drifting . . . in a trance . . . floating over the road. My car feels like a big boat. And even though I know where I am, I don't feel like I'm there. I feel lost . . . totally disoriented.

I haven't driven on a highway in five years, and it still scares me just to think about it. The hard part is explaining to other people why I won't drive anywhere. There are just so many excuses you can make up.

Other Visual Flooding Problems

Visual flooding also accounts for the fact that some phobics are frightened by fast strobe lights but unaffected by slow blinking lights; the fact that some phobics panic when they look at a moving train but are unaffected by the sight of a slow or stationary train, and so on. Even crowd phobias and social phobias are often the result of visual flooding.

AUDITORY PHOBIAS

The CVS is responsible for filtering and fine tuning all auditory input. If this process is impaired and the brain cannot adequately compensate, any or all types of auditory flooding and deprivation may trip the fight or flight alarm.

Sensitivity to auditory flooding and deprivation is determined by the nature and extent of the inner-ear dysfunction. Some individuals with auditory processing problems are sensitive to all loud noises and noisy environments. Others are sensitive to specific noises, such as ringing, screeching, rumbling (a combination of noise and motion), high pitches, low pitches, garbled noise (which, in itself, often stems from a CVS processing problem), and so on. Still others are only sensitive to auditory-deprivation environments such as water (underwater), tunnels, subways, underground garages, and empty streets. And some unfortunate individuals are sensitive to all of the above.

Two Types of Auditory Problems

Auditory processing problems, like visual processing problems, play two roles in the development of phobic behavior:

- They are responsible for many pure auditory phobias, such as the fear of screeching noises or explosions.
- They aggravate underlying compass, balance, motion, and other sensory problems normally kept in check by auditory compensation.

In other words, auditory flooding and deprivation effects often destabilize other inner-ear problems that rely on compensatory auditory information. Although the fear is being triggered by noise, or the lack of it, the real problem can be traced to one or several other faulty inner-ear mechanisms. Keeping this in mind, consider the following cases:

Alana J.

Alana has been in a discotheque only once in her life. That was enough. Her balance and orientation problems were aggravated by auditory and visual flooding, and the result was a nightmare. She recalled:

> I'll never forget what happened to me the first and last time I went to a disco . . . and believe me, it was the *last* time. The music was booming out of these giant loudspeakers. It made me light-headed and dizzy. Then my heart started pounding . . . I couldn't hear it, but I could feel it.
>
> Suddenly I had to get out. But as I ran for the door, they turned on those strobe lights. That freaked me out completely. It was as

though I was hallucinating. Nothing seemed real. I pushed my way through the crowd screaming, "Please let me out of here!" By the time I got to the exit, I had completely fallen apart. I was breathing a mile a minute . . . I was sweating like crazy.. I was crying . . . I've never been so scared in all my life.

Brenda S.

Although many noises make Brenda anxious, she is most frightened by the sound of thunder. She comments:

I hate thunderstorms. They scare me to death. I just freeze. If I'm home working, I get paralyzed . . . especially if I'm alone. The sound of the thunder goes right through me, like a knife. If it's dark out and I can see the lightning bolts, that's even worse. The two together are enough to give me a heart attack. My husband teases me . . . he says that my dog and I must have the same problem. My dog runs under the bed and won't come out until the storm has passed . . . I feel like doing the same thing.*

MOTION-RELATED PHOBIAS

There are many different types of motion: vertical, horizontal, clockwise, counterclockwise, etc. Though our eyes, ears, and proprioceptors provide the brain with some motion-related information, most of this information comes from the small structures within the vestibular system. If the CVS is impaired, any or all motion input may be improperly processed. This can result in a hypersensitivity or hyposensitivity to any or all types of motion.

Motion Sensitivity and the Motion-Sickness Response

If you are hypersensitive to motion, the motion-flooding effect of a moving car, a rocking boat, or even a rocking chair (de-

---

* The dog's reaction suggests that there may be a universal component to the fear of thunder (see Chapter 15).

pending upon your sensitivity) can provoke dizziness, nausea, vomiting, and retching, as well as anxiety and other fight or flight symptoms. This combination of motion-flooding and fight or flight symptoms is commonly referred to as motion sickness.

Just as these symptoms are indicative of motion sickness, the other symptoms previously discussed are, in turn, indicative of compass sickness, balance sickness, vision sickness, and auditory sickness. And just as these other sensory sicknesses can provoke fear or panic, so can motion sickness. Your impulse is to get off the boat, bus, plane or out of the car before you get sick. Vomiting occurs only when you are unable to escape the motion-flooding environment in time. Similarly, fainting, falling, or even vomiting may occur when you are unable to escape other sensory flooding environments.

In motion-flooding environments, anxiety and other fight or flight symptoms are usually dwarfed by the all-consuming nausea, vomiting, and retching. As a result, we don't usually think of motion sickness as having any relation to these other sensory sicknesses. But there is really a very significant relationship. They are all a by-product of the same problem: an inner-ear dysfunction.

Motion Hypersensitivity and Related Phobias

Hypersensitivity to motion, and the susceptibility to motion sickness, can result in a wide variety of phobic behavior, including a fear of cars, buses, boats, planes, trains, amusement-park rides, elevators, escalators, bicycles, conveyor belts, swimming (especially in the ocean), jogging, and even walking (or all of these). Consider the following examples:

Ann-Marie F.

Ann-Marie is an eleven-year-old fifth grader who was referred to me for dyslexic evaluation. During my conversation with her and her mother, I learned that Ann-Marie is fearful of everything that has to do with motion: planes, trains, elevators, escalators, cars, swings, running, and so on. She is even afraid to get a haircut because she panics when the chair in the beauty salon moves up and down. Interestingly, the one thing that doesn't make her panic is riding her bike. But even in this instance, she gets motion sick if she rides in a circle.

Norman H.

Norman has a motion-related fear of flying. He describes his problem as follows:

> In my business, I have to fly. If I had any other choice, believe me, I would take it. If the flight is smooth I can usually handle it . . . although I'm never really relaxed. Every time I see that fasten-your-seat-belt sign come on, I grip the handles of my chair. As soon as there's turbulence, I freak . . . especially if I can't see out of the windows. I never fly at night or when it's raining, and I try to avoid all wintertime flying. When the weather is rough, those planes just get bounced around like little toys.
>
> A friend of mine was recently on a flight where the plane suddenly dropped several hundred feet. He said that for a split second he could actually see his coffee cup in front of him, suspended in midair. He thought it was funny. I almost got sick just listening to his story.

Since individuals may be oversensitive to one, several, or all types of motion, they may also have phobias related to one, several, or all types of motion. Furthermore, since vibration is motion, motion-sensitive individuals may also have vibration-related panic episodes and phobias.

Compensating for Motion Flooding

Motion flooding does not always trigger motion sickness and phobic behavior. Often the brain is able to compensate for motion overload by fixing the eyes on something that isn't moving, such as the horizon. This visual fixation suppresses fight or flight and motion-flooding symptoms.

It is therefore not surprising that motion-sensitive individuals would rather drive than be driven and would rather sit in the front seat than the backseat (unless they are also sensitive to visual flooding). Sitting in the backseat makes it much harder to visually fixate and therefore harder to suppress anxiety and other motion-sickness symptoms.

Many motion-sensitive individuals grow out of their symptoms. This permanent compensation is possible for other sensory problems as well, and is another reason sensory phobias sometimes improve spontaneously over time.

Motion Hyposensitivity and Related Phobias

If an impaired inner-ear system is overfiltering motion input, the brain may be starved of any or all types of motion-related information. The brain can often compensate for this by making you rock yourself or move around. But the inability to compensate may trigger anxiety, fear, or even panic. The motion-deprivation effect of being tied down, stuck, trapped, or unable to move (literally or symbolically) are all capable of provoking this kind of response. Even the anticipation of motion deprivation can trigger claustrophobic anxiety once this response has been imprinted.

OTHER SENSORY PHOBIAS

Thus far, I have discussed the most common sensory phobias. But as I have said before, *any* type of sensory processing problem may lead to phobic behavior. A tactile malfunction, for example, can lead to the fear of being touched . . . hypersensitivity to certain odors can provoke dizziness and panic . . . the inability of the skin to "breathe" can trigger anxiety . . . and so on. Hopefully, increasing clinical experience will shed even more light on the many sensory mechanisms underlying the phobic disorder. No doubt there are many more insights to be gained.

Coordination-Related Phobias

Commenting on the role of the cerebellum as a motor information processor, Nobel-prize winner Sir John Eccles wrote:

> . . . the computational machinery of the cerebellum is engaged in a continuous on-going correction of movements in much the same way as occurs for a target-finding missile.

Many times a malfunction in our motor circuits—the guided-missile system that steers, coordinates, and fine tunes all of our movements (voluntary and involuntary) and thoughts in time and space—also contributes to the development of phobias. I call these coordination-related phobias *guided-missile phobias*.

Consider again, if you will, the fear of stairs. Many people who are not afraid of looking down from a high window or rooftop are deathly afraid of walking up and down a small flight of stairs (or even a small stepladder). Why would someone fear falling down three steps and not fear falling from a fifteen-story window?

When you speak to these individuals, you quickly discover that their fear reflects far more than an imbalance problem. They will tell you, "I don't trust my feet" . . . "I'm afraid of tripping and falling" . . . "I'm afraid of missing a step and falling" . . . "I can't judge the distance between the steps." These people are not just afraid of falling, they are afraid of their own poor coordination—their malfunctioning guided-missile system. This is clearly illustrated in the following case:

Holly R.

When Holly is sitting or standing still, she can look down from considerable heights without being affected. If, however, she has to walk down even the smallest staircase, she is terrified. She commented:

> You know those portable steps they use at airports? When I see them wheeling those steps up to the plane I get a lump in my throat. By the time I reach the aircraft exit I'm hyperventilating. If I'm by myself, and I can concentrate really hard and take my time, I somehow manage to get down. But if someone is talking to me or something is distracting me, the result is total panic.

See-through or open-backed steps are particularly frightening to Holly, as they are to many phobics. She once ran onto a fire escape during a fire in her building and froze at the sight of the open metal stairs. She eventually had to sit on the staircase and work her way down step by step.

Holly's fear of stairs has had a tremendous effect on her lifestyle. She is afraid to go anyplace where she might encounter steps, and she makes up tons of excuses to avoid going anywhere or doing anything that might give her a problem. She recalled:

> Recently my husband and I took a tour of a U.S. aircraft carrier. It was the biggest mistake I ever made. All over the ship were these small metal staircases. I had to leave the tour and work my way down each staircase on my behind. I was petrified the entire time.

She is also terrified of walking across bridges and walking on bumpy, uneven roads. Furthermore, she avoids escalators. She explains: "I just can't figure out which foot goes first."

ARE YOU UNCOORDINATED?

The word "uncoordinated" brings to mind images of hands that can't catch a ball, arms that can't throw, legs that move awkwardly and ungracefully, and feet that trip over each other. But

motor uncoordination reflects far more than these spastic movements. It entails the coordination of our eyes, hence our depth
perception; the coordination of our mouths, hence our ability to
talk, eat, etc.; the coordination of our involuntary muscle system,
hence our ability to swallow, digest, breathe harmoniously, etc.;
the coordination of our thoughts, hence our ability to construct
complex ideas from simple ones; and innumerable other processes. When any of these processes are dyscoordinated, phobic
behavior may result.

Why Aren't All Uncoordinated People Phobic?

Obviously you can be uncoordinated without being phobic.*
Underlying the development of most coordination-related, guided-
missile phobias are either or both of the following contributing
factors:

■ An impaired anxiety filter: When guided-missile functions are
   impaired, performing such functions often generates anxiety,
   especially when poor performance could lead to embarrassment, frustration, or danger. (If, for example, you have poor
   hand-eye coordination, trying to catch a ball can make you
   anxious since you may fear getting hurt or being embarrassed.)
   But if your anxiety filter is impaired, the brain may be unable
   to properly regulate and dampen anxiety. Without this control,
   your anxiety may quickly escalate into considerable fear, even
   outright panic.
■ A sensory filter malfunction: Many guided-missile phobias really
   stem from a combination of motor and sensory malfunctions.
   For example, certain escalator and stair phobias result from a
   combination of balance and depth perception problems; certain

---

*Many poorly coordinated individuals are extremely accident-prone. Yet even in
situations where they should be anxious or afraid, they are not. This appears to reflect a
malfunction in either the anxiety filter or the imprinting mechanism (or both).

driving phobias represent a combination of coordination and motion-sensitivity problems; etc.*

COMMON GUIDED-MISSILE PHOBIAS

There are innumerable guided-missile phobias. Some of the most common include:

- Driving phobias (due to a fear of getting hurt because of poor depth perception and/or poor driving skills).
- Sports phobias (due to a fear of being ridiculed because of poor coordination, a fear of getting hit by a ball you misjudge, a fear of tripping and falling while running, etc.).
- Social and school phobias (due to a fear of being embarrassed by or ridiculed for dyscoordinated speech and/or movements).
- Escalator phobias (due to a fear of not being able to get on or off without falling).
- Elevator phobias (due to a fear of not being able to get in or out of the elevator before the door closes).
- Tunnel and bridge phobias (due to a fear of not being able to keep the car within its narrow lane).

As you can see from the previous chapters, these phobias are not always coordination related. Often they are the result of sensory problems. This clearly illustrates that a variety of inner-ear problems can lead to the same fear, even though the basis of that fear is entirely different.

---

*In a sense, *all* guided-missile phobias involving movement may be attributable, at least in part, to a sensory malfunction. In order for our guided-missile system to properly regulate movement, the brain has to know the location of the various parts of the body at all times. This information is provided by the proprioceptive system, with its many sensors located throughout the body. But, like all sensory information, proprioceptive information is also regulated by the CVS. (This has been established for some time. In fact, it was C. S. Sherrington, one of the greatest neurologists of all time, who, in 1906, referred to the cerebellum as "the head ganglion of the proprioceptive system.") If the processing of proprioceptive information is being disrupted by a malfunctioning CVS, the guided-missile system cannot function properly. This paves the way for the development of coordination-related phobic behavior.

Compensating for Guided-Missile Phobias

You have seen many examples of how the brain compensates for sensory malfunctions. The brain is equally capable of compensating for malfunctions in the guided-missile system.

The most common form of compensation for motor dysfunction is increased concentration. If, for example, your hand-eye coordination is poor, you concentrate harder on the tennis ball you are trying to hit; if you are klutzy, you concentrate harder on the movement of your legs and feet when you climb a staircase (or hold on to the banister), etc.

For this reason, anything that interferes with your ability to concentrate can aggravate your coordination problems and increase your level of anxiety. Concentration mechanisms may be disrupted by loud music, distracting lights, darkness, someone talking to you, etc.

Guided-missile problems are also often aggravated by any increase in task difficulty—motor flooding, in a sense. Consider, for example, the fear of swallowing pills. Most individuals who are afraid to swallow pills do not trust their swallowing reflex. As a result, swallowing even a tiny pill can trigger fears of choking and make them anxious. But a far more difficult task— swallowing a large pill or capsule—terrifies them and can even bring on full-fledged panic.

Let's examine the guided-missile phobias of several more patients:

Angie S.

Angie has severe visual coordination problems. As a result, she is afraid to drive. She recalls:

> I remember saying to the man who was giving me driving lessons, "Where should I look?" because I didn't know where to look when I was driving. In order to see where I was going I would start following the curb line. But I wasn't looking straight ahead, I was looking at the ground. And he said, "You have to look in front of you." But I couldn't see. By looking at so much, I couldn't focus on anything. I need to use the relationship of the hood ornament to the curb to know that I am in a lane.

Harriet O.

Harriet's impaired guided-missile system makes it almost impossible for her to coordinate her thoughts. This problem has led to the development of a writing phobia. She explains:

> Nothing terrifies me more than having to write a paper. I just can't collect my thoughts and write them down in a structured fashion. Sometimes just looking at a blank piece of paper makes me panic so badly I actually throw up.

Although Harriet has an I.Q. of 165, she has been unable to graduate from college because of this problem.

Bruce W.

Bruce suffers from severe chronic anxiety—a strong sign of an impaired CVS anxiety filter. He also has considerable motor and rhythmic dyscoordination. The combination of these two inner-ear problems has led to the development of a variety of phobias.

Bruce is, for example, afraid of playing sports. "The thought of being ridiculed is enough to make me panic," he explained. "As a kid I was terrified of going to camp for this very reason." He also fears dancing. "It's not that I don't like to dance," he told me, "it's just that I can't dance in front of anyone. I always think people are going to laugh at me. That makes me panic." In addition, Bruce has always been afraid of talking to people— a problem that can be traced to his speech dyscoordination.

Nora K.

Nora is afraid of going into her own bank to deposit or withdraw money. She explained:

> It has to do with my handwriting . . . it's atrocious. If a teller asks me to write something or sign something, I panic. My writing is so terrible it's embarrassing. As you can probably see, I have quite a coordination problem.

Nora's explanation reveals that her phobia is codetermined by coordination difficulties and a malfunctioning anxiety mechanism. In other words, her poor coordination leads to embarrassment, embarrassment provokes anxiety, and anxiety escalates into total panic.

THE ORIGIN OF "JELLY LEGS"

If your guided-missile system is functioning properly, your muscles should become tense when the fight or flight alarm is sounded; your legs should be ready to run. When just the opposite happens—i.e., jelly legs—it indicates a malfunction in the system that is being aggravated by the state of alarm. Some agoraphobic fears are actually triggered by jelly legs. Individuals who are susceptible to fluctuations in muscle tone sometimes experience a spontaneous weakening of the legs. This caving in triggers fears of falling, fainting, injury, losing control, and so on, and can lead to panic.

CHAPTER 15

Universal Phobias

While fear of elevators is only as new as the elevator itself, certain fears have always been known to mankind, regardless of how sophisticated or primitive the society. These so-called universal phobias include the fear of snakes, mice, insects, knives, etc.* Although psychoanalysts generally view these phobias as having sexual and/or aggressive connotations, I believe there is a very different explanation for them.

A PART OF OUR EVOLUTIONARY HISTORY

All animal species are known to inherit a wide variety of reflex behavior patterns, including breeding patterns, feeding patterns, attack patterns, avoidance patterns, etc. As humans, we are no different. We have inherited our crying reflex, our sucking reflex, our grasping reflex and our breathing reflex, to name just a few. These reflex motor patterns were imprinted in our genes during a long evolutionary process that focused on the survival of the fittest.

Many of these reflex patterns are known to fade soon after birth. Consider, for example, the grasping reflex. If you stroke the inside of a newborn baby's hand with your finger, the infant will instantly grasp that finger with a display of strength that is totally disproportionate to its size and weight. This reflexive grasp

*Note that these universal phobias do not include a fear of snakes that results from a snakebite, a fear of knives that results from a stab wound, or other phobias related to a specific trauma. These Type 1, realistic phobias are discussed in Chapter 17.

is so strong, in fact, that you could practically lift the baby out of the crib by raising the finger it is holding (though I don't recommend it).

It has been postulated that this amazing grasping reflex is a vestige of our ape ancestry—a time when this powerful grasp was needed to navigate from tree to tree. Not long after birth, it fades. To say that it has disappeared seems foolish. There is little doubt that this survival mechanism, being of little use in a world where few humans continue to swing from trees, is repressed in the brain by more practical human impulses.

A PRIMITIVE REFLEX

Another fascinating primitive motor reflex is one we have already discussed in great detail: the fight or flight response. Various studies have shown that the fight or flight reflex of many animals is instinctively triggered by a variety of specific stimuli, including certain scents, sounds, colors, and visual configurations, such as the shape of various insects and other animals.

Although the human animal has developed to the point where it is often able to use its judgment instead of these primitive fight or flight reflexes, there is no reason to believe that these more archaic defense mechanisms simply disappeared. On the contrary, it is far more logical to assume that we still carry them around with us, buried somewhere deep in our brain where they are kept in check.

AN INNER-EAR PROCESSING PROBLEM

What if there is a malfunction in the processing center of your brain (i.e., the CVS)—the area primarily responsible for the inhibition of our primitive defense mechanisms? It is quite conceivable that such a malfunction could render you incapable of suppressing these programmed responses. Therefore, in the presence of a primitive trigger, such as a spider or a snake, your brain would automatically trip the fight or flight alarm.

This mechanism would certainly explain the universality of many puzzling phobias. Interestingly, the existence of such a mechanism is supported by the observation that numerous repressed reflexes, including various sexual and emotional responses, are released when the CVS is damaged. (Some of these other maladaptive responses may even be at the root of neurotic, Type 2 phobic behavior.)

Universal-like Phobias

It is also quite possible that other universal-like phobias, such as the fear of birds and the fear of frogs, are sometimes the result of a similar mechanism. In such instances, there appears to be a flaw in the universal reflex itself. As a result of this flaw, the brain responds to a likeness of a universal trigger instead of, or in addition to, the appropriate universal trigger.

The following cases illustrate the universal mechanisms often responsible for phobic behavior.

Diane V.

Diane has a typical universal fear of bugs. She told me:

I won't walk anywhere near trees. The sight of a caterpillar is enough to give me a heart attack—even a photograph of a caterpillar makes me panicky. Once, when I was young, a small caterpillar fell out of a tree and onto my head. As soon as I felt it, I started tearing at my hair and screaming: "Oh, my God! Get it off of me! Get it off of me!" I was shaking my head frantically, pulling at my hair and screaming, all at the same time. My father must have heard me because he ran over and tried to calm me down. I kept screaming and he kept saying, "It's only a bug!" Then he slapped me. I don't think I ever forgave him for that.

Vicky F.

Vicky has a universal-like fear of birds. Her husband recalled the first time he learned about her phobia:

> We had only known each other for a few weeks. We were walking down the street in New York City and suddenly Vicky let out a bloodcurdling scream. Then she jumped up onto the hood of a parked car. I couldn't believe it. It was like what you see in the movies when a mouse runs across the room . . . only there was no mouse. Her face was all contorted. I kept asking, "What is it?" She couldn't say anything . . . all she could do was point at the ground. But I couldn't see anything. Finally she sputtered out, "A b-b-bird." I looked down again, and then I saw it. A little bird was walking in the gutter. I have to admit, I thought the whole thing was a bit strange.

CHAPTER 16

Miscellaneous Type 3 Phobias

Concentration problems, speech problems, reading problems, academic problems—all of these are quite common when the inner-ear system is impaired (see Chapter 9). These various inner-ear-related symptoms often lead to embarrassment, frustration, even danger. This in turn provokes anxiety. An intact CVS anxiety filter is able to regulate and control this anxiety, but if this response is maladaptive—if anxiety is severe or uncontrollable—phobic behavior may develop.

SOCIAL PHOBIAS AND STAGE FRIGHT

When words or thoughts become scrambled, you may have a great deal of difficulty expressing yourself. This can make you extremely uncomfortable in social situations. You may, for example, think: "I can't speak to these people . . . I'll probably sound stupid and make a complete fool of myself." If your anxiety filter is impaired you may be unable to control the anxiety triggered by your feelings of insecurity. The result: social phobias, stage fright, and more.

Naomi M. is a patient whose social phobias and stage fright have haunted her most of her life. Her explanation clearly reveals the underlying Type 3 mechanisms responsible for these fears:

> I'm really terrified of talking to more than one person . . . for me, five is a crowd. As a child I played sick every time a book report was due. I just couldn't bear the thought of getting up and talking in front of all those people . . . I was afraid I'd make a fool of

myself. I hid from everything . . . I had excuses to get out of everything . . . it was horrible.

As I got older it became worse. I wouldn't take a better job if it meant I had to talk in front of more people. I'm so self-conscious I can't even get up from my seat at a ball park without panicking . . . I always think everyone's looking at me and that they'll see how stupid and clumsy I am.

Naomi admitted that she was a poor student in school and always felt dumb and ugly. Clearly, these insecurities provoked anxiety whenever she thought she would be in the spotlight. This anxiety would mushroom into fear and lead to Naomi's various avoidance mechanisms.

SCHOOL PHOBIAS

When inner-ear-determined academic difficulties create anxiety, the result is often school phobia. Note how Karen, now twenty-four, describes why she was school phobic:

In first grade I was pretty good in reading. At that time the material wasn't too difficult. But I found writing the alphabet, words, and numbers completely impossible. I can recall my mother becoming very impatient with me—and me crying hysterically. It was then that my temper tantrums began. Eventually I mastered writing the alphabet. But believe it or not, the simple process of writing was all but impossible for me.

Nothing much happened in the second grade. But the third grade brought addition, subtraction, and lots of numbers. I was fairly good at understanding math, but I had difficulty doing addition and subtraction without using my fingers. And the multiplication tables in third grade required continuous practice and reinforcement; otherwise my memory of them would just wash away.

I was fourteen when my school phobia began, or at least became obvious. During this time my homework and schoolwork became a disaster. I was failing all of my subjects. And although I did my homework, I could never understand or remember what I was reading.

I can't begin to tell you how completely isolated I felt at this point in my life. I couldn't do anything right. And the other kids just kept laughing at me. So I was afraid to do anything at all.

Clearly, Karen had many very good reasons for being afraid of school. Her school phobia was anything but irrational.

ADDITIONAL TYPE 3 PHOBIAS

The following cases have been selected to give you some idea of the variety of phobias determined by a malfunctioning inner-ear system. Although some of these cases are unusual the majority of them are typical, and all of them are extremely insightful.

Anne M.

Anne's impaired inner-ear system makes it difficult for her to organize and express her thoughts. This problem has influenced the development of several phobias, including a fear of telephones. She writes:

> When you are unable to organize and express your thoughts you become isolated, a hermit . . . you feel worthless. Depression sets in and you become incapacitated . . . unable to function.
> I had become afraid to talk to people. I feared the words would come out backwards or not come out at all. And I feared sounding and appearing stupid. I reached the point where I avoided speaking on the telephone. My mind would blank out . . . I could not get the words out. Eventually the ringing of the telephone was enough for panic to set in. It was terrible.

Mary B.

Due to a malfunction in her auditory filter, Mary has difficulty distinguishing foreground noise from background noise (auditory scrambling). When she speaks to people face-to-face, she is able to compensate for her hearing problem by looking at their expressions and reading their lips. But when she talks on the telephone, she is unable to compensate. All she hears is garbled noise. This sensory scrambling makes her feel stupid and anxious, and her anxiety quickly escalates into total panic. Mary commented, "When I'm home alone, I disconnect the phones."

Jean D.

Jean has always had dyslexic reading difficulties—she would scramble words, mispronounce words, etc. Her embarrassment at her inability to read provokes uncontrollable anxiety and panic. She writes:

> I thought I was agoraphobic because I felt like running out of the house or building where a meeting was being held. In retrospect, I wasn't afraid of the space or the people but of the possibility that I would have to read.

Raymond T.

Raymond's tortured existence is the tragic result of an inner-ear disturbance that was not properly diagnosed and treated. During his first visit to my office, he told me:

> I'm really afraid of life. The reality of it scares me to death. I can't read or write. Merely filling out a job application is enough to put me into a sweat and cause me to panic. I have to avoid everything that involves reading and writing, and things that make me feel completely inept and stupid. As a result, I've drifted into marijuana, cocaine, and other drugs merely to escape these horrible feelings. I've always known that drugs aren't the answer, but it's the only solution I've been able to find . . . except suicide.

CHAPTER 17

Type 1 and Type 2 Phobias

Up to this point, my discussion has focused almost entirely on Type 3 phobias and their mechanisms. But as I said in the beginning of this book, there are *three* types of phobias: realistic (Type 1), neurotic (Type 2), and physiologically determined (Type 3). Now that you are more familiar with the wide variety of Type 3 mechanisms that can influence phobic behavior, you are ready to examine other phobias and their mechanisms in greater detail.

TYPE 1 VS. TYPE 3 PHOBIAS

- Anyone who has a car accident *might* develop a fear of driving.
- Anyone who gets stuck in an elevator *might* develop a fear of elevators.
- Anyone who is bitten by a dog *might* develop a fear of dogs.
- Anyone who is mugged at night *might* develop a fear of the dark.
- Anyone who gets hurt in a fall *might* develop a fear of falling.
- Anyone who is attacked or abused in school *might* develop a fear of school.

On and on the list of realistic, Type 1 phobias goes. It makes sense that a severe traumatic experience could lead to the development of phobic behavior. Yet as you certainly must realize, not everyone who suffers from such an experience becomes phobic. Fearful for a short time? Yes. But permanently phobic? Definitely not.

To some degree, the severity of the trauma determines whether or not a lasting phobia will develop. It is, for example, not surprising to see a man who has been in a car accident develop a fear of driving. Nor is it surprising to see a man who has been brutally stabbed develop a fear of knives. In fact, one would almost expect phobias to appear after these experiences. Yet not all serious stabbing victims develop a long-lasting fear of knives. And not all victims of serious car accidents develop a fear of driving. On the other hand, some people develop a terrible fear of knives after sustaining a minor, self-inflicted injury. And some develop a terrible fear of driving after being in a minor car accident. Certainly, some other hidden factor, or factors, must be influencing the development of these phobias.

Why Are Some People More Susceptible Than Others?

There is no denying that some individuals are far more capable than others of shrugging off a traumatic incident. Indeed, some people seem almost able to forget the incident entirely. This ability to inhibit the memory of a traumatic event, and with it the anxiety provoked by reminders of that event, seems to determine whether or not intense, prolonged fears will develop. But what determines an individual's ability to suppress these memories and anxieties?

An Emotional Predisposition

Emotional history plays some role in the development of realistic phobias. The more experience someone has had coping with trauma, the greater is the likelihood that he or she will be able to handle a new trauma. But this still doesn't explain why two inexperienced individuals may react entirely differently to the same trauma. Clearly, there is yet another factor involved—something that predisposes certain individuals to the development of phobias, while helping others to resist.

A Type 3 Predisposition

Clinical evidence suggests that the crucial determining factor in the development of most realistic phobias is a malfunction in the CVS anxiety filter—our anxiety control mechanism.

If the inner ear is impaired and this filter is not working properly, you may be unable to dampen and control the anxiety triggered by reminders of the original traumatic experience. Furthermore, you may be constantly haunted by perseverating memories of that trauma. As a result, phobias develop. Since these phobias really have realistic *and* physiological origins, I refer to them as *mixed* phobias.

Occasionally, underlying inner-ear problems are actually responsible for precipitating traumatic incidents. For example, you may have been in a car accident because of poor coordination skills, or you may have fallen from a horse because of a poor sense of balance. Although these phobias may have been triggered by realistic traumas, they also have mixed origins.

There are, of course, some pure Type 1 phobias. But more than 90 percent of those phobias considered to have entirely realistic origins probably stem from some combination of Type 1 and Type 3 mechanisms. In other words, the vast majority of phobias initially triggered by a realistic trauma are really mixed phobias.

MIXED PHOBIAS: SOME EXAMPLES

The following cases illustrate the influence of an underlying inner-ear dysfunction in the development of realistically triggered phobias.

Bonnie Y.

Bonnie developed a fear of needles when she was ten years old. She recalls:

It all began after a horrible medical malpractice-type incident. As a child in elementary school, I wanted pierced ears. The family doctor did give me them, but by torture: he put a needle through each earlobe without using novocaine or any other anesthesia. I think my piercing screams could have been heard ten miles away.

Following this incident, Bonnie developed such a severe fear of needles that even a photograph of a needle would make her panic. She was particularly terrified of blood tests and for years refused to take any injections unless it was a medical emergency.

Listening to Bonnie's story, it would have been easy for me to conclude that her needle phobia was a pure Type 1 phobia. But diagnostic testing revealed the presence of an underlying inner-ear dysfunction. I suspected this was not a coincidence. Treatment with vestibular medications resulted in a considerable improvement in her condition, thus confirming my suspicions. Bonnie is still not fond of needles, but she is no longer terrified of them.

Edward C.

When Edward was fourteen he and his two brothers went to see a particularly frightening horror film. His mother recalls:

Ever since he saw that film Edward has been afraid of ghosts, afraid of scary movies, and afraid of walking around the house at night.

Once again, it would have been very easy for me to assume that Edward's fears had an entirely realistic basis. Yet one has to wonder why neither of his brothers, especially his younger brother, developed any of these fears. When Edward came to my office he had been suffering from these fears for more than a year. Diagnostic testing revealed the presence of an underlying CVS dysfunction, and a trial of medications was prescribed. Edward's mother recently reported:

Edward recovered from all of his fears almost immediately after starting medication. He sat with the family and watched a scary movie just the other night and actually enjoyed it. This would not have been possible before treatment.

Marion L.

Marion's driving phobia developed after her first car accident.
She recalled:

> I've never been too crazy about driving. I never felt I had control
> of the car. It was always hard for me to keep in my lane, especially
> on narrow roads. I couldn't trust my reflexes either, so I was always
> braking way ahead of time just to be on the safe side. But I had to
> drive if I wanted to work.
>
>   Then the accident happened. It was totally my fault. I hit the
> brakes without looking into my rearview mirror, and the guy behind
> me plowed right into my trunk. Fortunately I wasn't hurt, but I was
> really shaken up. It more or less confirmed everything I'd always
> worried about. I haven't been able to get into my car since.

Marion's tests revealed clear-cut evidence of CVS dysfunction.
Her inner-ear problems had no doubt been responsible for her
poor coordination and reflexes, which in turn led to her accident
and subsequent driving phobia.

TYPE 2 VS. TYPE 3 PHOBIAS

Before the physiological basis of phobic behavior was discovered,
it was generally assumed that neurotic mechanisms were responsible for the majority of phobias. According to Freudian theory,
when phobias develop in individuals who have not been subjected
to any known or conscious (i.e., realistic) danger, one must
assume:

- That the panic and anxiety still represent a true signal of danger.
- That this reaction must therefore be due to an unknown or
  unconscious emotional danger or conflict that is about to act
  up and overwhelm you.
- That the triggers—elevators, cars, bridges, etc.—are symbols
  provoking fear and avoidance, and are reflections of the unconscious conflict and stress that is about to erupt.
- That frequently these symbols denote a sexual and/or aggressive significance.

■ That the sexual and/or aggressive trauma created during childhood was repressed and thus forgotten, and has recently been triggered or activated by current events.

Let's examine how these assumptions are usually applied to phobic analysis.

Psychoanalyzing Phobic Behavior

If a married woman is fearful of leaving home and walking on the street, a psychoanalyst might assume that:

■ Walking alone in the street is symbolic of the actions of a prostitute.
■ The unconscious conflict reflects the following mixed emotions: "Should I or shouldn't I have an affair and act like a prostitute?"
■ The fear of leaving home and walking the streets alone is a defense against the desire to act out these sexual impulses. Therefore the phobia serves an important adaptive role.

In other words, the woman would like to have an affair, or group of affairs, but this wish is held in check by counterforces—i.e., pangs of guilt and a resultant fear of street walking. A psychoanalyst might further assume that the above sexual conflict was first initiated during childhood (an Electra conflict).

If this same woman, or some other woman, is fearful of driving and/or traveling too far from home, a psychoanalyst is trained to reason as follows:

■ Driving and/or traveling from home triggers anxiety, thus signifying some unconscious danger.
■ Traveling from home (via some vehicle, such as a car) is symbolic of a desire to leave husband and home.
■ The traveling fear represents an unconsciously determined adaptive mechanism to prevent this individual from leaving her husband and/or children.

■ A similar conflict may first have occurred during early child-hood when the woman wanted to run away from her parents and siblings but was prevented from doing so by pangs of conscience, fears of being alone, etc.

Consider one more example. If a woman is frightened by elevators, buses, trains, and stairs, a psychoanalyst might reason as follows:

■ Moving elevators, buses, trains, and walking up and down stairs are motion symbols that trigger anxiety.
■ Motion is probably symbolic of intercourse, or even mastur-bation.
■ The unconscious conflict, dating back to childhood, must sound something like this: "I'd like to masturbate and have sexual intercourse but I'd feel too guilty and might even be punished by 'castration' or death."
■ The shape of the triggers—buses, trains, etc.—may also rep-resent more specific genital symbols, such as the penis, vagina, etc.
■ The fear of moving vehicles and motion represents an uncon-scious attempt to prevent, or keep in check, forbidden sexual desires.

Interesting? Yes. Accurate? I wonder. These Type 2 mecha-nisms are to a great extent incapable of accounting for the specific shapes, forms, variable intensities, combinations, onset, and dis-appearance of most phobias. In other words, given the personality profile and background of any individual, psychoanalytic theory has been unable to explain or predict the specific phobias or combination of phobias to which he or she might be heir. Nor can it predict which patients will develop phobias and which will not.

Psychoanalysis therefore fails to satisfactorily explain why one patient is afraid of cars, another of buses, another of trains, another of planes, another of heights, another of wide-open spaces, and another of various combinations of the above. Nor does it explain why still others fear crowds, social events, department stores, tunnels, or nothing at all.

TYPE 2 PHOBIAS: TYPE 3 PHOBIAS IN DISGUISE?

In certain cases severe psychological conflicts from childhood may indeed be capable of single-handedly giving rise to phobic behavior in adult life. But clinical evidence strongly suggests that these conflicts are not the only factor, and are probably not even the key factor in the development of most phobic behavior. On the contrary, they appear to be totally irrelevant in many, if not most cases.

What, then, is the key factor? A *physiological* predisposition stemming from an impaired inner-ear system. In fact, clinical evidence suggests that 90 percent or more of all phobias believed to be of purely Type 2 origin actually stem from either:

- a *combination of* Type 2 and Type 3 mechanisms (or Types 1, 2, and 3). Often the stress from neurotic factors aggravates and reinforces underlying inner-ear problems such as disorientation, motion sensitivity and/or imbalance. In other words, the woman who fears walking alone on the street probably has some underlying balance and/or disorientation problem that is being aggravated by the neurotic stress; the woman who fears driving her car probably has some underlying disorientation and/or coordination problem; the woman who fears elevators, buses, and trains probably has some underlying motion-sensitivity problem; etc.; and/or . . .
- a malfunctioning CVS anxiety filter that is unable to properly dampen and control the anxiety triggered by a reminder of some underlying neurotic conflict (also a combination effect); or . . .
- purely Type 3 mechanisms. Usually phobias viewed as neurotic are in reality sensory, guided-missile, universal, or other typical Type 3 phobias.

OTHER PSYCHOLOGICAL THEORIES EXPLAINED

It is often suggested that other psychological factors, aside from the neurotic sexual and/or aggressive conflicts from childhood, can be responsible for the development of phobic behavior.

One popular theory suggests that children may learn to be phobic by copying the fears they see displayed by parents, friends, or relatives (for example, a child who sees his mother panic in an elevator and senses her terror may develop his own fear of elevators later in life). This "mimicking" of phobic behavior may indeed be responsible for the development of some mild anxiety states. It may also influence the development of phobic behavior. But clinical evidence has made it plain that true and lasting phobic behavior is not likely to develop unless there is an underlying physiological predisposition.

Since CVS dysfunction is so frequently inherited, there is no doubt that the child who successfully mimics his parent's phobic behavior has the same underlying inner-ear dysfunction that is responsible for his parent's phobias. This would explain why only one of several children may mimic the parent's fears, or why a child could even develop entirely different fears.

Some clinicians feel that an acute psychological trauma, such as divorce or the death of a loved one, can create phobic behavior. There is no question that the stress from a psychological trauma can produce considerable anxiety. But clinical evidence indicates that this anxiety will develop into an unrelated phobia (i.e., anything other than the fear of divorce, fear of marriage, or fear of death), or perhaps any phobia, only when it is inappropriately regulated by a malfunctioning CVS anxiety filter.

In other words, these acute psychological traumas can trigger phobic behavior when an underlying physiological predisposition is present, but they cannot create phobic behavior when no CVS dysfunction is present (with the possible exception of extreme psychological trauma—such as severe chronic anxiety, shell shock or prolonged sensory torture).

MIXED PHOBIAS: MORE EXAMPLES

You are now ready to examine several rather complicated case histories. As you read these cases, note the mixing of Type 1, Type 2, and Type 3 mechanisms.

Paula R.

When I first examined Paula, I learned that she had many phobias, including a fear of crowds, heights, loud noises, diseases, driving in the front seat of a car, elevators, escalators, and stairs. Her mother recalled:

> Paula was a very nervous child. I know children have all kinds of fears, but I'll never forget the first time I saw her freeze up on a staircase. We were going down these steep steps into the subway, and Paula just came to a halt. I kept saying, "Come on, everybody else can do it." Then I realized she was covered with sweat. I really though she was going to be ill. Actually, a similar thing happened to her father. He suffered from paroxysmal tachycardia (racing heart). His first attack came when we were going down a steep set of marble steps. But he would never admit that he was phobic.

Paula's most unusual phobia was a fear of bread. Her mother explained:

> When Paula was a little girl she nearly choked on a piece of bread during dinner. Her father and I were arguing at the table and didn't notice for a moment. She was terribly shaken up. I suppose that's why she won't eat bread. Her association of the bread, her choking, and our arguing makes her almost retch every time she looks at bread.

Paula had her first panic attack when she was eighteen. Her mother commented:

> We were going through a very bad period. My marriage was breaking up. There was a lot of stress and strain—it was a very disagreeable divorce. I was full of tension, and Paula absorbed it like a sponge. We were all at a restaurant and it was very noisy. My husband and I were arguing, adding to the commotion. Suddenly Paula gasped,

"I can't swallow . . . I can't breathe." I kept asking, "Why can't you breathe?" I didn't realize that she was having a panic attack.

Her attacks became more frequent. Her job was extremely stressful—totally unsuitable for her. She had to cut out tiny little labels and stick them on library books. She would often cut herself with the scissors. The whole thing made her very nervous, and she would start hyperventilating.

Paula's examination revealed numerous signs of CVS dysfunction. She had articulation difficulties, memory problems, a short concentration span, and poor gross and fine coordination. Her handwriting was slow and dyscoordinated, and she had numerous academic difficulties, including poor mathematical skills and difficulties using punctuation. Diagnostic tests confirmed the presence of CVS dysfunction, and treatment was started. Paula's mother recently wrote:

> Since starting medication, Paula has been free of anxiety and phobic behavior, such as: hesitation and dread of using escalators and elevators, fear of diseases such as cancer, sleeping with the bedroom door closed, and sitting in the front seat of the car.
>
> Paula recently took an escalator to the twelfth floor of a building in Chicago with no adverse reaction. She used to experience extreme discomfort and sudden severe perspiration due to her fear. She now displays new confidence. A stability of mood and a feeling of happiness and well-being are also evident.

Angela D.

Angela developed several phobias shortly after she got married. Though she had managed to live with them for many years, her growing concern recently brought her to my office. She told me:

> For years I couldn't walk across big intersections or empty parking lots. I always thought my fear of intersections had something to do with my mother. A very meek woman, she was terrified of crossing most streets. Even when I was a little girl she would make me hold her hand and walk her across. It was very frightening. I think she had once been hit by a car, and that was why she was so afraid. But she would never talk about it.

When I got married I moved away from my mother's neighborhood. Then all of a sudden I couldn't walk across intersections by myself. At first I couldn't understand it. I never had a problem when I lived in New York City. I just couldn't figure it out. I was very happily married, and I loved my new house.

Eventually I came to realize that it had something to do with the guilt I had over leaving my mother. As I said, she was a very meek woman—very sensitive and very vulnerable. Anyway, I would get to an intersection and just freeze. I couldn't cross, so I'd try to find some other way to get to my destination. Then the same thing started to happen in parking lots. I couldn't get out of my car . . . I was just frozen. Once I had to get to an important doctor's appointment, and I didn't know what to do. Finally I parked my car near a wall and crept toward his office, clinging to the wall the entire time. This was terribly upsetting for me, especially since there didn't seem to be any rational explanation. I could understand my problem with intersections, but not this.

Several years ago my mother passed away. All of a sudden I was able to cross big streets by myself. I would just say to myself, "She's gone now . . . you can cross the street." And I could! But the fear of parking lots continued.

Recently, I was walking down the street and I started to black out. I got really light-headed, then my heart started pounding. I didn't know what had hit me, but I was scared. Fortunately my husband was with me. I held on to him until I gained control of myself. Now I was afraid of walking anywhere by myself. That was when I decided to do something about this.

As I listened to Angela's story I developed a strong suspicion that her problems were due to an impaired balance mechanism that was being aggravated and reinforced by the stress from her guilt. Our conversation revealed numerous other signs of CVS dysfunction. She was nonathletic, she didn't like to read, and her driving skills were poor (causing a number of small fender benders). In addition, her memory often failed her, her concentration span was short, she was easily distracted, and she was prone to worrying obsessively about many unimportant problems. Diagnostic tests confirmed the presence of an inner-ear dysfunction, and treatment was started. Angela recently wrote:

My fear of parking lots has vanished. I can walk across giant empty lots—like the ones in Roosevelt Field—without any problem. Often I purposely park far away from the stores just to test myself. My fear of passing out on the street is also gone . . . it disappeared almost immediately.

My whole sense of balance feels different since I started the medications. I never realized how bad it used to be. I used to fall once in a while—especially on stairs—but I never associated this with my sense of balance. I haven't tripped or fallen since I came to your office. Also, I've had no dizziness or light-headedness. As I said, I just feel more on-center. I know it sounds strange, but lately I've also been wondering whether or not my mother actually had the same thing I had—only worse. It would certainly explain a lot of things.

Stacy B.

Stacy's case clearly illustrates how the presence of realistic, neurotic, and physiological factors can produce an assortment of mixed phobias. She recalls:

I've always been afraid of heights. I can't look down. I feel like I'm going to fall over or jump. High waves are one of my biggest fears. I'm always afraid that we're going to have a tidal wave. The movie . . . *Krakatoa, East of Java* . . . that seemed to have started it. I began having dreams of people drowning, or of me not being able to save someone. The other day I had a dream that I was on a ship and the ship split. Water was flowing in through the middle. I was on one side and everyone else was on the other side. I'm getting scared just talking about it .

I've also always had this fear of getting old and dying. I'm really afraid of old people. When I see them, like on a bus or something, I panic. Not an uncontrollable panic . . . but bad. I'll be thinking, "Oh, my God, I'm going to get old and die." Then my heart will start to beat really fast and my hands will start to sweat.

But my biggest fear has been the fear of going crazy. That is uncontrollable. My mom was put in a mental institution when I was little. I didn't see her for twenty-one years, and I really didn't know what was wrong with her . . . the hospital lost all of her records. The first time I saw her again I really freaked out. She had only one tooth in her mouth . . . it was sad and horrible.

After seeing her, everything got worse. Most of the time I worried that I would go crazy, too. I got really depressed. I was unable to sleep. Then I won two scholarships in the same week, and I had to choose between the two. That's when I lost it. I started having major anxiety attacks. I would wake up and my heart would be beating like crazy and I'd be sweating. I'd wake up my roommate and say, "I'm dying, I'm dying." She would say, "You're awake and you're fine . . . go back to sleep." I'd run to the closest emergency room, but by the time I got there I would be okay. It was as though I was flipping out . . . I just couldn't understand it.

I was very close to the nurse in school, and I started going to her office regularly. I kept telling her, "I think I'm going to crack up." And she would say, "You're normal, you're fine. You're not going to crack up." And I would ask, "How do you know I'm not going to crack up?" The more she told me I wasn't going to crack up, the more anxious I became.

Other things got bad, too. I'd always had a pretty good memory. But all of a sudden I couldn't remember anything. People would say to me, "Hi! How've you been?" And I couldn't remember where I had known them from. I was forgetting everything . . . appointments, schoolwork . . . everything. And I couldn't concentrate on anything.

I also started getting lost everywhere. One day it took me three hours to find the subway that I'd been on a million times. I couldn't read street signs . . . I couldn't make sense of anything I was reading. Then I became afraid to walk on the street. I used to do everything by myself. Now I was afraid to go out alone.

The first doctor I went to—at the hospital—gave me Thorazine. I needed to take something because I was just flipping out. It put me in a weird state . . . like "stretched out." An hour felt like a day. And it didn't help. The next doctor said, "You're not schizophrenic. I don't want you taking that anymore." Then another doctor suggested Lithium. But that didn't really work either.

By the time Stacy came to my office she had been through a battery of doctors and a vast array of medications. But she was still in terrible condition. Her story indicated the possible presence of an underlying CVS dysfunction, and this was quickly confirmed by diagnostic testing.

As I explained to Stacy how the inner-ear system could be responsible for many of her problems, she began to sob hysterically. Finally she blurted out, "I knew I wasn't crazy!" Her boyfriend reassuringly added, "I told you that you weren't crazy." Then he turned to me and said, "Thank you, doctor. This is the happiest moment we've had in two years."

CHAPTER 18

Type 3 Phobias and Their Mechanisms: A Summary

The phobic disorder is as varied and complex as its underlying mechanisms. Because the number and combination of these mechanisms is infinite, so, too, are the many faces of phobic behavior. In this chapter I have listed the most common Type 3 phobias, along with a summary of their typical underlying mechanisms (including decompensatory mechanisms). As you read these summaries, please note that this analysis is by no means inclusive. The Type 3 mechanistic possibilities are, as I have said, endless.

Often your reasons for being afraid, and the way you feel when you are afraid, are what distinguish a Type 3 phobia from a Type 1, Type 2, or mixed phobia. For this reason, these summaries include the subjective feelings typically associated with Type 3 phobias.

Although it is virtually impossible to closely examine every known Type 3 phobia, I have tried to include the vast majority of them. I apologize if your particular phobia(s) or phobic mechanism(s) has been left out or overlooked. Hopefully you will be able to use your newly acquired insight and your intuition to fill in any gaps that may be important to you.

As you read this chapter, notice how many different mechanisms or combination of mechanisms can account for the same phobia. Perhaps now, more than ever before, you will understand why a phobic classification system or treatment regimen that does not focus on these underlying mechanisms is shortsighted, simplistic, and even dangerous.

FEAR OF HEIGHTS

When the inner ear is impaired, your sense of balance—your internal gyroscope—is frequently affected. Imbalance problems are triggered and magnified by reaching heights where falling and injury, or the anticipation of such, is possible. This fear may be restricted to realistic possibilities, such as an open rooftop, a ladder, a bridge, a platform edge, a gangplank, or an open window. But it may also be present when you look down from a height through a closed window or see-through elevator, or when you look up at a tall object. Typically, the visual perception of the height triggers and magnifies partially compensated feelings of imbalance. Frequently, the visual deprivation effect of great height also triggers and magnifies orientation problems.

Type 3 fears of heights are usually associated with some or all of the following feelings: dizziness, light-headedness, off-balance or off-center feelings, vertigo, motion sickness, spinning, faintness, floating sensations, a magnetic pull toward the bottom or a repellent recoil from the bottom, a fear of jumping, and various fight or flight symptoms. Some individuals in a tall building actually fear that the building will crumble—a displacement of their inner feelings of imbalance.

FEARS OF SMALL, ENCLOSED SPACES AND OTHER "TRAPS"

Elevators, planes, cars, rooms without windows (or windows that don't open), basements, closets, the dark, tunnels, being underwater, movie theaters, and other shielding environments physically deprive the brain of vital sensory information (visual, gravitational, auditory, etc., or some combination). This can trip the fight or flight alarm and lead to fears of being trapped (claustrophobic anxiety).

Individuals who suffer from these deprivation-related fears dread being trapped in a room, or anywhere, without a window, door, or some other visible means of escape. Many will not go to a classroom, movie theater, or lecture hall unless they can sit on an aisle seat or near an exit. They need to know that they can get out if they suddenly are overcome by a fear of losing control, screaming, passing out, or dying. When there is no visible means of escape, the inner, deadly feelings of being trapped are reinforced, and anxiety and panic escalate.

Most people who fear small, enclosed spaces are also sensitive to the smothering effects of crowds. Many are uncomfortable when people get too close—get "in their face." Some even feel uncomfortable wearing goggles, glasses, masks, tight clothes, and jewelry because of the smothering feelings these objects provoke. These smothering feelings are also frequently experienced when bathing. As a result, many so-called claustrophobics prefer to shower.

Even in a wide-open space you may feel trapped—frightened that you will never get back to home base. In other words, you are trapped in the middle, even if the middle is wide-open and uncrowded. These trapped sensations can also occur when you are stuck on a wide-open highway or in a traffic jam . . . when you are stuck in the middle of a crowd or in the middle of a line . . . when you are stuck in a broken elevator . . . when you are stuck in a social situation you can't leave . . . when you are stuck living in a high-rise apartment building with hundreds of people living above you, etc. In each of these cases, being trapped (literally or symbolically), or the anticipation of being trapped, produces anxiety, and the inability to escape magnifies that anxiety.

Interestingly, analysis has revealed that many individuals with these fears were hyperactive, overactive, or overly energetic as children. Though their overactivity may have decreased to the extent that it is no longer visible to others, they still feel like a racing motor inside. These individuals need to be in motion and cannot be held down or trapped for too long without feeling overwhelmed and panicky.

One of the most fascinating ramifications of this fear of small, enclosed spaces is the way it can lead to a fear of death. While most people fear dying, not everyone fears it for the same reasons. For some CVS-impaired individuals, dying represents the ultimate trap—being buried in a coffin, the smallest enclosed space a human being can fit into, six feet underground. Although you will be dead at the time, and it shouldn't really matter, the very thought of coming to such an end can terrorize someone who is afraid of small, enclosed spaces.

Many claustrophobics are obsessed with death, dying, illness, etc., and are constantly trying to figure out ways to avoid this terrifying consequence. They wonder, "Should I be cremated? . . . Should I donate my body to science? . . . Should I be frozen?" But none of these possibilities seems to provide them with an acceptable solution. Although these obsessions could easily be diagnosed as having purely psychological origins, this is clearly not the case.

CROWDS

Crowds tend to create the sensation of being trapped in a small, enclosed space. The sensory deprivation, as well as the feelings of being smothered, stuck, or trapped, can effect a rapid escalation in anxiety.

Improper filtering of background noise is another basic Type 3 mechanism that is responsible for crowd phobias. Individuals who cannot block out or inhibit background acoustics often become overloaded, discombobulated, and anxious in a busy restaurant, noisy stadium, crowded party, etc. Trying to carry on a conversation under such circumstances is even more distressing, since background noises merge with the conversation and result in auditory blurring.

Improper filtering of the visual, olfactory (smell), and motion input furnished by a crowd can also be overwhelming—provoking dizziness, imbalance, and panic. For example, specific or intense odors may destabilize certain people, thus contributing to restaurant phobias (as well as other phobias characterized by destabilizing scents). Various visual and/or color patterns created by stationary or moving crowds can also provoke dizziness, nausea, and severe anxiety when this visual input is improperly processed.

Since most people are usually more sensitive to one sensory input than to another, the exact nature of the crowd phobia will vary accordingly. For example, individuals whose symptoms are triggered by moving visual input will fear and avoid crowded supermarkets, busy moving traffic, crowded city streets, and other situations where flickering and changing colors and/or shapes overwhelm the visual filter. These same individuals may feel completely comfortable in a crowded restaurant in which everyone is seated and movement is minimized.

Some crowd phobias stem from imbalance problems. One of my patients, for example, feared crowded department stores, grocery stores, and streets because she was afraid of being knocked down and trampled by the mo ing crowd. This woman's sense of balance was severely impaired, and it didn't take much to tip her over. Hence, her seemingly irrational fear had a very rational basis (interestingly, this fear of being knocked down was also at the root of her fear of dogs).

FLYING

When you are flying in a giant metal bird thirty thousand feet above the earth's surface, you have relinquished control of the plane—and your life—to the pilots, mechanics, and crew (unless, of course, you are flying the plane). This is enough to make most people uncomfortable or fearful. But putting your life in someone else's hands provokes and magnifies inner feelings of losing control already present in many phobic individuals, and the subsequent out-of-control feelings become unbearable.

Fears of crashing and/or falling are especially prevalent when you look out of a plane window or think about how high up you are. Altitude frequently triggers anxiety, vertigo, and motion-sickness responses similar to those some individuals experience atop a high mountain resort. Some individuals feel better when they look out of a window and see land and clouds, because they are able to get a visual fix. Others feel much worse, the visual perception being just a reminder of how high up they are.

Feelings of being trapped (claustrophobic anxiety) are also provoked and magnified by being confined within an enclosed plane, since the individual knows he is unable to get out or off at conscious will. (Obviously this same mechanism is triggered in a closed moving train, elevator, bus, and so on.) For some individuals, feelings of being trapped set in as soon as the airplane door is closed. For others, these feelings don't set in until the plane has taken off and there is no turning back.

Some people panic only if they are seated in the middle of a row of seats where their feelings of being trapped are intensified. As a result, they always require an aisle seat, or even a seat next to the door. Some individuals who are not afraid to fly over land are terrified of flying over water, or of landing on a runway that is surrounded by water. This usually indicates an underlying fear of water, or of drowning. Although most people who have this fear are poor swimmers, some are not. These strong swimmers are not afraid of the water per se but of being trapped underwater in the airplane.

Some phobics fear acceleration and deceleration. This highlights the difficulties some people have with monitoring and controlling speed—regardless of whether the speed is experienced in a plane, car, or train. Many of these individuals have difficulty stopping, starting, and directing their bodies on target, and displace these coordination-related difficulties to the vehicle in which they are traveling.

In addition, individuals with CVS dysfunction may be sensitive to turbulence (motion sensitivity), and/or the rapid changes of electromagnetic forces experienced when traversing varying time zones at high speeds. All too often we assume that fears with a common name have common determinants. As the fear of flying illustrates, this assumption is frequently erroneous.

DRIVING

For some individuals, the flickering, blurring, or hypnotic effects created by objects that pass in front of them or next to them (or in their mirrors) while they are driving overloads their visual circuits and triggers anxiety or panic. Usually this visual flooding is destabilizing orientation and balance mechanisms. As a result, a variety of compass- and balance-related symptoms often surface.

Typically, the greater the driving speed, the worse is the effect (it's easier for the eyes to track visual information at lower speeds). Highway driving is therefore worse than driving on slower, local roads. Some phobics feel trapped when they are on a highway that has no immediate exit in sight. Traffic jams tend to provoke similar feelings. As a result, expressway driving is typically avoided. By using local roads, the navigational process is slowed down, easing the strain on the sensory system. Meanwhile, knowing that you can pull over and get out of the car at any time lessens anticipatory worries of being trapped.

Many people do not have the coordination skills and reflexes required to drive a car safely—even one with an automatic transmission. In fact, they have more difficulty driving a straight line than walking one (and curves and turns may be difficult or impossible to negotiate). When visual coordination is poor, you may have difficulty judging the speed and direction of oncoming cars. Furthermore, you may not be able to judge how far you are from the car in front of you, the one beside you, or behind you—even how far you are from adjacent streets, fences, guardrails, walls, and pedestrians. This can provoke tremendous anxiety. If you have CVS-induced tunnel vision, you may be unable to look straight ahead and see the periphery at the same time. Not knowing what is happening on either side of your narrow field of vision can also generate tremendous anxiety.

All coordination-related problems are magnified by high-speed highway driving. Motion sensitivity also underlies the development of some driving phobias. While some individuals are sensitive to the vertical motion of a car on a bumpy road, others are sensitive to the changes in motion brought on by acceleration and deceleration. Sensitivity to the speed of the vehicle can also magnify underlying fears of losing control, crashing, etc.

Considering all of the possible Type 3 mechanisms that can contribute to the development of driving phobias, it is no wonder that these phobias are so common.

ELEVATORS

A fear of elevators can stem from any or all of the following Type 3 mechanisms (or some combination):

- The sensory deprivation effect of the small, enclosed space aggravates underlying compass and/or balance problems, provoking anxiety, dizziness, light-headedness, disorientation, etc. As anxiety mounts, fears of becoming stuck or trapped surface and become magnified.
- The smothering effect of a crowded elevator (a sensory effect) can provoke anxiety, disorientation, dizziness, feelings of being trapped, etc.
- The movement of an elevator (especially sudden movements, bumps, acceleration, and deceleration) can trigger anxiety and panic in motion-sensitive individuals.
- In glass elevators the visual perception of height, or the hypnotic visual distraction created when the elevator is in motion, can destabilize partially compensated balance and/or compass and/or motion-sensitivity problems. The result is anxiety, dizziness, disorientation, etc.
- Coordination difficulties—especially poor depth perception (visual dyscoordination)—can provoke fears of being crushed by the elevator doors when entering or exiting.

STAIRS AND ESCALATORS

Stair phobias can result from imbalance problems, coordination problems, motion sensitivity, or any combination of the three. If imbalance problems are wholly or partially responsible, individuals will typically have other imbalance-related fears, such as the fear of heights. If coordination problems are present, even one or two steps can provoke anxiety, fear, or panic.

Walking down steps is generally more difficult than walking up, because the eyes are forced to look at the large wide-open space below, or at the flickering effects created by the rows of steps. These visual distractions destabilize visual compensation.

In addition, the tug of gravity magnifies imbalance symptoms. Going up steps can also provoke anxiety or panic if the eyes are mesmerized by the pattern of the steps in front of you.

Walking up open-backed steps can be particularly terrifying because your eyes are forced to look through the steps at the objects or wide-open space below. Some individuals with poor depth perception actually feel as though they are falling through these open-backed steps. Stair phobias are often magnified when the stairs move, i.e., on an escalator. The evaluation of Type 3 escalator phobias has revealed the following:

- Down escalators are frequently more terrifying than up escalators because of the tug of gravity and because you are forced to look at the wide-open space below. Both of these factors aggravate imbalance problems.
- Many individuals with coordination and/or balance problems fear that they will not be able to get on or off an escalator without falling.
- The motion of an escalator can upset or terrify motion-sensitive individuals.
- Certain phobics fear being trapped or stuck in a crowd in the middle of an escalator.

While some phobics avoid staircases and escalators whenever humanly possible, others hold on to the railing for dear life. Many stair phobics actually sit on the staircases and inch their way down step by step. Others run up and down stairs and escalators in order to get off them as quickly as possible.

WIDE-OPEN SPACES

The fear of wide-open spaces is often just the fear of fear itself, produced when chronic anticipatory anxiety makes you afraid of leaving your home. In this highly sensitized condition, the slightest bit of sensory shielding or flooding can trigger panic.

But even when chronic anticipatory anxiety is not present, certain wide-open spaces—such as giant intersections, large empty parking lots, wide-open fields, deserted streets, big department stores, empty highways, sports arenas, etc.—can trip the fight or flight alarm. Typically, this reflects underlying gyroscope and/or compass disturbances. When the sensory-deprivation effect created by the wide-open spaces aggravates balance and/or compass problems, you may feel off-balance, weak-kneed, dizzy, disoriented, light-headed, out of control, etc. Such symptoms can easily provoke anxiety, fear, or panic.

When crossing a large, busy intersection, balance problems can be intensified by the flooding effects of moving cars, changing lights, honking horns, etc. This can produce more anxiety and vertigo, as well as a realistic fear of getting hurt or killed if you happen to trip, fall, become dizzy, pass out, or have a momentary memory lapse.

One of my patients (Susan S. in Chapter 1) feared crossing the street because she could not remember whether green meant go or stop. In addition, she could not accurately determine the speed, position, or even the direction of the various moving vehicles. Accordingly, she would freeze before crossing, or just dash across the street while praying that she would make it safely to the other side. This clearly illustrates how entirely different Type 3 mechanisms can result in the same fears.

BRIDGES

A wide variety of Type 3 mechanisms—either alone or in some combination—can result in bridge phobias. For example:

- Coordination problems may result in the fear that your car will go over the side of the bridge or crash into another car.
- Imbalance problems may make you feel as though the bridge itself is going to collapse.
- Visual overload from the flickering effect created by cars, signs, lines, bridge uprights and cables, etc., can destabilize an impaired CVS compass and/or gyroscope that relies on visual information for compensation.
- The visual deprivation effect of the wide-open space surround-

ing the bridge can destabilize visual compensatory mechanisms, triggering and magnifying feelings of imbalance and/or disorientation.

The fear of bridges may also reflect an underlying fear of heights (provoked by looking down), a fear of the water, motion sensitivity (the swaying of the bridge makes some individuals motion sick), or a fear of getting stuck or trapped on the bridge (claustrophobic anxiety).

TUNNELS

Tunnels are sensory-deprivation environments that physically deprive the inner ear of various types of sensory input. If the CVS is impaired, the absence of important visual and/or auditory and/or electromagnetic information can destabilize compass and/or balance mechanisms to the point of provoking panic, disorientation, confusion, disassociation, and fears of being stuck or trapped. In addition, the flickering patterns of oncoming cars, tunnel lights, lines, signs, etc., can destabilize visual compensatory mechanisms, further aggravating the impaired CVS.

Other Type 3 mechanisms that can lead to tunnel phobias include the following:

- If the tunnel rests beneath a body of water, individuals with water phobias may fear drowning.
- Inner feelings of imbalance may be responsible for an outer feeling that the tunnel is going to collapse.
- The physical strain of keeping a car in a tight lane for an extended period of time can make coordination-impaired individuals fear they will lose control of the car and crash into a wall or another vehicle.

The inability to see the end of the tunnel further intensifies feelings of being trapped, lost, or disoriented. Typically, sighting the end of the tunnel helps considerably because it shows an escape from the trap (psychological help) and also provides the deprived CVS with more visual information (physiological help). But if these fears are purely coordination related, you may continue to panic or be frightened until you are actually out of the tunnel—i.e., until the coordination task is complete.

NOISES

When a malfunctioning auditory filter renders an individual highly sensitive to sound, a variety of noise-related phobias may result. Many crowd phobias and social phobias, for example, stem from a hypersensitivity to noise. Typically, this underlying factor is overlooked. Auditory processing problems can also result in a sensitivity to specific sounds or pitches. This type of dysfunction typically accounts for the fear triggered by the sound of screeching brakes, ringing telephones, racing cars, tire blowouts, barking animals, birds, thunder, etc.

BRIGHT LIGHTS

An oversensitivity to light reflects the inability of the CVS to properly filter incoming visual signals. This underfiltering can make a 100-watt bulb look like a 1000-watt beacon, and trigger panic. As stated earlier, this oversensitivity to light, typically referred to as photophobia, is one of the few sensory phobias that has long been recognized as a vestibular disorder.

MOTION

Individuals predisposed to motion sickness or motion-related anxiety will avoid or dread motion-related tasks or vehicles. Thus people fear flying, driving, running . . . even walking, depending upon their sensitivity. Certain elevator and escalator phobias are also motion related, resulting from the same mechanisms as other more obvious motion-related fears.

Some individuals are extremely sensitive to acceleration and/or deceleration. This sensitivity to changes in motion is sometimes responsible for driving phobias, flying phobias, etc. Since vibration is motion, various vibration-related fears and panic episodes can also result from a hypersensitivity to motion. Motion sensitivity is often responsible for various swimming and water-related phobias (discussed separately).

SOCIAL GATHERINGS

Social gatherings may trigger anxiety and panic because these situations tend to overload the brain with visual and/or auditory and/or olfactory input. The crowds at a social gathering can also provoke feelings of being trapped. Any of these could result in anxiety, disorientation, light-headedness, off-balance feelings, and even a sudden urge to run out of the room, go home, and so on.

Many individuals incapable of properly filtering out background noise have difficulty hearing and participating in conversations because everything they listen to gets blurred out. As a result, they become embarrassed, feel stupid, and want to get out of, or avoid, social situations. Individuals with speech disturbances also feel stupid and embarrassed in social situations, and tend to have severe social anxieties, fears, and phobias (especially when their anxiety is not properly filtered).

Memory problems, coordination problems, and various other inner-ear-related disturbances can also make an individual feel self-conscious, embarrassed, stupid, humiliated, clumsy, or ugly in social situations. If these thoughts perseverate, and/or anxiety is improperly filtered, fears and avoidance can result. Sometimes even handshaking difficulties stemming from left-right confusion can lead to social phobias.

Unfortunately, the feelings of stupidity, clumsiness, ugliness, etc., that result from CVS-induced speech, hearing, coordination, and memory dysfunctions further complicate an already serious problem. If such feelings are to be treated properly, it is crucial that both the therapist and the phobic be aware of the physiological roots of these problems.

SLEEPING

The examination of thousands of CVS-impaired individuals has clearly revealed that abnormal eye movements occur when these individuals stand or lie in certain positions with their eyes closed. In fact, the presence and quality of these eye movements is a key diagnostic indication of inner-ear dysfunction. (See Chapter 22.) When abnormal eye movements are severe, closing your eyes can result in dizziness, nausea, retching, etc. Opening your eyes, on the other hand, and concentrating on a fixed object (as one does when motion sick) generally results in compensation and the subsequent disappearance of these symptoms. By avoiding sleep and other activities that require closing the eyes, these unpleasant symptoms are circumvented.

When inner-ear dysfunction is present, closing the eyes may also provoke the release of terrors and nightmares related to falling, floating, and spinning (signs of balance and compass disturbances). The desire to avoid these unpleasant experiences can also lead to insomnia.

SEX

Occasionally the stress, excitement and/or motion from inter-course triggers fears of fainting, losing control, or dying, as well as vertigo and motion-sick responses. Coordination dysfunction or obsessive worries about sexual performance can also lead to sexual fears and avoidance.

SWIMMING AND WATER

Many inner-ear-impaired individuals are afraid of the trapped and/or disorienting sensations provoked by underwater swim-ming—especially if they have to close their eyes. Some actually lose their way underwater and swim down when they want to swim up. This can be particularly terrifying, and is very dangerous.

Some patients have reported that they won't swim if they can't see the bottom of the pool. In essence, a watery void is like a dark room or a wide-open space, all of which provoke similar anxieties and fears. While many people become disoriented and/ or feel suffocated in the water, others cannot learn to coordinate swimming movements and breathing patterns adequately, and therefore fear drowning.

Certain individuals are so sensitive to motion that they become anxious or motion sick in the water. In fact, some extremely motion-sensitive individuals become anxious, panicky, or nauseous just looking at waves, rolling tides, even ripples. Some people with impaired balance mechanisms feel discombobulated even when they float with their heads above water. One of my patients used to panic every time her feet didn't touch the bottom of the pool.

Fear of swimming can lead to various drowning-related phobias such as fear of boats, fear of flying over water, fear of driving over bridges, fear of driving through underwater tunnels, etc. For some individuals, merely looking at a lake, swimming pool, or ocean provokes terror, while other highly sensitive individuals may even dislike drinking water.

SPORTS

Sports and coordination phobias are prevalent in CVS-impaired children and are often witnessed in adults as well. Many people who appear disinterested in, or afraid of, sports have underlying coordination difficulties. Disinterest is therefore merely a defensive attempt to avoid frustration, embarrassment, and humiliation. In fact, the anticipation of embarrassment is enough to provoke tremendous fear in certain individuals.

Some sports phobias result from a coordination-related fear of being hurt. In fact, many CVS-impaired individuals do get hurt (they get hit by balls, trip frequently, fall easily, etc.). Fears of swimming (discussed separately) and gymnastics are particularly common because both may involve coordination problems and/ or balance- and/or compass-related difficulties. Fear of driving (also discussed separately), one of the *most* common phobias, is also frequently coordination related (either entirely or in part).

TRAVELING

Individuals with an impaired internal compass and/or impaired memory often fear going too far from home and are anxious about getting lost. Accordingly, they prefer traveling with someone whom they trust will get them back and forth safely. In fact, many will not travel at all without their "savior." (Some school phobias stem directly from these mechanisms.) These phobics are not necessarily emotionally dependent but are merely compass dependent.

Trapped feelings are also often triggered when traveling. Typically, this happens midway between home and your destination, when you become unsure whether it is safer and faster to head back before it is too late or proceed forward. Individuals who suffer from this problem constantly find themselves turning around and running or driving home, regardless of how much they want to reach their intended destination. Furthermore, short walks may become as difficult as long trips. Obviously new situations and destinations will trigger the greatest anxiety, because these situations provide the least number of orienting and guiding clues, and also deprive you of psychological crutches such as your home or friends.

The specific Type 3 mechanisms responsible for your traveling phobia are often reflected in the vehicles you won't travel in. If you are only afraid of traveling by boat, this may reflect a motion-related phobia; if you are only afraid of traveling by car, this may reflect a vision-related phobia, and so on. These possibilities must always be investigated.

SCHOOL

School phobias are commonly a reaction to the frustration and hardship experienced because of CVS-induced academic difficulties. Schoolwork is such torture to the dyslexic mind that the mere thought of going to school provokes anxiety or terror. These feelings are often magnified when teachers or peers criticize, torment, ridicule, or insult the struggling student. Specific academic phobias, such as fear of reading, fear of writing, fear of math, fear of tests, etc., also typically stem from the anxiety provoked by dyslexic difficulties. The student who is unable to organize his or her thoughts, for example, may fear writing; the student with visual problems may fear reading; the student with memory problems may fear taking tests, etc.

An impaired inner-ear compass makes it very easy for some children to get lost on the way to and from school. An impaired CVS balance mechanism can make crossing busy intersections on the way to school dangerous and terrifying. Both of these problems can result in school phobias. Speech problems, lack of athletic skills, and other coordination-related difficulties are also a source of embarrassment and frustration for children, and frequently lead to a dislike or fear of school. These phobias can also stem from an underlying fear of crowds, noise, bright lights, stairs, odors, being trapped (in an auditorium, classroom, etc.), etc. If treatment is to be effective, it is important to ascertain what, if any, underlying fears are present.

FEAR OF THE DARK

When it is dark, visual compensatory mechanisms are strained or blocked. The inability to zero in on, or clearly target, surrounding objects results in the release of balance-, compass-, motion-, and coordination-related anxieties and fears normally held in check by visual compensation. Some individuals get dizzy and disoriented in the dark, others lose their balance, others get nauseous, others fear that "things" are coming at them (and fear getting hurt), while others are just afraid or panicky. All of these symptoms are indicative of underlying CVS dysfunction.

PUBLIC SPEAKING

Bright, hot lights are capable of flooding visual circuits and generating anxiety. A crowded room can flood visual, auditory, and olfactory circuits, and generate anxiety. The pressure of performing typically generates anxiety. Put these three together, and you have a situation that can easily overwhelm someone with an impaired CVS. The result is stage fright, which is typically characterized by dizziness, light-headedness, immobilization, off-balance feelings, and a fear of losing control and/or fainting. Fears of speaking and performing are not always limited to the stage. These same symptoms can arise in a small, enclosed room, or in any number of flooding or shielding environments known to destabilize the CVS.

Sometimes concerns about embarrassment or humiliation are magnified by an impaired anxiety filter. This can also lead to a fear of public speaking and/or performing. Some fears of public speaking stem from speech problems. When CVS motor dysfunction affects speech, causing stuttering, stammering, slurring, slow speech, and other dysrhythmic speech patterns, you may be filled with dread at the thought of having to speak in front of a crowd. In fact, the thought of speaking in front of just one person may provoke anxiety, fear, or panic.

Memory dysfunction can also lead to stage fright, especially when you have difficulty remembering words or thoughts fast enough . . . or at all. Of course, any combination of the above mechanisms is also possible.

FEAR OF SWALLOWING AND OTHER FEARS OF REFLEX FAILURE

When CVS dysfunction is present, normal reflexes may become dyscoordinated. When you do not trust your reflexes, a variety of fears may result, including fear of swallowing, fear of choking, fear of suffocating, fear of heart failure, fear of dying, etc. These fears can be aggravated by wearing a mask, taking a bath, swallowing a pill, etc.

GERMS AND DISEASES

The fear of diseases and disease-carrying organisms, as well as the repetitive hand-washing, bathing, and cleansing habits that result, seem to stem from CVS-induced perseveration. In other words, a malfunctioning inner-ear system prevents you from erasing or properly dampening concerns over illness and infection. Instead, these concerns stick in the mind and magnify, creating obsessive worries and fears. This in turn triggers compulsive cleansing behavior.

INSECTS, SNAKES, MICE, KNIVES AND OTHER UNIVERSAL PHOBIAS

Fears of sharp objects, insects, snakes, mice, and various other animals probably represent built-in release phenomena—instinctive fight or flight responses imprinted in the brains of our evolutionary ancestors. While some species in the animal kingdom continue to rely on these instinctive reactions, such responses were covered up and neutralized during the evolution of the human species. But if the central inhibitory system—the CVS—is impaired, these responses may surface when provoked by the appropriate triggers.

Other universal-like phobias, such as the fear of birds and the fear of frogs, may be similarly triggered if the universal reflex itself is improperly programmed. Although people with these fears are often ridiculed, they are actually suffering from a physiologically determined maladaptive reflex response over which they have little or no control.

PART IV

DISCOVERING THE BASIS OF PHOBIC BEHAVIOR

CHAPTER 19

A Most Fortunate Accident

Nothing would please me more than to be able to claim that my discovery of Freud's "missing link"—the physiological origin of phobic behavior—resulted from brilliant theoretical deduction. But the truth is that this discovery occurred somewhat by chance. In this chapter I would like to share with you the events that led me to this most fortunate "accident."

HOLES IN THE THEORIES

I have practiced psychoanalytically oriented psychotherapy since completing my psychiatric residence at Kings County Hospital in 1963. Almost from the very beginning, I felt that important insights were missing from the traditional Freudian approach to understanding and treating phobic behavior. For example, Freudian theory could not predict or explain the following:

- The form and shape of the vast majority of phobias.
- The varying combinations and intensities of distinctly separate phobias occurring in any one patient.
- The onset and remission of phobias.
- Treatment success and failure in phobic patients, regardless of treatment techniques and motivation.
- The personality profile predisposing individuals to phobias.

In view of the obvious limitations of Freudian theory in practice, many clinicians were forced to seek and develop alternate methods of treatment. Some researchers discovered that antidepressant medications sometimes significantly and rapidly reduced phobic symptoms. Others discovered that many phobias appear to have hereditary origins. Still others came to believe that the only way to successfully treat phobias was to ignore the underlying causes and conflicts that allegedly existed and focus instead on desensitizing phobics to their triggers and their overwhelming anticipatory anxiety.

In my clinical experience with medical theories that seem to be mutually contradictory, either/or approaches are seldom complete. Only theories capable of encompassing and explaining *all* sub-theories, however contradictory and antagonistic they appear to be, are generally able to provide patients with the best chance of success.

As a budding Freudian-trained psychiatrist, my best asset, in retrospect, was my feeling that if I couldn't understand or accept traditional concepts and theories, it was my fault. To come to terms with my difficulties, I had leading psychoanalysts privately supervise my treatment of neurotic and psychotic patients during my psychiatric residency (paying for this assistance by moonlighting).

Although this expert clinical supervision helped me to understand the theory and practice of psychoanalysis, I continued to feel that important explanations were missing. The theories that supposedly explained the clinical facts of phobic life seemed too complicated to be valid in all instances. These theories were perfectly understandable, but something seemed to be wrong with them. Furthermore, often it appeared that clinical facts were forced into theoretical molds where they simply did not belong.

My observations made me feel uneasy. And my doubts made me switch from one training analyst to another. To my great dismay, I often found that the same clinical data was interpreted in entirely different ways by different analysts. In other words, the interpretation of phobic symptoms, instead of being absolute and identical for all analysts, was often merely a function of who was doing the interpreting.

How was I to deal with this dilemma? Who was I to believe? Couldn't an incorrect assessment of phobic mechanisms lead to therapeutic errors and delays—even treatment failures? Having only minimal clinical experience in examining and treating phobics at the time, I could not scientifically decide which, if any, of my teaching supervisors were right. Forced to use my instincts, I continued to switch from teacher to teacher until I finally settled for several whom I felt had a better grasp of the data. But an irritating anxiety, based on two of my own unresolved conflicts, persisted:

■ Why did the interpretation of clinical data by psychoanalysts teaching in the very same psychoanalytic training institute differ so?

■ How is a psychiatric resident-in-training to objectively judge the validity of what he is taught without having acquired sufficient clinical experience and personal clinical insight?

MY OWN PSYCHOANALYSIS

I could come up with only one answer. I would undergo psychoanalysis and see firsthand how the experts worked, and how their patients responded. Sadly, my first analyst died after several years of therapy, and I was forced to switch to another. But, almost immediately, it became apparent that both analysts had significantly different treatment styles, and to my great dismay, even different views on the exact same symptoms. My attempt to find consistency in the practice of psychoanalysis had again failed.

Many of the clinical interpretations made by my analysts were amazingly insightful and therapeutically beneficial. But many others fell flat, and remained so even in retrospect. These mixed results forced me to arrive at two very simple truths:

■ All psychological theories are incomplete, regardless of how brilliantly conceived and worked-through they appear to be.

■ All who attempt to understand and apply Freudian theory in practice are subject to both emotionally determined and intellectually determined errors, regardless of one's best intentions.

In other words, one's psychoanalyst is not infallible, regardless of how famous and erudite he (or she) is, and regardless of how perfect one would like him to be. He is limited not only by his own interpretations but by the very theories from which he draws these interpretations.

Only years later did I ask my colleagues about their own personal experiences with their training and teaching analysts. Many were equally bewildered by what had transpired, yet few openly spoke about their personal experiences, frustrations, disappointments and criticisms. After all, we were all psychiatrists or psychoanalysts . . . no one wanted to cast aspersions on the profession to which we had dedicated our lives.

At the same time, every psychiatrist must somehow handle his or her professional conflicts. Accordingly, some psychiatrists denied their anxiety and confusion and "confidently" went on to practice as their teachers had; others overreacted and shifted their allegiance to an opposing school of psychoanalytic thought; still others became interested in drug therapy, hoping to accomplish faster and better results for larger numbers of patients; and some adopted behavior modification and desensitization techniques, often to the chagrin of their colleagues. This last group was initially viewed by defensive psychoanalytic conservatives as scientific traitors—betrayers of the Freudian truth.

As for me? I remained loyal to Freudian principles, but I silently questioned both my personal psychoanalytic experiences and my clinical observations of patients. Of all paths to choose, this was no doubt the most difficult.

MORE EXPERIENCE YIELDS MORE DOUBTS

The vast bulk of my private psychiatric practice was initially comprised of phobic and anxiety-ridden patients. For many years I attempted to understand and treat their diverse symptoms as best I could, while continuing to seek out private supervision by well-known psychoanalysts. Some of my patients improved, others did not. And no matter how hard I tried, I never really developed a meaningful understanding and insight into the nature and origin of the vast majority of phobic symptoms. Instead, I was often left with feelings of frustration and emptiness.

Too often, my teachers believed they completely understood the origins of, and mechanisms determining, phobic behavior. To prove it, they often quoted from Freud and his brilliant disciples. But these quotations did not explain the gaps that seemed to exist in phobic theory. This only intensified my scientific doubts. To make matters worse, my teachers often falsely attributed my doubts to unconscious forces of resistance that were attempting to deny the underlying truth. In retrospect, it is clear that they were the ones who were resisting.

In order to better understand my patients, and the existing theories, I studied more. But the harder I studied, the less certain I became. Clearly, I had expected, even hoped for the opposite to happen. It seemed logical to me that the better I knew the theory, the better I would be able to understand phobic symptoms. And the better I understood the symptoms, the more effective my therapeutic approach would become. Not so! Studying only enabled me to become more familiar with the thoughts, convictions, and theories of others. It did not lead me to see and feel the clinical-theoretical correlations my teachers dogmatically insisted were there.

In spite of everything, I plodded ahead, continuing to gain clinical experience while rereading the Freudian literature. Although I could see and rediscover for myself the many psychological mechanisms so magnificently and brilliantly described by Freud in his twenty-four volumes, I did not become the Freudian convert I so desperately wanted to be. Freud's original writings appeared to be scientifically sound and exciting, but the phobic theories proposed by his disciples often left me cold.

There was no denying it . . . the excitement triggered by true insight was still missing far too often when I studied these theories . . . and when I treated my patients. I still did not feel that I really knew the underlying mechanisms responsible for the phobias and related symptoms expressed by so many of my patients.

THE DYSLEXIA CONNECTION

From day one of private psychiatric practice, I began examining and treating learning disabled children. I needed an income while my private practice grew, and the New York City school system needed an interested psychiatrist to treat the learning disabled within their schools.

Once again, I read through all of the available psychiatric and psychoanalytic literature available on learning disabilities and dyslexia. Many of these theories linked reading disorders with such emotional causes as Oedipal conflicts, sibling rivalries, sexual and/or aggressive fantasies having to do with the eyes, competitive difficulties, fear of success, child-rearing difficulties (pampering, overpampering, abuse, etc.), classroom abuse, etc.

To my dismay, I eventually found much of this scientific literature to be in error—some of it even fictitious. Popularly quoted sources had obviously never examined more than a handful of cases, if that. And despite their limited clinical experience, these very same experts wrote long-winded explanations of learning disabilities, implying an understanding that was not feasible.

After having examined several thousand dyslexic patients, I came to realize that all psychological theories concerning the origin of learning disabilities or dyslexic symptoms were substantially incomplete and/or in error. Some theories even seemed significantly, if not totally independent of the dyslexic reality, often stating cause-and-effect correlations between symptoms of learning disabilities and psychoanalytic theories that simply did not exist.

This discovery hit me hard. I was still scientifically naive, thinking experts were right and students such as myself must be wrong (although I had indeed been practicing for several years). Yet I knew I was not wrong about my evaluations of the traditionally espoused psychoanalytic theories concerning learning disabilities and dyslexia. After all, I had now studied thousands of cases . . . I knew what could not be! I also knew that much of what was written about the psychology of learning disabilities and dyslexia had little to do with science—at least little with what I knew and felt science to be.

Only after recognizing that the neurological theories concerning dyslexia were as biased and erroneous as the psychological ones did it dawn on me that scientists did not always have the grasp of their science that they should have had . . . that I was taught they had. Only then did I begin to look more seriously for new concepts to fill the scientific void I had felt once before during my determined study of psychoanalysis. Only then did I begin to search for the key that would ultimately unlock both the dyslexic and phobic riddles.

SOLVING THE FIRST RIDDLE

My first priority was to use the clinical evidence gathered from thousands of my dyslexic patients to develop a clearer, more accurate picture of the dyslexic disorder. Until now, dyslexia was naively assumed to be a learning disorder *necessarily* characterized by one, or both, of the following:

- Severe reading problems.
- Scrambling and/or reversals in letters, numbers and words (evident in spelling, writing and reading).

Therefore it was also assumed that if there was no scrambling, reversal, or reading problem, there was no dyslexia.

Not so! There are literally millions of dyslexics with *no* scrambling or reversal problems and *no* reading problems. These are only two symptoms of dyslexia. There are *dozens* of others, including concentration problems, memory problems, directional problems, balance problems, etc. And any or all of these may be present in a given dyslexic individual. These many symptoms are discussed in more detail in Chapter 9 of this book, and in even greater detail in my books *Smart But Feeling Dumb* and *A Solution to the Riddle Dyslexia*.

Redefining dyslexia was only half the battle. The second, far greater challenge was determining the true physiological and/or psychological origin of the disorder. At the time, the prevailing neurological theory was that dyslexia was due to a disturbance within the cerebrum—the "thinking" brain.* It was on this assumption that I first focused my research efforts. After reviewing my data on one thousand consecutively examined dyslexic patients, it was revealed that only one percent of these cases showed evidence of cerebral dysfunction (low I.Q., difficulty comprehending and formulating meaningful speech, epilepsy, left- or right-sided weakness, etc.). Regardless of how carefully I searched for this evidence, the figure did not change.

Much to my surprise, however, more than 750 of these 1000 patients exhibited distinct evidence of balance and coordination difficulties—i.e., guided-missile problems—including one or more of the following:

- Delayed ability to sit, crawl, walk and/or talk.
- Difficulty skipping, hopping, running, and/or participating in sports.
- Fine-motor-coordination disturbances, such as difficulty tying shoelaces, buttoning buttons, zippering, holding a pencil, using crayons, coloring within guidelines, and/or awkward use of knife and fork.
- Dyscoordinated speech functioning, i.e., slurring, articulation impairments, stuttering and/or stammering.
- Difficulty with balance and coordination, evidenced in delays in learning how to ride a bike or walk a balance beam.

In addition, neurological examinations performed on each of the 750 patients revealed clear and distinct corroborating evidence

---

* One particular cerebral theory that has received considerable attention over the past forty years is the association between dyslexia and left-handedness. My research has clearly demonstrated that there is no significant correlation between the two. This becomes obvious in light of the fact that 90 percent of all dyslexics are right-handed. The errors prevalent in this and other popular dyslexic theories are discussed in detail in *A Solution to the Riddle Dyslexia* (pp. 88–93).

of coordination, balance, and rhythmic difficulties—problems indicative of a cerebellar-vestibular dysfunction. In light of this completely unexpected evidence, I was forced to conclude that there was no significant correlation between dyslexia and cerebral dysfunction. The only correlation that seemed to exist was between dyslexia and inner-ear dysfunction.

Fascinated by my preliminary findings, but not entirely convinced (after all, this evidence went against virtually everything I had learned up to this point), I examined a second series of dyslexic patients. This time, I looked specifically for signs of vestibular and/or cerebellar dysfunction (the first time I looked for signs of cerebral dysfunction, so I was concerned that my efforts might not have been thorough). Close examination of this second series of patients indicated that more than 95 percent of these cases exhibited signs of inner-ear dysfunction. I was stunned.

To independently corroborate my findings, I sent a significant number of cases for neurological reevaluation at a major metropolitan hospital. These neurological studies revealed that 96 percent of these cases showed signs of cerebellar-vestibular dysfunction. I then sent a large group of my patients for special physiological testing called electronystagmography (see Chapter 22). Test results from New York University Medical Center, New York Hospital, Mount Sinai Hospital, Lenox Hill Hospital, and Manhattan Eye, Ear and Throat Hospital revealed that 90 percent of these cases showed definite evidence of inner-ear dysfunction, further confirming my clinical findings.

MEDICATIONS DISCOVERED

Faced with this startling discovery, I set out to find a new means of treating dyslexia. For a long time it had been known that certain antimotion-sickness medications, antihistamines, and other pharmaceutical agents were useful in treating inner-ear problems such as motion sickness. I reasoned that if these medications helped the inner-ear system to handle motion input, they might also help it handle various other sensory input.

Initial experimentation with these medications proved to be far more successful than I had anticipated. Frankly, I had only hoped that dyslexic reading problems might improve with medication. But to my absolute delight, a whole series of sensory and motor symptoms improved—including visual, auditory, and tactile functioning.

Furthermore, treatment with these medications also produced the following, thoroughly unexpected results:

- Smart dyslexic children and adults who invariably felt dumb and ugly, and who avoided a variety of academic, social, and motor tasks, suddenly experienced a new state of confidence and well-being (physical and mental).
- Anxious, panicky, moody, irritable, depressed, antisocial, and temper-prone dyslexics often experienced a dramatic reversal of their symptoms, developing a sense of tranquility and quiescence new to their personality profiles.
- Obsessive and compulsive individuals plagued by repetitive thoughts and actions reported feeling "free," often for the very first time.
- Dyslexics with various psychosomatic symptoms such as tension headaches, nausea, dizziness, vomiting, retching, abdominal complaints, fatigue, ocular squinting and tics, bed-wetting, soiling, excessive sweating, night terrors and/or nightmares, and insomnia unexpectedly reported relief from, or the complete disappearance of, these symptoms.

My greatest surprise came when dyslexic patients reported that their school phobias, motion-related phobias, direction-related phobias, balance-related phobias, and coordination-related phobias disappeared or were significantly alleviated by these medications. When these improvements were initially reported to me, I assumed they all had a psychological basis. In other words, I had believed that these symptoms resulted from the frustrations and anxieties experienced by dyslexics in their attempts to live, compete, and succeed. Therefore, by relieving the academic, memory, concentration, overactivity, and distractibility symptoms that characterize dyslexia, it was only natural that these stress-related phobic and mental symptoms should improve. Indeed, this had been my conviction for many years.

With increasing experience, however, it slowly became apparent that not all of the above improvements were of a secondary, psychological nature. Indeed, the very same inner-ear mechanisms found to be a major determinant in causing dyslexic academic symptoms also seemed to be implicated in emotional and behavioral symptoms—i.e., phobias, anxiety states, mood disorders, obsessions, compulsions, etc.

I had always been aware of the prevalence of phobic behavior among dyslexics. But these unexpected clinical results seemed to suggest that dyslexia and phobic behavior were linked in a way that neither I nor any of my colleagues had ever imagined. I wondered: Was it truly possible that phobic symptoms and dyslexic symptoms were both a direct result of the same inner-ear and/or cerebellar dysfunction? The implications and ramifications were mind-boggling, almost overwhelming.

PHOBIC BEHAVIOR: A PRELIMINARY INVESTIGATION

In an effort to understand this puzzling array of new findings, I set out to reexamine the entire phobic disorder in light of its possible relation to dyslexia. I began by reevaluating my dyslexic patients who were school phobic.

One of the most important things I noticed in these cases was that many dyslexic children who developed school phobias did so only after kindergarten—in first grade, second grade, third grade . . . even in high school and college. This observation clearly challenged traditional psychoanalytic concepts that attributed school phobias to maternal pampering and seduction (babying). If this traditionally espoused separation-anxiety concept of school phobias was universally true, or even true for the majority of school phobics, then most children should develop school phobias when they start school—i.e., in nursery school and kindergarten. Furthermore, the incidence of school phobias should dramatically decrease with advancing grade level as children learn to function more readily on their own. But this was not the case. In fact, the opposite was true.

Although a minority of school phobics were found to be over-pampered, emotionally immature, and tied to their parents, the vast majority were not. Indeed, the vast majority of school phobics avoided school only because they could not cope academically or physiologically with new and confusing school-related circumstances. As a result, the incidence and intensity of school phobias often mushroomed with advancing grade level. These increases were in proportion to the escalating complexity of academic content, the distraction and confusion triggered by larger classes and schools, and the resulting anxiety and frustration.

Were it not for my clinical experience with thousands of dyslexic children, and my ability to study their responses to frustrating subject matter, and to school in general, I would never have understood or even recognized this paradox. Yet once I had recognized the connection between school phobias and *physio-logically* determined academic frustrations that increased in proportion to advancing grade level, this paradox was no longer paradoxical. In fact, it was predictable. But this necessarily implied that school phobias were not usually triggered by separation anxiety.

Suddenly I also understood why many of my older dyslexic patients frequently cut school when they were in high school and college. They also suffered from tremendous school-provoked frustration and anxiety. But they were older and more able to avoid the frustration and feelings of stupidity that resulted from an inability to cope academically. Although these older children were now labeled antisocial and behavior disordered, they were in reality school phobic.

I even came to realize that some pampered children with school phobias were pampered only because their parents intuitively realized there was something physically wrong with them. These so-called pampered children were often hyperactive, overactive, or distractible; they frequently had significant memory disturbances; they had various directional and orientation problems; and their balance and coordination functions were often poorly developed. Moreover, the "pampering" parents of these school-phobic children did not invariably need years of intensive analysis and family therapy. They just needed to be told in simple terms what was really wrong with their children's learning, orientation, balance, and coordination skills.

Many of these school-phobic children were called stupid, dumb, retarded, or klutzy by siblings, classmates and teachers. All of them inwardly felt this way—even under the best of circumstances, when their parents were supportive and pampering rather than critical or abusive. The frustrations inherent in their school situation were just more than they could handle emotionally. Is it any wonder they became school phobic? Is it any wonder their parents became concerned, overconcerned, or even pampering?

Frequently, concerned parents argue with each other about the best way to handle their child's academic and concentration difficulties, as well as the resulting school phobia. Needless to say, these arguments cause or intensify marital problems. All too often, misguided therapists insist that these arguments cause the child's school phobia, rather than the reverse. In other words, sincere parental interest and frustration resulting from a child's school phobia frequently triggers marital discord. Marital discord alone is seldom found to trigger school phobias.

Many therapists who espouse the overpampering or smothering view of school phobias ignore many crucial contradictions. For example, why, in a given family of several pampered children, would only one child become school phobic—especially when that child was not the one most pampered? Why, outside of school, are some school phobics the most independent children? And why do abused children also become school phobic in proportion to their advancing grade level and academic frustration?

Needless to say, abused and neglected children are not pampered! With no one to complain to or to protect them, these children are frequently forced to act out their underlying academic frustrations and anxieties by cutting classes, lying, drinking, and resorting to drug abuse. Sad to say, their school and academic phobias were never properly recognized and treated. Instead, these children were merely referred to as disturbed or sociopathic—labels that prevented proper treatment. In a very real sense, these children were doubly abused.

SCHOOL PHOBIAS: THE TIP OF THE ICEBERG

It wasn't long before my reevaluation of school phobias led to additional insights into other types of phobic behavior. For example, some school phobics also feared getting lost in shopping centers, beaches, and other crowded, unfamiliar environments (including school). Many in fact did get lost. But these children did not want to get lost, as psychoanalysts assumed. Their parents did not want to get rid of them, as psychoanalysts assumed. Their parents didn't even want to pamper them, as psychoanalysts assumed.

Upon neurophysiological examination, these children were found to have orientation and navigational difficulties. They would quickly forget how to get back to home base. Their inner-ear-related compass and memory functions were defective. Accordingly, they not only feared new and/or big schools but any situation in which they could not readily recall, and thus find, their way back home. Interestingly, similar memory problems tended to characterize their reading, spelling and math, resulting in typical dyslexic learning difficulties. Furthermore, upon detailed examination and questioning, their mothers, fathers, siblings, and even their emotional lives were no different from those of children who never developed fears of getting lost.

My understanding of the association between phobias and dyslexia continued to grow, aided in part by a reevaluation of my own children. My daughter Laura, for example, who was belatedly diagnosed as dyslexic, was always fearful of heights and escalators. Furthermore, when she was a child I could not get her to set foot in the ocean without making her cry (despite all attempts at bribery). Initially, my Freudian training forced me to wonder:

- Were Laura's sexual and/or aggressive feelings threatening her emotional tolerance and stability?
- Was she defying me by not liking the ocean as I did?

But now I wondered, "Could Laura's inner-ear dysfunction, clearly visible in her dyslexic symptoms, also be influencing her phobic behavior?"

Soon I had come to realize that many dyslexic children, in addition to having school phobias, were frightened by heights, elevators, escalators, bridges, cars, buses, planes, swimming, sports, and so on. Once again, I was forced to wonder:

- Was it possible that the various motion-related phobias were of inner-ear origin?
- Was it possible that fears of heights and bridges, fear of falling out of a window, fears of falling into a pool, etc., were due to a *physiological* dysfunction in the inner-ear balance mechanism?
- Was I treating two groups of patients: dyslexics *and* phobics? Or was I, as I had suspected for some time, treating two different manifestations of the same underlying physiological problem?

By the time these questions occurred to me I knew I had stumbled onto an explanation for the puzzling inconsistencies in popular phobic theory. I had found a simple and exciting scientific truth, the implications of which were barely imaginable. All that remained for me to do was make sure my hunches were in fact scientifically valid.

PHOBIAS AND DYSLEXIA: AN UNDENIABLE CONNECTION

Fortunately, I had the records of thousands of dyslexic patients as well as countless phobic patients to analyze and reexamine. What I found particularly fascinating was the way in which my phobic patients suddenly opened up to me when I questioned them about possible dyslexic symptoms. For the very first time, they revealed memory, concentration, reading, writing, spelling, and math difficulties, as well as associated feelings of clumsiness (motor dyscoordination), stupidity, and ugliness.

After careful questioning and examination, it was revealed that almost every one of my phobic patients had a history of other inner-ear-related symptoms. And all had neurological evidence of CVS dysfunction. (I was to realize later that those without any apparent dyslexic history had always managed to compensate for their CVS-related difficulties, or had acquired CVS dysfunction later in life.)

Once again, I was stunned by my findings. Yet I was also elated beyond words, for suddenly I realized that there was now true hope for suffering phobics. Interestingly, phobias have always permeated dyslexic case histories. They were just never seen or heard before. They were, instead, blocked out of scientific view by denial and bias. The reverse is true as well. Dyslexic symptoms have invariably characterized phobic cases in psychiatric treatment. Unfortunately, these dyslexic symptoms were overlooked or attributed to distinctly separate origins. Once again, scientific bias and denial were responsible for this truly amazing oversight, which I, too, had been guilty of.

But as a result of this research, the presence of phobias in dyslexic cases and the presence of dyslexic symptoms in phobic cases can no longer be scientifically denied or blurred out. Once and for all, it has been established that these two seemingly different sets of symptoms are both part and parcel of the same underlying physiological problem: an inner-ear dysfunction.

CHAPTER 20

Additional Insights into Phobic Behavior

Valid scientific theories are always interconnected with an unlimited and unrecognized number of variables and thus have no confining horizons. Therefore, the number of unexpected clinical insights increases in proportion to the validity and scope of the working theory.

Incomplete theories, on the other hand, are most often derived from too few, and inadequately studied, clinical cases. Accordingly, related clinical symptoms and syndromes are frequently viewed as disconnected and/or unrelated, and the insights that could and should have evolved are seldom, if ever, seen.

Prior to this research, the number of new clinical/therapeutic insights resulting from the traditional theories concerning phobias, panic states, anxiety states and dyslexia were significantly disappointing. Interestingly, the new but seemingly disjointed observations reported by other researchers can only be united and understood using cerebellar-vestibular theories.

In retrospect, two traditionally accepted, but erroneous medical convictions were responsible for the limited insights into phobic behavior:

- Erroneous assumption #1: That phobias, anxiety, and panic episodes were emotionally determined and emotionally triggered symptoms, thus not influenced by physiological events.
- Erroneous assumption #2: That dyslexia was due to a cerebral dysfunction present from birth and was therefore always of a congenital, nonacquired nature.

These convictions biased the observations and thinking of clinicians and researchers to such an extent that obvious and clear-cut scientific realities were unwittingly blocked out of view. Thus, for example, numerous occurrences following ear infections, mononucleosis, and concussion states in children were unseen or overlooked, including the following:

- Normally walking one- to two-year-olds suddenly became unable to walk, or even crawl.
- Older children suddenly verbalized feelings of dizziness and imbalance associated with fears of heights, stairs, and motion-related activities.
- Emotionally steady children suddenly became fearful of the dark, leaving home, going to school, socializing, crowds, new places, going to sleep, etc.
- Academically normal or superior students suddenly experienced typically dyslexic difficulties with their reading, writing, spelling, math, orientation, concentration, anxiety level, balance, coordination, etc.
- Normally speaking two- to seven-year-olds suddenly developed impaired speech or lost their speech functioning altogether.
- Antihistamines given for asthma, allergies, etc., frequently resulted in a noticeable improvement in phobic and dyslexic symptoms—symptoms that recurred when the medication was discontinued.

Over a period of twenty years, and through the examination of more than fifteen thousand phobic and dyslexic patients, it became slowly but definitely apparent that a variety of infectious, metabolic, toxic, allergic, and physical traumas may impair a child's CVS functioning and result in acquired phobias and/or dyslexia. As these observations crystallized, I began to wonder: Might concussions and related infectious states in adults also be capable of impairing CVS functioning sufficiently to effect the sudden appearance or intensification of phobic and/or dyslexic symptoms? After all, don't postconcussion and whiplash patients frequently complain of such typical inner-ear symptoms as dizziness, loss of balance, slurred speech, headaches, blurred vision, concentration problems, poor memory, reading problems, etc.? The correlation was suddenly all too clear.

Careful questioning revealed that a majority of postconcussion/ whiplash patients—even those with minimal injuries, where there was no loss of consciousness—suffered from a variety of phobic and/or dyslexic symptoms. Careful neurological testing and examination of these patients also revealed that the vast majority had clear signs of inner-ear dysfunction. Of great significance is the fact that CVS dysfunction—and the resulting mental, academic, and behavioral states—were invariably missed by examining physicians more interested in diagnosing and treating the necks, backs, joints, and limbs of these patients. And if these patients complained of phobic and/or dyslexic symptoms, physicians, and even the patients themselves, often attributed the origin of these symptoms to emotional and/or legal determinants.

In retrospect, it is clear that a whiplash injury sufficient to damage the spinal cord and nerve roots may also "whip" the brain and cause it to snap against the hard, bony skull. This could easily result in injuries to the central nervous system—including the CVS—without loss of consciousness.

Interestingly, the onset of the phobic/dyslexic disorder among these patients also brought with it the onset of decreased self-esteem, regardless of age. Suddenly they began to feel weird, crazy, stupid, ugly or klutzy, as do most phobics and dyslexics. Unfortunately, this decrease in self-esteem was mistakenly viewed by many examining clinicians as the cause of the phobic and/or dyslexic disorder rather than the result.

As my research continued, I began to understand that many other factors, aside from concussions and whiplash, could result in acquired inner-ear dysfunction in adults. In fact, virtually all of the metabolic, toxic, allergic, infectious, and physical disturbances that disrupt CVS functioning in children were found to be capable of causing or intensifying phobic and/or dyslexic symptoms in adults as well.

Examining the histories of more and more patients, it eventually seemed natural for me to ask the following questions:

- Couldn't obstetric difficulties during delivery and/or the traumatic use of forceps cause fetal concussion states, and result in impaired CVS development and functioning?

- Couldn't malnutrition during pregnancy result in a metabolic failure of the CVS to develop properly and thus contribute to delayed or impaired inner-ear functioning?
- Couldn't toxemia during pregnancy, and related toxic states within the pregnant mother, impair the developing fetal CVS?
- Couldn't prematurity slow down or arrest the normal development of the inner-ear system?
- Couldn't the traumatic twisting of the head and neck during delivery result in fetal whiplash and injuries similar to those seen in older children and adults?
- Couldn't the above considerations explain the high incidence of dyslexia, learning disabilities, and minimal brain damage reported in conjunction with the above-mentioned states?
- Couldn't the inner-ear dysfunction resulting from the above-mentioned states give rise to phobias, panic episodes, anxiety states, as well as related mood and mental disorders in both children and adults?

Careful and detailed clinical research performed over a period of many years led to clear-cut, affirmative answers for all of the above questions. Eventually I came to the simple conclusion that inner-ear dysfunction and its related phobic and dyslexic symptoms is always acquired. Sometimes it is genetically or traumatically acquired before or during birth, and sometimes it is acquired after birth through one of the many possibilities discussed in Chapter 6.

I could no doubt go on and on. After all, you must realize that these insights came to me over a period of more than twenty years, during which time I examined more than fifteen thousand patients. Those years had their ups and downs. There were moments of tremendous clarity and moments of terrible confusion. But through it all, these theories have grown and developed— improved with age, so to speak—and proved themselves to be increasingly capable of accounting for the wide and once-puzzling array of symptoms that characterize phobic behavior. As I have said before, this is the true test of any theory. But, of course, all of this is merely my opinion. Hopefully by the time you have completed this book, you will be ready to form your own.

PART V

FINDING HELP

Getting the Help You Need

Long before the physiological basis of phobic behavior was discovered, most clinicians still thought they knew what phobias were all about. I was no exception. But with our limited understanding of phobic behavior, we could never ask patients the right questions. And we never heard the right answers, even when these patients were desperately trying to tell us what was wrong. We only heard what we thought was important. But what we thought was important was only truly valid for a small minority of cases.

It isn't my intention to blame therapists for their lack of success with phobic patients. We were all limited by our own training, and we did the absolute best we could given the information we had at our disposal. But now we have new information . . . information that clears up most of the mystery and confusion surrounding phobic behavior . . . information that answers questions that have puzzled even the most competent clinicians.

HELP FOR YOU *AND* YOUR PHYSICIAN

Hopefully the role of the inner-ear system in the development of phobic behavior will no longer be ignored. But much of that is in your hands. When you discuss your phobic symptoms with your physician, you have to assume that he or she will not be familiar with the relationship between phobias and the inner-ear system—especially since this research has only begun to receive serious attention within the past few years. For this very reason, I have written the following chapters for you and your doctor.

To ensure that you receive a proper diagnosis and proper treatment, it is crucial that your doctor sees the information in the next two chapters. But I also feel that it is important for you to be familiar with the proper procedures for diagnosing and treating Type 3 phobic behavior. For one thing, it will take much of the mystery and magic out of the procedure. But far more important, it will make you more capable of helping yourself and helping others who suffer.

A HOLISTIC APPROACH

In diagnosing and treating phobic symptoms of inner-ear origin, two things must be recognized:

- Although all Type 3 phobias share a common underlying denominator, each case has its own unique characteristics. Therefore each case requires a unique understanding if adequate diagnosis and treatment are to be assured.
- Although these symptoms have a physiological origin, they may be precipitated, intensified, or reinforced by emotional and/or traumatic scarring. In fact, unless phobic symptoms are nipped in the bud, it is more than likely that some psychological complications will develop. Considering the hardship and fear experienced when trying to live with these debilitating symptoms, these complications are only normal.

In light of these two points it should be clear that any attempt to treat phobias with *only* medication or *only* psychoanalysis or *only* behavior modification may be overly simplistic and limited in its effectiveness. What we need is a *holistic* approach to the diagnosis and treatment of phobic behavior. Only a holistic approach can ensure that all phobics get proper medical attention.

CAN ANY DOCTOR HELP ME?

Many different types of physicians are capable of helping you to obtain proper diagnosis and treatment. ENT (ear, nose, and throat) physicians, especially those with neurological training (neuro-otologists), are more familiar with evaluating and treating inner-ear dysfunction. Psychiatrists, on the other hand, have more experience treating the psychological complications associated with phobic behavior. But any interested physician, including your internist or family doctor, can help you if he or she is willing to follow the guidelines presented in the following two chapters.

In order to follow all of these guidelines, most physicians will require the help of other specialists and/or a hospital laboratory. This is only normal. Very few physicians are capable of performing all diagnostic and treatment procedures single-handedly.

CHAPTER 22

Proper Diagnosis

Successful treatment begins with proper diagnosis. This is true for all disorders, and phobias are no exception. For too many years phobic diagnosis has stopped at the analyst's couch. I have said many times that the psychological component of phobic behavior is important and must be carefully evaluated. But it is just one aspect of a multidimensional problem. More often than not, it is not even the key aspect.

PROPER DIAGNOSIS: THE KEY INGREDIENTS

If phobic behavior is to be properly diagnosed, a more comprehensive, holistic approach is necessary. This diagnosis should include all of the following, if possible:

- Patient history
- Phobic mechanism evaluation
- Physical and neurological examinations
- Electronystagmography
- Blurring-speed testing
- Bender Gestalt and Goodenough drawing tests (used primarily in diagnosing children)

Let's take a close look at each of these diagnostic techniques.

PATIENT HISTORY

In order to properly evaluate the nature and origin of phobic behavior, a complete history of the patient is needed. This history should include all of the following:

Symptoms

Every patient must be asked to describe their fears in as much detail as possible. It is vital that this information not be limited or biased to conform to the patient's or the doctor's expectations. In other words, this information must be elicited freely and with minimal distortion on both your part and that of your doctor. With this information, a tremendous amount of preliminary insight can be gained; without it, much is lost. Let me give you an example that clearly illustrates the importance of symptomatic evaluation.

If a man who fears heights spontaneously claims that he is afraid of falling when looking down from a ladder, bridge, or building, this fear is probably the result of an inner-ear dysfunction. If this same man feels dizzy or motion sick when looking down or feels magnetically pulled toward or repelled from the bottom, these clues add additional weight to a Type 3 diagnosis.

On the other hand, suppose this fear developed after the man fell from a tree. If so, there is clearly a realistic component to the fear. It is possible that the phobia has an entirely realistic basis, especially if the trauma was unusually severe. But if the original realistic trauma was precipitated by an underlying imbalance or coordination problem (e.g., he fell out of the tree because he has a poor sense of balance), or reinforced by a maladaptive anxiety mechanism, the phobia has both Type 1 and Type 3 origins. This mixed phobia needs to be treated accordingly. Other diagnostic tests will help to clarify this possibility.

The fear of heights and the fear of falling may also have an unconscious symbolic significance. These fears may, for example, represent a fear of failure or a fear of falling down from a high level of attainment . . . or even an unconscious desire to fail that is derived from a guilty conscience. But to justify these assumptions, the patient must freely and spontaneously offer evidence that substantiates this. Just because the fear exists, you cannot automatically assume that it stems from an unconscious emotional conflict. If neurotic evidence is present, other diagnostic tests will determine whether the fear is entirely of Type 2 origin or Type 2 *and* Type 3 origins.

It is also theoretically possible for a person with an emotionally determined need to fail (Type 2) and an inner-ear-determined balance problem (Type 3) to develop a fear of heights after a traumatic fall (Type 1). In this case, all three determinants are somewhat responsible for the phobia. From a therapeutic point of view, all three factors may require treatment if this fear is to be dissolved.

Associated Symptoms

After evaluating the chief or primary complaints presented by a patient, it is important to evaluate all associated symptoms. Are other fears present? What are their characteristics and origins? How long have they been present? What triggered their appearance? It is also exceptionally important to determine whether or not there are other symptoms of inner-ear dysfunction. This is the precise purpose of the Self-Test presented in Chapter 2.

Never assume anything. If a patient exhibits numerous symptoms of inner-ear dysfunction, it is highly probable that he or she has a physiological predisposition to phobic behavior. But the presence of inner-ear dysfunction does not automatically prove that all phobias present are entirely of inner-ear origin. Review the cases and information I have presented. Do they not show that some phobias can be partially, if not purely of Type 1 and/ or Type 2 origins? Although this may be true only for a minority of cases, it is a possibility that cannot be overlooked.

Perhaps an example here might help to illustrate the importance of associated symptoms in the diagnosis and treatment of phobic behavior. One of my dyslexic patients, Louise N., was terrified of bridges. Although most people with a Type 3 fear of bridges typically have at least one or more other fears, Louise did not. Still, I mistakenly assumed that she was able to compensate for her other fears and that her fear of bridges was *entirely* of inner-ear origin. But this fear did not respond favorably to medication even though Louise's various dyslexic symptoms did quite well.

At this point I performed a more thorough investigation of Louise's history. Eventually I discovered that her father was almost killed in a car accident while driving over a bridge. Although Louise was only four years old at the time, the memory of the trauma still played an active role in her subconscious, causing and contributing to the maintenance of this symptom. Only when this traumatic component was recognized and treated did Louise begin to improve. Therefore, just because CVS dysfunction is present, it doesn't rule out the possibility that other factors are also contributing to the presence of phobic behavior. Only a careful investigation of the patient's history will tell for sure.

Genetic Factors

Fears often run in the family, as do the other inner-ear-related symptoms we've discussed. This is usually (see next section) due to the passing on of a defective genetic blueprint of the inner-ear system. In some cases, several family members may have identical phobias. In other cases, the fears may differ. As you can see in some of the cases presented, the same defective blueprint may also give rise to phobic symptoms in one family member and only "dyslexic" symptoms in another. These possibilities result from the action and interaction of various other factors known to affect an impaired inner-ear system.

Although an accurate family history is often difficult to obtain, it is extremely useful when trying to determine the exact nature of a patient's phobias.

Learning Factors

At times children identify with, or unconsciously learn to mimic, their parents' phobic symptoms. They then exhibit similar, if not identical fears. Usually the phobic child has an inner-ear-related predisposition to phobic development (from heredity, or from some acquired basis). As a result, the unconscious mimicking of a parent's phobias comes naturally and sinks in deeply. But it's quite possible that if the child didn't have a role model to mimic, phobic symptoms might never have surfaced.

The complexity of learned phobias often requires a combination of treatments since medications alone may not be able to overcome the psychological component influencing this behavior.

PHOBIC MECHANISM EVALUATION

Once you have obtained a thorough history, you are ready to make a preliminary determination of the possible Type 1, Type 2 and/or Type 3 mechanisms responsible for each specific phobia. This mechanistic evaluation is important for two reasons:

- It is the only way to ensure that all components of the phobia receive adequate treatment.
- Phobic mechanisms give patients tremendous insight into why they are afraid. This insight enables them to control both their physiologically triggered fear and the resulting psychological fall-out.

This second reason may not seem very important to some clinicians. But if you talk to phobics, you quickly realize that most of them have grave concerns about their mental and physical health. Some phobics are afraid they are having a nervous breakdown or going insane. Others fear they are dying or have a brain tumor. Most feel weird, stupid, or crazy. For these patients, the ability to understand why they are phobic is often more helpful than any form of treatment.

PHYSICAL AND NEUROLOGICAL EXAMINATIONS

Each and every phobic patient deserves a careful physical and neurological examination, especially when you consider the fact that 90 percent or more of all phobias may have at least some physiological basis.

The Physical Exam

When I conduct a physical examination I look for any evidence of medical problems, past or present, which may have precipitated or aggravated a patient's inner-ear dysfunction. Among the most important things to look for are:

Thyroid problems	Diabetes
Hypoglycemia	Multiple sclerosis
Mononucleosis	Irregular periods
Ear infections	Premenstrual syndrome
Allergies	TMJ problems
Menopausal changes	Drug use or abuse

As I have said before, any of these problems can trigger phobic symptoms. Furthermore, treating these problems (if possible) often results in the immediate improvement or disappearance of phobic symptoms.

The Neurological Exam

When the inner-ear system is impaired a variety of specific balance, coordination, rhythm, and reflex disturbances may result. A thorough neurological examination is necessary to detect these disturbances and verify the presence of an inner-ear dysfunction. A proper neurological examination should also investigate the possible presence of other central-nervous-system (CNS) disturbances. All of the structures of the CNS have feedback connections. Therefore a disturbance in any vital CNS structure can disrupt normal inner-ear functioning, rendering an individual far more vulnerable to phobias and anxiety states.

The neurological examination is an especially important part
of the diagnostic procedure because it helps to establish the presence of an inner-ear malfunction while simultaneously ruling out
any other neurological problems. But as in any test for inner-ear
dysfunction, the physician must know what specific abnormalities
he or she is looking for.

**Table 1: Common Neurological Indications of Inner-Ear
Dysfunction:
Frequency Distribution in Patient Samples**

Neurological Indication	% of Examined Patients (approximate)
Ocular fixation and tracking difficulties	75%
Tandem difficulties	65%*
Romberg difficulties	80%*
Hypotonic disturbances	10%
Finger-to-thumb sequencing difficulties	90%*
Dysdiadochokinesis	85%*
Speech disturbances	20%

*Frequency reflects results from eyes-open and eyes-closed testing.

Signs to Look For

In Table 1 you will find the most common neurological signs
of inner-ear dysfunction present among patients I have examined.
For the benefit of those who are totally unfamiliar with the procedure in a neurological examination, let me briefly explain how
some of these signs are detected:

■ Ocular (eyeball) fixation and tracking difficulties: A pen or
pencil is held several inches in front of the eyes and the patient
is asked to follow its movement from side to side. Patients
may have little difficulty following the smooth movements of
the pen, but if it is suddenly stopped, the eyeballs usually

continue to move or jiggle back and forth when inner-ear dysfunction is present.

■ Tandem difficulties: Tandem walking is the process of walking a straight line by putting one foot in front of the other in a heel-to-toe fashion. Poor heel to toe placement, poor foot or leg coordination, swaying, or loss of balance are typical signs of inner-ear dysfunction.

■ Romberg difficulties: The Romberg position is assumed by standing up straight and holding your arms directly in front of you. Inner-ear disturbances become particularly obvious when patients are asked to lift one leg and hold their balance, or do both of the above with their eyes closed. (Irregular nystagmus-like movements are often present in the eyes-closed and occasionally even in the eyes-open Romberg position.)

■ Hypotonic disturbances: Hypotonic disturbances are signs of poor muscle tone such as double-jointedness, flat feet, toeing-in or toeing-out, bad posture, knock-knee, etc.

■ Finger-to-thumb sequencing difficulties: In this test the patient is asked to touch each of his (or her) fingers to his thumb in rapid succession. Inner-ear dysfunction will typically result in missed finger-to-thumb contact, out of order contact, etc.

■ Dysdiadochokinesis: Dysdiadochokinesis is the inability to perform rapidly alternating movements. One simple way to test this is to have the patient hold his or her arms straight in front and rotate the palms up and down with ever-increasing speed. When CVS dysfunction is present, a variety of dysrhythmic or awkward movements may be evident.

Over the years it has been noticed that certain signs of inner-ear dysfunction are far more obvious when patients are asked to perform some of these neurological tests with their eyes closed. In retrospect, these findings should not be surprising. Disorientation, dyscoordination, imbalance, vertigo, etc., are often suppressed or compensated for by visual fixation and concentration. It makes sense that these signs will be more obvious if the patient's eyes are closed.

To ensure accurate test results, I recommend including eyes-

closed Romberg, tandem, finger-to-thumb and dysdiadochokinesis testing in all neurological examinations. (Frequencies in
Table 1 include results from eyes-closed testing.) Physicians should
also try to disrupt other compensatory concentration mechanisms
by talking to the patient during testing (patients with inner-ear
dysfunction have great difficulty talking and overconcentrating
on task performance at the same time).

ELECTRONYSTAGMOGRAPHY

When the tail of a fish is bent to the right, its eyes automatically
move to the left; when the tail is bent to the left, the eyes move
to the right. These interlocked tail and eye movements are an
adaptive mechanism controlled by the fish's vestibular system.
What is the purpose of these movements? To keep the fish in
balance with its underwater world.

A woman sits in a swivel chair with her eyes open. When the
chair is swiveled to the right her eyes move to the left, then
suddenly snap to the right; when she is swiveled to the left her
eyes move to the right, then suddenly snap to the left and in line
with the rest of her head. If this woman lifts her head up quickly
her eyes will roll down, then suddenly snap up; if she bends her
head down her eyes will roll up, then suddenly snap down and
in line with the rest of her head. This odd pattern of eyeball
movements is known as nystagmus. Like the eyeball movements
of the fish, nystagmus helps us to maintain a sense of visual
balance in an ever-changing visual world.

To help clarify this, think of what happens when you slip and
start falling to the right . . . your left hand juts out and tries to
restabilize your balance. Well, the same thing happens to your
eyes when your visual world shifts to the right—your eyes temporarily shift to the left to help maintain your visual balance.
Then they readjust to your new position.

If the woman in the chair closed her eyes, the exact same
eyeball movements would occur every time she was turned. They
would also occur every time she raised and lowered her head. If

you looked carefully, you could actually see the movements of the eyeballs behind her closed eyelids. In other words, the eyes automatically react to a change in balance, regardless of whether or not they actually see that change. This suggests that although nystagmus is a visual aid, it is not necessarily vision dependent. Nystagmus is in fact an automatic, reflex response controlled by the human balance center: the inner-ear system.

Since the vestibular system triggers and controls nystagmus, a defect in this system should result in a similar defect in nystagmus. Clinical evidence proves that this assumption is absolutely correct. In fact, defects in nystagmus are such a frequent by-product of vestibular dysfunction that they are the most accurate means of diagnosing this dysfunction.

Nystagmus is evaluated using a technique called electronystagmography (ENG). ENG measures the beats of the eyeballs in much the same way an electrocardiogram measures the beats of the heart. Electronystagmographic testing is discussed in detail in Appendix A.

BLURRING-SPEED TESTING

It is clearly established that the CVS guides the movements of the eyes. Therefore it is directly responsible for our ability to track visual information. When the inner ear is impaired, visual tracking difficulties are often obvious, manifesting themselves in a variety of reading and other vision-related problems. Sometimes, however, these visual problems are not so obvious, especially since we frequently learn to compensate. But even visual fixation and tracking difficulties that are being compensated for can be revealed through the use of a 3D Optical Scanner—an instrument I devised many years ago to help screen for CVS dysfunction in elementary school children.

The 3D Optical Scanner is a fairly simple machine. Basically, it projects a series of moving objects (such as elephants) on a screen or wall (see Figure 2a in Appendix B). Patients being tested are asked to look at the moving objects while keeping their head still and minimizing all efforts to concentrate. The speed is slowly increased. This effects a concomitant increase in the speed at which the eyes reflexively follow these objects across the screen (this tracking is called the optokinetic tracking reflex). Ultimately the moving objects will reach a speed at which the eyes are no longer capable of keeping up. At this point, blurring occurs (Figure 2b in Appendix B). The point at which this happens for a particular individual is his or her blurring speed. The average CVS-impaired individual has a blurring speed one-half that of a normal, nonimpaired individual.

In the second part of the blurring-speed tests patients are asked to look at a stationary sequence of objects. While they do this, a series of vertical lines (resembling the posts of a picket fence) moves across the screen in front of these objects. Normally, individuals are able to fixate clearly on the stationary objects despite the moving foreground, but individuals with inner-ear dysfunction may see blurring or movement of these stationary objects. Furthermore, the eyes of impaired individuals often lose their targets, wander from foreground to background, or confuse the two.

These two simple tests, if performed properly, can diagnose CVS dysfunction with an accuracy of 95 percent.

Single-Targeting and Tunnel Vision

Examining physicians should note that some patients can affect their scores by single-targeting objects. When patients single-target, they fix their eyes on one or two objects rather than on the entire series of objects. This can increase blurring speeds considerably.

To control for single-targeting, patients must be clearly instructed to look at all objects simultaneously and use minimal effort to concentrate. Furthermore, they must periodically be asked how many of the objects they are looking at and how many of them they can see clearly at one time. The answers to these questions will make it clear whether or not the patient is single-targeting.

Some patients are incapable of looking at more than one object at a time because they have inner-ear-determined tunnel vision. The above questions will enable physicians to identify this problem during testing.

BENDER GESTALT AND GOODENOUGH DRAWING TESTS

As I mentioned earlier, inner-ear dysfunction can cause dysgraphic and/or angulated handwriting, poor artistic skills, poor copying skills, or all of the above. Most adults eventually learn to compensate for these problems, at least to some extent, with practice and increased concentration. But children who have not yet learned to compensate, as well as adults who are unable to do so, will show visible evidence of these problems when asked to perform the following two tests:

Bender Gestalt Drawings

In the Bender Gestalt drawing test, patients are asked to copy the eight drawings shown in Figure 3 in Appendix B. If the patient is older than six or seven, his drawings should closely approximate the originals. But the drawings of inner-ear-impaired children, and some adults, typically show some combination of rotation, drifting, angulation, articulation, and general coordination errors (see Figure 4 in Appendix B). In the past, psychoanalysts mistakenly assumed that psychological factors were responsible for these drawing errors. But my research has clearly demonstrated that this is usually not the case. On the contrary, these errors are often the result of specific malfunctions in the spatial and coordination skills required to copy the drawings. In other words, these errors indicate underlying gyroscope, compass and/or coordination problems—problems that have an inner-ear origin.

During these drawing tests, inner-ear-impaired individuals frequently tilt and shift their heads, their bodies, the copying paper, and even the Bender Gestalt copying cards. These adjustments are a compensatory attempt to orient and stabilize a malfunctioning internal gyroscope, and are similar to the head tilting and body shifting that characterize dyslexic reading habits.

The Bender Gestalt test was originally designed to evaluate children's perceptual and coordinational development. Later, psychologists and psychiatrists began to offer psychological explanations for many of the unexplainable variations and errors in the drawings of their patients. Some clinicians suggested that if the drawings angled downward the child was depressed, and if they angled upward the child was elated. In many cases these assumptions clearly didn't correlate with other clinical evidence.

Not until recently, however, has anyone considered the possibility that these angulation errors could reflect a *physiologically* unstable internal gyroscope, coordination difficulties, and other inner-ear-related problems. In other words, no one considered the possibility that the child was physiologically off-balance, uncoordinated, etc. Although this analysis seems obvious, it still meets with tremendous resistance from clinicians bent on imparting more serious psychiatric undertones and overtones to these simple drawing errors.

Goodenough Figure Drawings

In the Goodenough drawing test, the patient is asked to draw the figure of a person. No other instructions are given. When inner-ear dysfunction is present, various inner-ear-related errors may be seen in the patient's drawing (see Figure 5 in Appendix B). For example:

- Figures are frequently titled, reflecting underlying gyroscope problems.
- Oversimplified stick figures are often drawn, reflecting a coordination-related inability to draw.
- Details such as hands, fingers, feet, and toes are omitted, simplified, or hidden—reflecting fine-coordination problems that make drawing these intricate details difficult.

As in the Bender Gestalt drawings, psychologists and psychiatrists often make dangerous assumptions when analyzing the Goodenough drawings. For example, when the figure is tilted many clinicians automatically assume that the patient is psychologically off-balance. The fact that the patient may be physiologically off-balance is never even considered. If fingers or hands are absent or hidden, many clinicians automatically assume that the patient has masturbation guilt and castration anxiety. The possibility that these appendages may be too difficult for the patient to draw is not even entertained.

These psychological interpretations are possible and may be totally accurate in some cases. But physiological determinants—such as balance, compass, proprioceptive and coordination problems—are usually at the core of these drawing errors.

DO YOU HAVE AN INNER-EAR DYSFUNCTION?

When diagnostic tests are properly performed, the presence or absence of inner-ear problems should be obvious. If you have any questions about your test results, be sure to discuss them with your physician. Regardless of your diagnosis, there should be no doubts in your mind.

More than 90 percent of all phobics tested show clear-cut signs of inner-ear dysfunction. If you are among those 90 percent, you are now ready to take the next step toward becoming phobia free: Type 3 treatment. If you are among the small minority of phobics who do not have an inner-ear dysfunction, do not despair. Type 1 and Type 2 phobics can also become phobia free once the mechanisms underlying their fears are clearly understood and properly treated. Treatment suggestions for all types of phobias are included in the next chapter.

CHAPTER 23

Treatment That Works

Phobic behavior is often extremely complex. Underlying physiological problems often trigger and reinforce psychological problems. These psychological problems then reinforce and magnify physiological problems in a vicious cycle. The result is a collection of symptoms and behavior patterns that are often extremely resistant to simplistic forms of treatment.

Multidimensional problems usually require a multidimensional treatment approach. Phobias are no exception. When psychotherapy, psychoanalysis or behavior modification leads to symptomatic improvements, it is often assumed that the phobia has been cured. But this is a very dangerous assumption, for these symptomatic improvements often mask the presence of an underlying physiological problem. This can lead to more serious troubles further down the road.

At the root of most phobic behavior is an inner-ear dysfunction. Therefore the first phase of treatment must focus on this dysfunction. Any treatment regimen that ignores this physiological problem is necessarily limited in its effectiveness. It simply is not getting to the core of the disorder. Unfortunately, far too many phobics find this out the hard way.

On the other hand, treating the physiological basis of phobic behavior is not always enough to free a paient from the phobic nightmare. All too often, the road to recovery is blocked by a variety of psychological factors that reinforce and compound the phobic problem. For this reason, the most successful treatment regimen often has three distinct components:

- Medications
- Behavior modification
- Psychoanalysis or psychotherapy

MEDICATIONS

No physician likes to dispense medication. But medications are almost always necessary when treating Type 3 phobias. Fortunately, most of these medications are extremely safe and are even available over the counter. But regardless of how safe the medications are, it is important for you to know as much about them as possible.

Phobic medications fall into two categories: *primary* medications and *secondary* medications.

Primary Medications

Primary medications specifically target the inner-ear system. These medications are the cornerstone of a successful treatment program—the key to conquering the phobic disorder. They include a variety of antimotion-sickness medications, antihistamines, vitamins, and stimulants known to improve vestibular functioning. These medications often result in rapid and dramatic improvements in phobic behavior and related anxiety symptoms. Furthermore, they often effect dramatic improvements in many or all of the inner-ear-related symptoms discussed in Chapter 9 —certainly a pleasant side effect.

For the benefit of your physician, the medications that have proved to be most effective in the treatment of phobic behavior are listed in Table 2 (see next page). *Note:* These medications, including those available over the counter, should be taken only under the supervision of a qualified physician.

The effects of the primary medications vary considerably from patient to patient. There is no way to predict how you, as an individual, will respond to each medication. For this very reason, it is important that you and your doctor not give up. If a particular medication is ineffective, patience and determination are essential if you are to ultimately find the medication or combination of medications that work best for you. Statistically, one out of four or five medications works best on any one patient. On an overall basis, 80 percent of all Type 3 phobics respond to these medications. Hopefully the development of new and better vestibular medications will one day lead to an even greater response rate.

It is important to be aware that antihistamines and seasickness medications have infinitely greater potency and effect than their names imply. Their purchase should not be taken lightly. In the right dosage these medications may help you tremendously, but if the dosage is too high, they may cause a variety of unpleasant symptoms. In rare cases, they may even intensify phobic symptoms. All dosages must therefore be carefully monitored by a qualified physician.

Table 2: Medications

This table of medications has been purposely separated from the rest of the text to emphasize a major point that cannot be sufficiently stressed: *No one should treat himself or herself, regardless of whether medications can be bought without a physician's prescription.* Only doctors are qualified to predict the benefits and/or side effects (sometimes serious) that can follow the use of the drugs and vitamins listed here, alone or in combination, in light of a given patient's height, weight, general physical condition, and sensitivity to chemical substances.

For the benefit of doctors who may be consulted by patients who have completed this book, I have listed the various chemical structures that have been used in clinically determined dosages and combinations during the past fifteen years when treating phobias and other disorders of cerebellar-vestibular origin.

PRIMARY MEDICATIONS

Chemical name	*Brand name*
Meclizine hydrochloride	Antivert
Cyclizine hydrochloride or lactate	Marezine
Dimenhydrinate	Dramamine
Diphenhydramine hydrochloride	Benadryl

Scopolamine	Transderm-Scop
Hydroxyzine hydrochloride	Atarax
Methylphenidate hydrochloride	Ritalin
Dextroamphetamine sulfate	Dexedrine
Pemoline	Cylert
Pseudoephedrine hydrochloride	Sudafed
Brompheniramine maleate	
Phenylephrine hydrochloride }	Dimetapp
Phenylpropanolamine hydrochloride	
Chlorpheniramine maleate	Chlor-Trimeton
Ergoloid mesylate	Hydergine
Deanol acetamidobenzoate	Deaner

In addition, the following are often helpful: vitamin B complex, ginger root, niacin, B_6, B_{12}, lecithin and choline.

SECONDARY MEDICATIONS

Chemical name	Brand name
Imipramine hydrochloride	Tofranil
Amitriptyline hydrochloride	Elavil
Doxepin hydrochloride	Sinequan
Trazodone hydrochloride	Desyrel
Phenelzine sulfate	Nardil
(And other similar Antidepressant medications)	
Diazepam	Valium
Alprazolam	Xanax
Chlordiazepoxide	Librium
Lorazepam	Ativan
(And other similar Antipanic medications)	
Thioridazine hydrochloride	Mellaril
(And other similar medications)	
Propranolol	Inderal
Atenolol	Tenormin
(And other similar Beta-Blocker medications)	

Physicians and interested clinicians may benefit further from reading the chapters on medication in my scientific text: *A Solution to the Riddle Dyslexia* (Springer-Verlag, 1980). In addition, *Anxiety and Its Treatments* by Doctors Greist, Jefferson and Marks, (American Psychiatric Press, 1986), magnificently and simply elaborates on the various antipanic, antidepressant, and Beta-Blocker medications useful for the treatment of phobias and panic attacks.

What Are the Best Dosages?

Contrary to what may be written in medical journals, *The Physician's Desk Reference*, and pharmaceutical books, my clinical experience with these primary medications clearly indicates that therapeutic dosages often have little relationship to such factors as age and weight. Each patient has his or her own specific sensitivity and reactivity to these medications—a personal threshold. As a result, a sensitive adult may need only one-eighth the recommended dosage, whereas a child may benefit from twice the average dosage.

Traditionally recommended dosages are usually too high for half the patients and not high enough for the other half. For this reason I start all patients on approximately one-quarter of the average therapeutic dosage. Their responses are observed and the medication either lowered or increased, depending on the results.

How Do These Medications Work?

No one really knows how the primary medications work. But they *do* work. I like to think of them as inner-ear fine tuners. These chemical fine tuners readjust impaired inner-ear mechanisms. As a result, sensory input and motor output are better tuned, sequenced, and coordinated. When inner-ear mechanisms work properly, the brain has no physiological reason to be alarmed.

It is important to understand that these medications do not cure the inner-ear disturbance. To date, there are no medications or surgical procedures capable of accomplishing this. Instead, these medications seem to teach the brain how to permanently compensate for the underlying disturbance.

Could This Be a Placebo Effect?

No one has ever tried to dispute the beneficial effects of the primary medications. The improvements resulting from these medications are as real as the patients themselves, and these patients are more than willing to talk to any doubting clinician. Some critics, however, may suggest that the benefits derived from these medications are a placebo effect. How do I know this isn't true?

Most of my phobic patients have been from pillar to post in search of help. They have tried every type of therapy imaginable. They have tried every type of medication imaginable. Most have even said every prayer imaginable. But no matter how desperate these patients were, nothing helped.

These patients have always wanted to get better. They have always hoped that each type of treatment they tried would rid them of their phobias. They would have been thrilled by any improvements . . . even placebo improvements. Yet few improvements were seen.

So why do these other types of treatment so often fail while primary medications continually bring about such clear-cut improvements? Clearly it is not because of placebo effects. Otherwise such improvements would have been noted with other treatments as well (and all primary medications would work for all patients). These medications work because they do something no other type of treatment does: they treat the inner-ear system, the physiological root of phobic behavior.

How Long Do Patients Have to Remain on Medication?

Most patients need to stay on medication anywhere from one to four years. Some require shorter periods of treatment, while others require longer periods. After one to four years of treatment, 80 percent of my successfully treated patients will continue to do as well off the medication as they did on medication.

To explain these observations I have assumed that the chemical readjustment of inner-ear mechanisms may become relatively stable or permanent when medications are used for a sufficiently long period of time. Similar observations are noted in all phases of medicine. For example, medication for high blood pressure may sometimes lead to a continued correction of high blood pressure despite discontinued use of the medication. Dysrhythmias of the heart and brain are often compensated for by using medications for relatively short periods of time. Stopping the medications does not often lead to recurrence of the symptoms, even though the problem has not been cured.

If a medical concept is to have a ring of truth and the weight of conviction, it should correspond and be compatible with other, similar observations. My observations regarding the medical treatment of phobic symptoms are in perfect harmony with the responses noted when various other medical disorders are similarly treated with medication.

What Short-Term Side Effects Are There?

The most common short-term side effects of the primary medications are fatigue, irritability, moodiness, and intensification of various inner-ear-related symptoms. All of these side effects are readily reversed by either reducing or discontinuing the dosages. *No side effects should be tolerated.* They all indicate that the dosage is too high or that the medication is inappropriate for the patient. All medications can and should be changed when side effects are noted.

Are There Dangerous Long-Lasting Side Effects?

The medications I have used to treat inner-ear dysfunction for the last fifteen years have been around for many, many years. They have been used safely for other conditions without any observable or recorded irreversible side effects.

Remember that the wrong dosage, or treatment without a doctor's care, can result in moodiness, tiredness, irritability, and even intensification of phobic symptoms. But if low dosages are administered by a doctor and patients are treated sensibly and carefully observed, both short- and long-term side effects can be minimized and avoided.

Doctors should note that long-term usage can, in some cases, lead to immunity. Should this occur, a slight change in medication may be required.

What Do I Tell My Patients Before They Start Medical Treatment?

Medications may cause side effects. For this reason they entail risk, however small. On the other hand, all untreated symptoms cause emotional (and sometimes physical) damage and pain. Unfortunately, nothing in life is without cost or risk. But no patient should agree to treatment before weighing the alternatives. No one should be told what to do. The possible advantages of treatment must be carefully considered by the patient and the doctor before a decision is made. When I present the facts of treatment to my patients, I may tell them what I would do, or have done, in treating members of my own family. But I tell them to think things out for themselves and to do whatever they feel is correct. After all, clinicians and experts are only professionally responsible for the well-being of their patients. Patients are totally responsible for themselves. Therefore they must be aware of the pain and consequences of professional errors and unknowns.

I respect patients who raise questions and express different opinions. And I work with them to the extent that I can, in the manner I would like my colleagues to work with me and with members of my family. All phobic patients need and deserve this kind of attention.

A VARIETY OF RESPONSES

After patients find the right primary medication, or combination of medications, many of their phobias just seem to disappear—often as quickly as they once appeared. Some of my patients tell me they feel as though their phobias never existed and can hardly believe how bad they really were. They get on elevators, drive, go swimming, etc., without giving it a second thought.

Although I wish all Type 3 phobics responded to primary medications in this way, many patients need a bit more coaxing to help them get over all of their fears. The explanation for this is simple. Once you have learned your phobias—once they have been imprinted in the memory banks of your brain—a phobic trigger provokes two types of anxiety: primary (physiologically determined) and secondary (psychologically determined). This secondary anticipatory anxiety aggravates and intensifies phobic symptoms and also makes you far more susceptible to subsequent phobic episodes.

While primary medications can alleviate primary anxiety, they do not always alleviate secondary anxiety. This secondary anxiety is sometimes sufficient to sustain phobic behavior. In other words, treating the inner-ear disorder is not always enough. When a phobia has been imprinted, the frightening memories can linger and continue to create anxiety long after the actual threat—the physiological malfunction—has been treated.

Overcoming Anticipatory Anxiety

The struggle to overcome anticipatory anxiety is experienced differently by every patient. Needless to say, the emotional support of friends, family, and physicians is always crucial. In fact, sometimes this emotional support is enough to eventually convince the patient that there is nothing left to fear. Unfortunately, this is not always the case. Regardless of how much emotional support they receive, some patients continue to be frightened.

If secondary, anticipatory anxiety persists, patients may need some type of behavior modification therapy and/or psychotherapy (both discussed later in this chapter) to break through the psychological resistance. Furthermore, the use of secondary medications may be necessary and helpful.

Secondary Medications

Secondary medications are used to control persistent, anticipatory (secondary) anxiety. The most effective secondary medications are the so-called antidepressants. Some of these have and similar antipanic medications are not just secondary medications but also function as *potent* primary medications and thus help control both primary and secondary anxiety.

In a similar fashion, the so-called antidepressants were initially but mistakenly thought to control phobias and panic attacks by eliminating underlying depressions and/or secondary anxieties. Once again, further research has clearly indicated that this group of medications also have potent primary properties. As a result, they have become traditionally sanctioned for use in phobias and panic attacks. Not too long ago, the use of these very same medications were viewed with great skepticism and triggered significant controversy among psychiatrists and psychologists.

Many of my patients who use antidepressants frequently notice improvements in such other inner-ear-related symptoms as distractability, poor coordination, dizziness, motion sickness, and bed wetting. These are the very same improvements produced by the antimotion sickness medications and even some antipanic drugs. Surprisingly, even some Beta blockers such as Inderal which control the secondary anxiety effects on the heart, blood pressure and respiration are used by inner-ear specialists for controlling dizziness.

It thus appears that *all* groups of medications found to be helpful in controlling phobias and panic attacks have one common denominator. They all control inner-ear functioning.

Clinical experience with the antimotion sickness medications and antihistamines, the antipanic medications, the antidepressants, and the Beta blockers indicate that phobias and panic attacks may occasionally be intensified if starting doses are too high or if patients are unusually sensitive to them. This side effect often misleads patients into thinking that they are getting much worse, going crazy, etc. To avoid these problems, the use of all medications must be carefully monitored by a qualified physician.

For the benefit of your physician, the secondary medications with potent primary properties are listed in Table 2, (see page 250).

Note: For best results, various groups of medications must often be combined.

Mixed Phobias and Medications

As I have said earlier, many phobias are not of purely Type 3 origin. They are created by a combination of underlying mechanisms: physiological (Type 3), neurotic (Type 2), and/or realistic (Type 1).

The first phase of treatment for these mixed phobias is the use of primary medications. Sometimes this is all the patient needs; without the support of an underlying physiological malfunction, neurotic and realistic mechanisms are often not strong enough to maintain phobic symptoms. But sometimes primary medications are not enough. Therefore, once physiological mechanisms have been adequately treated, it may be necessary to treat the other complicating factors before the patient can experience true relief. This may involve psychotherapy and/or behavior modification and/or secondary medications. Every patient is unique, so the response to treatment may differ. In all cases, patience, persistence, and careful medical supervision are required.

BEHAVIOR MODIFICATION

Behavior modification therapies are conditioning techniques that help patients to neutralize their fears. The theory behind these different behavioral therapies is that phobic anxiety can be reduced or eliminated if a patient is continually exposed to the source of his or her terror (in controlled circumstances, of course).

Behavior modification can be extremely useful as a support therapy when treating Type 3 phobias and mixed phobias of Type 1 and Type 3 (realistic and physiological) origin. When treating mixed phobias, behavioral techniques help to neutralize the memories of the realistic trauma while primary medications neutralize the underlying physiological component of the fear. Pure Type 1 phobias also respond best to these conditioning therapies.

Unless you are treating a pure Type 1 phobia, behavior modification should always be used in conjunction with primary medications (and, if necessary, secondary medications). Failure to use these medications will severely limit the effectiveness of these conditioning techniques and could, in some cases, lead to the intensification of phobic symptoms.

The following brief descriptions of the more popular behavior-modification techniques may be helpful for those who are totally unfamiliar with this form of phobic therapy:

Systematic Desensitization

The goal of systematic desensitization is to shrink anxiety through a process of continuous confrontation and positive reinforcement. When patients undergo systematic desensitization, the first thing they learn is how to suppress anxiety by using deep breathing, meditation, muscle control, and other relaxation techniques. Next, the patient is asked to rank a series of fearful situations in order to develop a hierarchy of his or her fears. For a patient who fears heights, this hierarchy might look something like this:

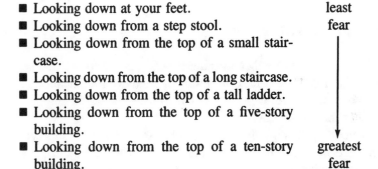

- Looking down at your feet.   least
- Looking down from a step stool.   fear
- Looking down from the top of a small staircase.
- Looking down from the top of a long staircase.
- Looking down from the top of a tall ladder.
- Looking down from the top of a five-story building.
- Looking down from the top of a ten-story   greatest
  building.   fear

Working with your therapist, you are instructed to imagine each of these scenarios, one at a time, in order of increasing fearfulness. At each step, you are to use the techniques you've learned to remain relaxed. If you become anxious at any point, you return to a less frightening image, calm yourself, and proceed forward once again.

Eventually you should be able to imagine the most fearful scenario and still remain calm. This process is repeated over and over to reinforce your sense of calm. Ultimately it is hoped that you will reach the point where you are capable of confronting the triggers you have feared without becoming anxious or panicky.

In Vivo Desensitization

For most patients, in vivo desensitization works even better than systematic desensitization. With this method, you actually act out each scenario of your fear hierarchy, one by one. In other words, first you look down at your feet, then down from the top of a small staircase, etc., repeating the process over and over again until you are finally able to look out of the top window of a ten-story building and remain calm.

As in systematic desensitization, relaxation techniques are used to help you control your anxiety level. If you become too anxious at any point, you return to a more comfortable situation in your hierarchy, relax, and begin working your way up once again.

Flooding and Implosion

Two other popular therapies are flooding and implosion. The theory behind these contextual forms of behavior modification is that the best way to overcome fear is to face it head-on and feel it rather than to neutralize it.

In flooding therapy the patient, under the therapist's supervision, is encouraged to directly confront his or her phobic trigger for a prolonged period of time (sometimes several hours). If you are afraid of heights, for example, the therapist may take you to the top of a tall building and instruct you to look down for as long as you possibly can. Avoidance or escape are discouraged. Eventually, the anxiety burns itself out and you are left mentally drained but hopefully not fearful.

In implosion therapy the therapist helps patients to imagine confronting their fears by verbally frightening them for a prolonged period. Covering your eyes, crying, or refusing to continue are not permitted, since these are all considered attempts to escape. Theoretically, the end result of implosion should be the same result anticipated from flooding: anxiety burnout, exhaustion, and no more fear.

Although I generally do not recommend flooding or implosion therapy for my patients, some of them have reported successes with each of these methods. *Note:* Neither of these two therapeutic approaches is advisable without the concurrent use of primary medications.

Modeling

Modeling therapy can be useful for phobics whose fears were influenced by watching and mimicking other phobics. In this therapy, the patient observes while someone else (usually the therapist) confronts and handles the fear-provoking trigger. If, for example, the patient fears cats, he or she might watch the therapist play with a large cat (or several cats). Hopefully the patient is eventually convinced that there is nothing to fear and is able to mimic the therapist and confront the same trigger.

Additional Help

Other helpful behavior-modification techniques include hypnotherapy, deep breathing, various relaxation exercises, and biofeedback. The success of each of these is no doubt due to its ability to help the patient suppress secondary anxiety.

While still other forms of behavior modification do exist, those listed here have proved to be most helpful to my phobic patients. If you feel that behavior modification may be helpful, therapists are best found through the recommendation of a physician or friend you trust and respect, or by contacting the Phobia Society of America, 5820 Hubbard Drive, Rockville, Maryland 20852 (Tel: 301-231-9350).

PSYCHOANALYSIS AND/OR PSYCHOTHERAPY

Few phobias have a purely neurotic basis. But some do stem from a combination of coexisting Type 2 and Type 3 mechanisms. In these mixed phobias, inner-ear problems are being reinforced and aggravated by the stress from symbolically triggered, deep-seated emotional conflicts. Let me give you an example.

Two Reasons to Stay Home

Suppose that a woman has an inner-ear-determined balance problem. Further suppose that this same woman is unhappily married and wants to leave her husband but fears and feels guilty about doing so (her guilt stemming, perhaps, from some unresolved childhood conflict). The stress generated by these emotional problems can reinforce her imbalance mechanisms and result in a fear of walking across wide-open spaces. By staying close to home, this woman is assured that:

- She won't fall.
- She won't leave her husband and be punished by her guilt.

Primary medications will alleviate this woman's imbalance problem, but they cannot alleviate the guilt and conflict she feels over her marriage. Therefore, even though the physiological component has been eliminated, the phobia may persist until she has worked out her marital problems. Remember, once a phobia develops, it takes on a life of its own that can be sustained by psychological factors alone.

When neurotic mechanisms reinforce and solidify phobias, making them more resistant to treatment, psychotherapy and/or psychoanalysis may be necessary in addition to primary medication. The purpose of this therapy is to expose and eliminate any deep-seated psychological conflicts that may be creating severe stress.

I have periodically observed that psychoanalysis alone can

improve or eliminate certain mixed phobias. This is not surprising. If the anxiety from an underlying emotional conflict is aggravating inner-ear dysfunction, one would expect that reducing or eliminating that anxiety could also reduce the intensity of the inner-ear problem. But more often than not, both types of treatment are needed before the patient can become phobia free.

Two Incorrect Freudian Assumptions

Unfortunately, classical Freudian therapists have always assumed that:

- Phobic behavior is entirely the result of unconscious emotional conflicts (usually sexual and/or aggressive) and therefore must be treated only with Freudian methods.
- Combining Freudian therapy with other forms of therapy decreases the chance of a cure.

In retrospect, both of these assumptions have proved to be incorrect. Yet this is no reason to dismiss Freudian therapy entirely. It is, as I have said before, extremely useful as a support therapy when treating mixed phobias of Type 2 and Type 3 origins. Furthermore, it is essential for treating pure Type 2 phobias. Freudian techniques can even be useful for treating Type 1 phobias if the initial realistic trauma has been buried deep in the patient's subconscious past.

TREATING THE REPERCUSSIONS OF LIVING WITH PHOBIAS

Anyone who has treated phobics knows that many patients develop severe psychological problems as a result of their phobias. Depression, withdrawal, denial, escape . . . these are just a few of the typical problems that develop from living a life of fear. Psychotherapy may not be capable of single-handedly eliminating phobic symptoms, but it can be invaluable in helping you to understand and overcome the psychological problems you may have developed and/or reinforced as a result of your phobias. I recommend it strongly for most of my phobic patients.

Neurotherapy

It has been my experience that most phobics feel better just knowing why they are afraid. In fact, this mechanistic insight is often crucial in relieving patients of their fears, anxieties, feelings of hopelessness, etc.

If clinicians want to see significant, long-lasting improvements among their patients, their approach to treatment should include some *neurotherapy*—a neurophysiological explanation of the mechanisms responsible for phobic symptoms. Until now, few clinicians have been capable of offering patients this physiological insight. But it is my greatest hope that this will change in the near future as the physiological basis of phobic behavior gains wider understanding and acceptance.

EVERY PHOBIC CAN BE HELPED

No two phobics are the same, and each responds somewhat differently to treatment. But every phobic can be helped.

If, after completing this book, you suspect that your phobias are due in part or entirely to an inner-ear dysfunction, use this book to get yourself proper help. Bring it to your physicians. Bring it to your therapist. And don't give up hope. Persistence, determination, and a positive mental attitude will ensure that you ultimately receive the treatment every phobic needs and deserves.

CHAPTER 24

Phobia Free

Phobias have always been defined as irrational fears. After twenty years of psychiatric practice, and after talking to and examining thousands of phobics, I am convinced that this is simply not the case.

Throughout this book I have attempted to prove to you that most phobic behavior is the very rational result of a common physiological disorder: a malfunction within the inner-ear system. Hopefully you are now convinced. In these final pages, you will find several more interesting, instructive, and insightful case histories. These cases will reinforce and highlight what you have just learned about the physiological basis of phobic behavior. But even more important, this material will add to your conviction that most phobic patients, if properly treated, can live phobia free.

Sheryl C.

Sheryl suffered in silence for four years before she finally found help for her crippling phobic condition. She recalled:

In November of 1980 I developed a severe case of infectious mononucleosis. It took me six weeks to get back on my feet. But little did I know what real damage this sickness had caused, or the agony I would experience for the next four years.

Until I developed mononucleosis, I had had no unusual or significant physical or emotional problems. However, after contracting this infection, I never quite felt the same—either physically or emotionally. I slowly began to recover my strength, but I always felt tired and had frequent headaches and nausea. And there was more than these symptoms . . . something was just not right with me. I couldn't put my finger on it (and certainly couldn't describe it to someone else, as hard as I tried), but I knew inside there was something wrong with me. I just wasn't the same.

Most of my symptoms were blamed on the mono, and I was told that in time I would recover. Shortly after, I began to become fearful of fainting or passing out in public. I was very dizzy and unbalanced. On one occasion, while sitting in a restaurant, I became so dizzy that I panicked and had to run out. Having experienced this all-consuming panic, I became intensely paranoid about eating out in public. The fear began to spread to several other areas. I was afraid to be in a room with people for fear I would become dizzy or feel faint. Along with feeling dizzy, I felt unbalanced, "off" in my perception of my surroundings. I felt as though I couldn't focus clearly, as if I were in a fog. Yet if I concentrated, I could see normally.

I tried to explain these physical symptoms to my physician, who reassured me that I was just not over the mono and probably under a lot of pressure. After all, I was about to be married. And my mother, who had suffered from Parkinson's disease for years, had just had two strokes and was being institutionalized. I had had the tremendous responsibility of caring for her at home alone for the past several years. She was now terminally ill with no hope of recovery. I accepted what the doctor said. It seemed logical, and he *was* the doctor.

I couldn't possibly tell the doctor about my fears—how could I? I wasn't sure what was happening myself. I was frightened, scared, and apprehensive about the future. I began to tell myself this would all wear off and go away.

I tried again and again to comfort and calm myself, but it wasn't helping. In fact, the symptoms and fears got worse. I felt I was slowly losing control of myself. What was I becoming? Even more agonizing was the fact that I was terribly embarrassed by my behavior in front of my family, fiancé, coworkers, and friends.

I fell apart under pressure. On the day of my wedding, I was so fearful and dizzy that I had to see a doctor. He gave me six prescriptions to get me through the day. Over and over, everyone kept telling me that I was just under too much stress and would be all right. But I had experienced tremendous pressure and responsibility taking care of my mother and working full time. What had suddenly changed me? If only I could make it through the wedding, then I could relax and everything would be fine.

My nerves did ease up somewhat after the wedding, but I was still not the same person I was before. All of a sudden I became fearful of work. I was afraid I couldn't handle the job or make it through the day. I felt dizzy and feared passing out. As soon as I got home from one day's work, I would begin to worry about making it through the next. I was afraid to drive downtown to my job. All I wanted to do was stay home where I felt safe. All these fears over a job I had been doing for over four years . . . it made no sense to me. Still searching for the key to my problem, I quit my job.

Later that year I took a college course, and by the spring of 1982, I was a full-time student. But in my second quarter I began to fear that I could not handle the work and pressure of college. As I sat in class one day, the room suddenly shifted. I was sure I would pass out. My heart was racing, my hands became sweaty, and my stomach was tied in a knot. All of a sudden I panicked. I was in the middle of the room in the first seat. How could I get out of this situation? Was I going to pass out? Who would help me? I was losing control of myself. In the midst of all my thoughts, I could barely hear the teacher talking. I had never felt so desperate. I had to hold myself to the chair in order to keep from running out of the room.

After class was over I seemed to settle down a little. But what about tomorrow, or my next class. I began to fear the panic that seemed to attack and consume me from all sides. The more I felt dizzy, the more I panicked. The more I panicked, the dizzier I felt. I made it through that quarter. Scholastically, I did very well. Outwardly, I appeared fine. Inside, I was falling apart.

The fears began to mushroom. I was afraid of heights for fear of falling . . . afraid of riding a moving escalator because it made me dizzy and unbalanced . . . afraid of the closed-in feeling of an elevator for fear I could not get out if I fainted. I feared going down stairs because I was afraid of falling forward . . . I was afraid of entering any public area that had a lot of activity because it made me dizzy . . . I was fearful of driving my car. I had always loved to drive, but somehow I could no longer handle so many objects coming at me, so many actions to coordinate.

From the fear of being in public came the fear of being in a room of close friends or family. From the fear of eating out in public came the fear of eating around a table with family and friends. No matter how hard I examined and rationalized the situation, I couldn't help myself. Over and over, I tried and tried to get myself over these fears. But I just couldn't.

Throughout these four years, I had repeatedly seen several different doctors, hoping each time someone would find something that would explain what was happening to me. But it was always attributed to stress and nerves. I began to fear that I might have a brain tumor or something they might be overlooking.

I talked with a psychologist and my pastor, but no one seemed to understand. They all assured me that I would be okay in time if I relaxed. Finally I concluded that I must be losing my mind. I had certainly lost control of myself. There was something wrong with me—I knew it—if only someone else could understand and help me.

My self-esteem was badly damaged by all of this. After all, how can a person feel good about herself when she might be emotionally or mentally ill. I had to keep so much pain bottled up inside . . . I couldn't share my prison with anyone . . . not even my husband. I was afraid that he, too, would think I was going crazy. And could I blame him? I couldn't even understand myself.

Through what might be called a coincidence, though I believe it was an answer to prayer, I saw you on a television show here in Cleveland. I was so shocked and stunned as I sat and listened to you describe the suffering I had experienced for the past four years of my life. Tears streamed down my face as I finally heard someone explain what I could never explain or put into words. Could there really be help? Only those who have felt the desperation of waiting and hoping for help can identify with how I felt at that moment.

My husband was shocked by my reaction. He hadn't realized just how serious my problem was. He watched the show many times (we taped it) and began to understand what had happened to me. He was extremely supportive and eager to help me in any way possible. Words cannot express what a blessed comfort that was in and of itself.

Sheryl came to my office shortly after seeing that television program. Her diagnostic tests confirmed the presence of an inner-ear dysfunction, and treatment was started. Several months later, she wrote:

My whole life changed the day I came to your office. Someone finally understood me. My problems were not in my head. I was not mentally ill. Best of all, someone felt they could help me.

I began taking the medication and noticed improvement within a week. Once the dizziness stopped, or at least lessened, so did my fears. There was a distinct and direct correlation between my dizziness, balance control, and coordination, and my phobias. It was as plain as black and white.

One by one, all of my fears have become controllable—many have been totally eliminated. Unfortunately, living with my fears for so long made me set up a destructive thinking pattern. Therefore, in addition to taking the medication, I had to reprogram my thoughts.

I have to keep reminding myself that I have nothing to fear, that I'm not going to pass out or go crazy anymore. But I'm really doing well. I can venture into stores again. I can enjoy driving more. I can go out in public and enjoy life again.

I've had my ups and downs on the medication. I still feel a bit dizzy at times, but most of the time I feel fine. I get discouraged once in a while, but I no longer despair. All in all, I've seen a lot of improvements. I'm no longer controlled by my fears . . . I've learned to control them. I am working again and thinking about going back to college. I can actually enjoy life. I'm happier and more relaxed. Most of all, I can forgive myself for my behavior. I can stop berating myself. I feel good about my future and much better about myself. I have hope, and that makes a world of difference to me.

Howard M.

I'm afraid to leave my house. I avoid leaving at all costs. Crowds bother me . . . big crowds . . . millions of people running around. I don't have faith in my own judgment. I get this strange feeling in my stomach, and then I get this tickling in my throat and start to cough. All the nerves in my body get tensed up and I feel weird . . . like I'm not part of this world. I feel like I'm in *The Twilight Zone*. You know . . . between light and shadow . . . in between two worlds.

These were the emotional words of twenty-six-year-old Howard M. as he sat in my office during his first visit. Howard had mustered all of his courage and flown across the country to be examined because he suspected his problems were inner-ear-related. During his visit, he recalled:

I was in first grade for two years at Catholic school. I was hyper, and I got into fights an awful lot. They didn't know how to handle me, so they flunked me the first year and kicked me out the second year. I had to go to public school, but in public school I couldn't handle the regular classroom. That just made everything worse.

School was not Howard's only problem. He continues:

I was afraid of everything. I was afraid of school . . . I was afraid of not being able to compete with other kids in sports . . . I was afraid of going places and traveling. I got the feeling I was different . . . that I was less competent . . . inferior. I would get plain mad at myself for not being able to do things everyone else could do. I was mad that my body controlled me and I didn't control it.

I'm afraid of crowds and crowded places like restaurants and grocery stores—especially large crowds. It's like overload. I don't feel comfortable with that much coming in, so I stay away. It drains me so I feel exhausted. I feel this anxiety coming over me . . . I have to take deep breaths, then I feel like running out. Sometimes I run so fast I bump into a wall or something without even seeing it.

When I got older and learned to drive, that scared me also . . . it still does. I can't judge distances well, and I get into lots of accidents. I also get lost constantly.

Howard's diagnostic tests confirmed the presence of an inner-ear dysfunction. One year later he flew to New York by himself to be reexamined. This is something he never imagined was possible. When asked what types of changes he had noticed since starting treatment, Howard replied:

Before I came here I was in my own little world. I was depressed . . . I drank a lot. Everything's different now. I wasn't able to drive unless somebody else was in the car with me . . . I didn't have the skills to do it. Now I have the skills. I drive all over town. I have no problems getting anywhere. I've made a 180-degree turn. I've even gone back to school, and I'm doing pretty well. I can read much easier now, and I comprehend what I read. And after I finish a book, my memory serves me much better than it used to.

Toward the end of our conversation, Howard summarized the pain of his youth and the new sense of hope he feels in the following words:

There would be times when I felt like I didn't belong in the same world with everyone else. I felt that I wasn't put together right. I felt that something was missing. I just belonged outside. I felt like somebody from another planet . . . or another universe.

It was pretty bad. At one point it was really bad. I was really depressed. I even had suicidal thoughts once or twice. Now I feel put together, just like everyone else. No differences at all. I don't feel self-conscious anymore. I used to feel there was so much to do in this world and so little time to do it. But now I know I can do it. It's a wonderful feeling to be part of the same world as everyone else.

Charlotte W.

Though Charlotte had always been plagued by numerous phobias, it was an agoraphobic relapse that finally brought her to my office. Here are some excerpts from our conversation:

Even as a child I was always afraid of heights. I never liked escalators; I even had trouble riding a horse . . . it seemed as though I was up too high. I can't look out of a high window. I feel it in my knees, my stomach, and in the small of my back . . . I get this crawling sensation . . . total anxiety. I break into a sweat. I know there is no danger. I know I'm in a room, on firm ground, and no one is going to push me . . . why would I jump? But it's almost like a compulsion . . . like a magnet is drawing me.

I've always been afraid to drive because I can't judge distances. If a car is a block away, I think it's thirty feet away. It's impossible for me to judge the speed of moving vehicles, and at certain speeds the cars look as if they're changing directions. They overwhelm me and seem to be coming directly at me. Furthermore, I can't read signs and drive at the same time. I need someone else to read the signs. I can't focus that quickly . . . everything blurs.

I can't drive on a highway at all. At slow speeds, I know that if I stay in my lane and the oncoming cars stay in their lane, we'll pass each other safely. But at fifty miles an hour, the cars look as though they're coming right at me . . . even if there is a divider in the road. Even when my husband is driving, I can't look at the oncoming traffic . . . I'm convinced the cars are going to hit us.

My problems got worse several years ago. I was shopping in Alexander's one day, and I got terribly dizzy. My heart started racing, and I broke out into an awful sweat. There were crowds of people around me, and I really felt sick. Since then, I've no desire to go back into any big stores by myself. I didn't know why I had the tachycardia. It was about the same time I was going through menopause, and I understand that kind of association is common, but it still didn't make any sense.

One day, shortly after the department store incident, I had an anxiety attack as I was leaving my house. I broke out into a sweat, and my heart started pounding. I was so dizzy, I thought I was going to pass out. So I just said to myself, "The hell with it, I just won't go out . . . there's nothing out there I need so badly."

The more I put off going out, the harder it became. Every once in a while I would try to leave the house. I'd get dressed and go to the elevator, but I couldn't do it . . . I just couldn't go out by myself.

The dizziness is what really kept me from leaving. I was afraid I would pass out somewhere. I felt unstable . . . vulnerable to everyone on the street. I could go out with my husband . . . but not alone. I had to know that someone would be there in case I passed out or fell.

Even when I was with my husband many things frightened me. I had terrible problems crossing the street. Turning my head from side to side to watch for cars made me dizzy and anxious. My husband would walk in front of me, and I'd put my hand on his shoulder and let him lead me. It was almost like being blind. Restaurants also bothered me. I'd have to sit at a table near the wall. Sitting in the middle made me panic . . . there were too many distractions. Sometimes the smells in a restaurant made me dizzy and panicky. Many smells have that effect on me . . . carpet glue can wipe me out.

Eventually I hired a contextual therapist to help me. It was through an outreach program, so she came to my home to get me. Otherwise I would never have done it. The therapist wanted to take me to the roof of my building, to the giant escalator in the Trump Tower, to the cable that crosses to Roosevelt Island, etc. She would stand me in front of open windows and I would keep saying, "It's organic . . . it's in my mind . . . this isn't helping." Finally, I gave up on it.

After about a year, the agoraphobia went away. It took a long time, but it went away. But now it's back again. That's why I had a driver take me to your office . . . I couldn't come here alone.

Charlotte's examination revealed numerous other signs of inner-ear dysfunction. She had, for example, significant reading problems, terrible concentration problems, a poor memory, poor math skills, and severe balance and coordination problems. Diagnostic tests confirmed the presence of an inner-ear dysfunction, and she was placed on medication.

Charlotte's response to treatment was dramatic. She recently commented:

The agoraphobia disappeared almost overnight. It was a miracle. Everything got better all at once . . . even my reading, concentration, and memory improved. I used to think I was a candidate for Alzheimer's . . . that feeling is gone.

For the past two years, my husband and I have taken the family to a resort in Vermont. The hotel room has a balcony that overlooks two hundred miles of mountains. Last year I couldn't set foot on that balcony; I couldn't even go near the window or look out. This year I could actually stand on the balcony without any problem. I was even able to go to the railing at those scenic overlook points and look out . . . I wouldn't even think about it half the time. This would have been impossible a year ago.

I used to have real trouble with escalators. Now I just hop on them, and I'm fine. I used to hate glass elevators too . . . the combination of height and movement was terrible. They don't bother me anymore either. Even my sensitivity to smells has improved. As a matter of fact, I'm wearing perfume . . . something I hadn't been able to do for years.

It's hard for me to believe, and even harder for my husband to believe, but my phobias are gone . . . they're just gone.

Ross S.

Ross S., a bright eleven-year-old, was referred to me because he was suffering from school phobia. When he first refused to attend school, he was hospitalized for three months at a neuropsychiatric hospital. No improvements were seen. Following his discharge, a school psychologist tried to take Ross to school forcibly in order to help him overcome his phobia—but to no avail.

It was said that Ross's mother was overprotective, and that as a result, Ross had difficulty separating from her. But he had no trouble separating from his mother to visit friends or to go to Disneyland. He only had difficulty separating when he had to go to school.

Recently, the school system attempted to take Ross's parents to court for their son's truancy. Yet no one had asked Ross *why* he hated school. Had they done so, they would have gotten the following reply: "I can't do well academically no matter how hard I try. And my clumsiness in sports as well as my C's and D's in school make me feel too stupid and clumsy to go on. I just can't take it." As a result of these related frustrations, Ross is convinced he is inferior and cannot possibly succeed in school.

Further questioning revealed that Ross becomes overly frustrated in a classroom. The noises and movements made by the other children distract him to such an extent that he has difficulty concentrating and functioning. As a result, he learns much better in a one-to-one situation where there are no distractions. In addition to his school phobia, Ross fears elevators, amusement-park rides, and bright lights. He is also significantly dyscoordinated and disorganized. For example, he has difficulty skipping, tying his shoelaces, zippering zippers, and playing sports; his drawers, his room, and his schoolwork are always a mess.

Discussions with Ross and his parents revealed that he also has all of the following typical dyslexic symptoms:

- Dyscoordinated and angulated handwriting
- Difficulty telling time
- Right/left confusion
- Extreme distractibility
- Head tilting and frequent blinking while reading
- Rapid reading fatigue
- Poor recall of addition, subtraction, and multiplication facts.

Diagnostic tests yielded conclusive proof of an inner-ear dysfunction, and Ross was placed on primary medications. Soon after he started treatment, his father called me to report immediate improvements. Ross had returned to school. His teachers felt he was performing much better, the school crossing guard noticed he was standing up straighter, and for the first time in his life, Ross was able to kick a ball in gym class.

As of this writing Ross has only been under treatment for several weeks. He has, no doubt, a long way to go. But his progress has been inspirational, and this book would not have been complete without his story.

Brad S.

Drug use or abuse often triggers phobic symptoms in predisposed individuals. Although Brad thought for some time that he was the only person in the world who suffered the way he had, his story is really quite typical. He recently recalled:

I'll never forget how it began . . . never. Basically, I had a toxic reaction to a hash brownie. It sounds so ridiculous in retrospect, but it wasn't ridiculous at the time . . . it was a living hell.

It was my senior year in college, and some friends were having a party. One of the girls had baked some terrific-looking hash brownies and everyone was greedily devouring them. I was not what you would consider a drug user. I had smoked marijuana a couple of times, like every other college kid, but that was the extent of it. But everyone was eating these brownies. Frankly, the whole thing seemed pretty harmless. I figured, one isn't going to kill me. I couldn't have been more wrong.

At first I was fine. The effect of the drug was kind of pleasant. Then everything got out of control. I was in the middle of a conversation when suddenly I was overcome by a horrible feeling of complete disorientation. It was really terrifying. I didn't know what was happening . . . I'd never felt anything even remotely like it before.

I left the room I was in immediately and went into a more well-lit room . . . I thought that would help me get my bearings. But it didn't. I had been in that apartment a dozen times, but now I felt as though I was in some strange place I'd never seen before. It took all of my energy to keep from "losing it" completely.

I left the party and went home. But that didn't help either. It was a cold, dark night, and the windows were full of frost. You couldn't see outside. Having my view closed off only made me worse . . . more disoriented and frightened. I felt as though I was in an apartment in New York City, even though I knew I was in upstate New York. It was almost as though I was hallucinating.

For two hours I tried to go to sleep. But every time I closed my eyes, my head started spinning . . . I felt as though I was falling through space. So I lay in bed with all of the lights on, afraid to close my eyes. I just kept telling myself, "It will wear off . . . you'll be fine."

When I woke up the next morning I felt better . . . not perfect, but better. I was supposed to go to New York City for the weekend, so I packed a suitcase and waited for my friends to pick me up. The drive started out fine, but as it got dark outside (it was a five-hour drive), I started to feel weird again. Then all of a sudden I started feeling really disoriented and frightened. I felt as though I was losing control again . . . as though I was going to pass out or go crazy. The noise level in the car seemed to get higher and higher. It was like being in a haunted house with all of these people cackling. Everything was terribly distorted. It took all of my energy to keep a handle on myself.

The next few days passed without a problem. Before I knew it, I was back in school and back to normal. I was sure my troubles were over. I was wrong. It was 8:00 A.M. on a Monday morning. I'd only been able to get three hours of sleep the night before. As I sat in the lecture hall, my mind began to drift. I could barely make out what the professor was saying. Everything seemed kind of hazy and blurry, the way it always did when I was overtired. The giant lecture hall seemed much larger than usual . . . it was as though I was in a different room. All of a sudden I got scared . . . then terrified. I jumped out of my seat and ran out of the room.

Outside I was able to calm down, but I was really upset. I just couldn't understand what was happening to me. Was I having flash-backs? Could you get flashbacks from hash brownies? Fearing the worst, I decided that the only smart thing to do was to go to the university hospital. The psychiatrist who saw me said I could be having flashbacks. He gave me a medication he gave to patients who had used LSD. I was desperate, and willing to try anything.

As soon as the pills—which I believe were tranquilizers—took effect, problems started. I was having dinner with two friends at a local restaurant, and I started to panic again. The restaurant was very dark, and I found it completely disorienting. I got up and went outside immediately. I walked around the parking lot, went back inside the restaurant, and left again. Finally, I asked one of my friends to drive me home.

I told the doctor what happened. He asked me to try one more medication. I did. It wasn't as bad as the first one, but it wasn't good. Obviously drugs were not going to help . . . at least not these.

Now I didn't know what to do. I was afraid to go to most of my classes. I was falling behind in my work. I was afraid of so many things . . . restaurants, labs, lecture halls . . . I was even afraid of being in my own apartment at night. I also became afraid of walking over the bridge between my apartment and the campus. I felt as though I might fall over the edge, or even jump. I didn't want to . . . I just felt as though I might lose control of myself. It was terrifying, uncontrollably terrifying.

I was quickly becoming a recluse, and I was extremely de-pressed. A life full of fear just didn't seem worth living. A few months ago I had been perfectly fine. Now my life was in ruin. Was I cracking up? Was I having a nervous breakdown? I didn't know what to think. I clung desperately to my past.

I don't even want to think about what might have happened if this had continued. But by an absolute stroke of luck, I met someone who had been through something very similar. I couldn't believe it . . . I couldn't believe someone else had gone through this. This woman told me that her problem turned out to be the result of a sinus infection. She said, "Go to another doctor . . . go to a dozen doctors . . . it has to be something physical."

I knew I didn't have a sinus infection . . . I'd never had a sinus infection. But I started going to doctors anyway. The first doctor I went to told me there was nothing physically wrong with me. I was devastated. To make matters worse, he started playing amateur psychiatrist. Clearly, he was convinced that whatever I had was inside my head.

The second doctor I saw was the head of internal medicine at the university hospital. After speaking with him for ten minutes, he said, "I've heard enough . . . I know exactly what your problem is. You are chronically hyperventilating. You're depriving your brain of carbon dioxide and it's making you light-headed, dizzy, and panicky. You can go to a neurologist if you'd like, but I'm sure this is what's wrong."

I immediately felt a billion times better. I could finally latch onto something physical. The doctor gave me breathing exercises, and I started doing them regularly. The exercises worked. I was able to go into classrooms, go out at night . . . I wasn't perfect, but I was a lot better. And the better I got, the less I thought about it. I had been obsessed with this thing. Now I was able to forget about it for hours at a time.

By the time I graduated from college, I was feeling close to normal. But a few problems lingered. I would panic if I had to drive through a long tunnel or over a high bridge. Highway driving also gave me problems . . . especially at night. For some reason, the breathing exercises just didn't help in these situations. Finally, I gave up everything but local driving. That took care of most of my problems . . . for almost ten years, anyway.

But this past summer I had a few unexpected scares. The first happened in one of those big glass elevators. As soon as the elevator took off, I found myself pinned to the door in sheer terror. It was totally unexpected . . . I'd never had any problems with elevators before. The second incident also happened in an elevator, a regular one. I went inside the elevator and the door closed, but the elevator didn't move. I hit all the buttons, but nothing happened. Then I couldn't get the door open. I flushed . . . then felt total panic. All of a sudden, the door just opened by itself. I ran out. No one likes to get stuck in an elevator, but my reaction just wasn't normal. This really bothered me. After these two incidents I started to avoid elevators. Then heights started to bother me more. Although I tried to deny it, I seemed to be having a slight relapse. Fortunately, that's when I heard about you.

Brad's examination revealed numerous other signs of inner-ear dysfunction. He had, for example, a poor sense of direction, a short concentration span, and an unstable memory. He told me, "I can remember concepts forever, especially if they paint a picture in my mind. But simple facts exit as quickly as they enter." Although he is a skilled tennis player, Brad admitted, "I have to work very hard at my game . . . my coordination and reflexes are marginal."

Diagnostic tests confirmed the presence of an inner-ear dysfunction, and a treatment program was started. Recently, Brad told me:

> Although the breathing exercises helped me tremendously, deep down I always knew that I had more than just a breathing problem. I was certain that the hash brownie had done something to me . . . something permanent. After all, I wasn't able to drive on a highway, through a tunnel, or over a bridge, regardless of how many breathing exercises I did. And the elevator episodes . . . they didn't make any sense at all. But I just blocked these worries out.
>
> But once you explained the significance of the inner ear, everything made sense. All of a sudden, nothing seemed as threatening . . . I started feeling better just knowing what my problem really was. It was the unknown that scared me more than anything . . . not knowing whether or not I really was in danger of losing control.
>
> As far as the medications are concerned, they've made a world of difference. Elevators don't bother me . . . highway driving isn't traumatic like it used to be . . . I can even handle bridges and tunnels. But as I said, it's the understanding that's made all the difference. I only wish someone had told me this ten years ago. I'd probably be a different person today.

Elaine R.

Several years ago, Elaine sustained a concussion during a mugging. As a result, she acquired a host of incapacitating phobias, as well as a variety of other inner-ear-related symptoms. She recalled:

> It all began one summer evening in 1978. While walking with a friend, I was brutally mugged and thrown against the side of a church pillar. As a result, I suffered a severe concussion.

Doctors assured me that my post-concussion symptoms would disappear in time and that I would be back to my normal self. But they were wrong. I didn't get better. Instead, I became steadily worse! In fact, due to my loss of balance and poor coordination, I kept falling, further injuring myself and sustaining additional concussions. As a result, my symptoms intensified and expanded. My life had become a nightmare.

My whole existence changed dramatically. I felt like Alice in Wonderland. Everything was topsy-turvy. I became terribly dyscoordinated. I headed in one direction and my body would wind up in another. If I intended to turn left, I'd end up right . . . sometimes smack into a wall or a door. I felt disoriented and confused all the time. And I didn't understand why.

And that's not the worst of it. I became phobic about everything. I had always been a fairly independent person. I was self-employed and enjoyed a satisfying and successful career in marketing. I played tennis and other sports, and just loved to travel worldwide. Unbelievably, I became unable to travel by car, bus, subway, or plane. I'd feel physically ill . . . nauseated, dizzy, and anxious. And very soon these feelings mushroomed into severe panic.

Closed-in or crowded places such as subways, elevators, and supermarkets began to fill me with terror. Even leaving my house became impossible. When I was outside, the street or ground beneath my feet began to look and feel strange . . . as though it was rocking and moving up and down simultaneously. Occasionally the floor in my apartment would appear to vibrate and I literally felt as if I was walking on air. When this happened, I would absolutely panic!

Heights became impossible, and looking down from them was even worse. My balance and coordination were too poor to navigate heights. And when I looked down, I'd see the ground tilted and shaking. This would make me feel more off-balance and dizzy than I was before.

Dizziness became a major problem for me. I constantly had a sensation of spinning. Walking, motion-related activities, trains, planes, and buses . . . even falling asleep made this feeling worse. Sometimes I'd wake up in my sleep with these horrible, dizzy feelings, grasping the sides of my bed to keep from falling off. During these episodes I'd feel sick . . . I'd be drenched with sweat and overcome by fear.

Soon after my accident I literally became housebound. Not only was I afraid of the floor moving, my balance and coordination were so bad that I was always afraid I would fall when I walked. Then I would get these crazy dizzy spells and become scared of fainting and passing out and losing control. Crossing the street became impossible . . . there was just no way I could get to the other side alive in traffic unless I was with someone.

And that's not all. I had always been an avid reader. And I was fortunate in being extremely visual . . . able to totally recall everything I read. Following my concussion, all of this changed dramatically. I couldn't remember anything at all, neither what I read nor what was said to me . . . not even what I was saying. I would literally stop talking in mid-sentence because I'd forget what I was about to say.

My mind and speech functioning became dyscoordinated. I found my mind racing faster than my tongue could follow. As a result, my speech became slurred and I had the greatest difficulty pronouncing even the simplest words. I was rambling on like an idiot at times. Do you know how humiliating that is?

Not only could I not remember the words, sentences and paragraphs I read, but the words would become blurry and jump all over the place. I would have to use a finger or marker when I read, otherwise I'd lose my place. And if I tried reading for any length of time, I'd become headachy and nauseous and severely dizzy.

I became filled with an inner anger that turned into depression and despair. I felt stupid, dumb, crazy, and hopeless. All of this made me feel like a freak. I developed a paranoid sensitivity. I felt as if everybody was looking at me and seeing right through me. I even let my appearance go to pot. I was so preoccupied and overwhelmed that I couldn't really care how I looked. And yet I was terribly embarrassed to be seen this way. On the one hand, it didn't really matter. And yet to be seen looking and feeling messy was dehumanizing.

I began to avoid old friends. After only a few minutes of conversation they'd ask, "Are you sick? Are you on drugs? Haven't you been paying any attention to what I've been saying to you? Don't you understand?" Their questions, annoyance, and lack of understanding further humiliated me. My friends used to call me "the computer" because my mind was so quick and sharp. I had a photographic memory. Now I was nothing more than a shaking vegetable.

I began to seriously wonder if I had suddenly become retarded, senile, or was having a nervous breakdown. I went to numerous doctors. All of them kept saying that my symptoms were in my head. I saw a psychologist and a neurologist. Initially both thought my problems were emotional. In total despair, I tried various diets and treatments, but to no avail. I even contemplated hypnosis. Then my neurologist suggested that I see you.

At first I objected. But my doctor said, "We have nothing to lose.'' To be honest, I really didn't think that anything else would work. But I was desperate. If there was only one chance in a million, I was willing to take it.

Elaine's story strongly suggested that she had acquired an inner-ear dysfunction from her fall. Diagnostic tests confirmed this, and she was placed on a trial of medications. When she failed to respond to this initial trial, the medications were changed. The second trial produced an allergic response, and her medications were changed again. The third trial proved to be successful.

Elaine's response clearly illustrates how similar primary medications can yield entirely different results. It also makes it clear why patients must work closely with their physicians and not give up hope. Elaine recently wrote:

As I have told you before, I began treatment with some misgivings. But I was determined to give it a fair trial. This was my last hope. Everything else had already failed.

The first medication I took produced no change. The second grouping had to be abandoned because I was allergic to one of the drugs. I felt terribly discouraged and depressed. In fact, I hit rock-bottom at this point. I couldn't work or even leave my apartment. Doctors and delivery boys were the only people I saw or spoke to. Some days I didn't even get out of bed. My depression was almost unbearable.

Although I felt extremely negative and discouraged, I called you again out of complete desperation. At this point, you again changed my medications and dosages. Almost immediately after taking the new medications, I felt greatly improved. I was euphoric! I called my neurologist, my office, friends, and anyone else I could think of to tell them of my almost unbelievable response. I began to function almost as well as I did prior to 1978.

By and large, most all my fears are gone. I am no longer frightened of riding the subways and buses. Heights no longer bother me. I can swim and play tennis without severe anxiety and dyscoordination. The ground no longer acts peculiarly . . . moving and swaying before my eyes. However, I am still afraid to be out alone at night. And I will not use the subways after 7:00 P.M. If I happen to be out and see a group of rowdy teen-agers who appear to be drunk or on drugs, I cross the street to avoid them. I am still afraid of being knocked down . . . or worse.

Most important, I am able to work again! I am able to concentrate, remember, and focus on the many details that are part of my work. I am now reading, writing, spelling, and feeling great with an internal steadiness and calmness that I thought I would never again experience. My speech is back to normal and I no longer slur my words, forget my thoughts, and misunderstand the remarks of others. Balance and coordination functioning has dramatically improved. In fact, my arms and legs once again appear to belong to me and now go where I want them to. I am no longer dizzy, and motion activities are tolerable . . . even normal.

I call my medications Dr. L's Mix—my own special brand of good fortune. Feeling very confident about my positive results thus far, I decided to stop taking my medications one day. I wanted to see if I still really need them or if my results were imaginary or a placebo effect. Within a relatively short period of time my symptoms returned. Feeling good on the medication made me feel normal. I even sort of forgot just how bad things had been. In fact, once you start feeling good, it's as if you've always felt that way.

But the reminders of my depression returned. I began to experience anxiety in the supermarket during rush hour, nausea while riding in the subway or in cars, trains or buses, and terror in crowded places. My speech became slurred, and words were difficult to recall and understand. While walking into the World Trade Center one morning, the floor squares began to move up, down, and sideways; I became extremely dizzy, nauseated. Waves of anxiety and fear suddenly enveloped me, building to a crescendo of intense panic. I felt impelled to race out! I suddenly remembered in great detail how I had felt before treatment.

I knew without doubt or reservation that my previous improvements were due entirely to the medication. After all, I had hit rock-bottom before taking the first two trials of medication. I was desperately wishing for help, and nothing positive happened. When I stopped taking the medications and my symptoms returned, I knew. And I knew even better once I resumed the medications. Once again, I experienced an incredible feeling of well-being . . . I was almost symptom free.

I have proved to myself, and to all of the other physicians who took care of me, that Dr. L's Mix works—regardless of how skeptical we all were (my neurologist aside). As a result, I want my story told so that others with similar problems will know they are not crazy and hopeless . . . so that physicians with similar patients will not just "yes" their patient's symptoms away and make their patients think that it's all in their minds . . . and so that other patients might not have to hit rock-bottom, consult endless experts, and get proper treatment merely by a stroke of luck.

Science is an electron in search of its orbit;
Theory is one of many orbits;
Fact is fiction in perspective;
The end is just a new beginning . . .

Appendix A: Proper Procedures for Electronystagmography

Comprehensive ENG testing is a crucial part of the phobic diagnostic procedure. When a patient is being prepared for electronystagmographic testing, five electrodes are taped to the face (surrounding the eyes). These electrodes will measure the horizontal and vertical beats of eyeball movements in much the same way electrodes taped to the chest measure the beats of the heart. It is recommended that patients refrain from alcohol, sleeping pills, tranquilizers, or sedatives for twenty-four hours prior to testing. Testing consists of three phases:

Phase #1: Positionals

Nystagmus occurs when there is a shift in your horizontal and/or vertical balance, or in the balance of your environment. It is the CVS's way of trying to adjust to that shift. Therefore, if you are standing, sitting, or lying perfectly still and your external environment is not shifting, *no* nystagmus or nystagmus-like movements should be present. (Nystagmus is defined as the regular, even beating of the eyes. When these movements are neither regular nor even, it is technically inaccurate to refer to them as nystagmus. Accordingly, I refer to them as "nystagmus-like" or "nystagmoid.") But if your inner ear is malfunctioning, there may be evidence of nystagmus or nystagmus-like movements even when your body and your surroundings aren't moving. The first series of ENG tests is designed to investigate this possibility.

When you are undergoing positional ENG tests, it is critical that horizontal and vertical eye movements be recorded. Be sure to mention this to your physician. All too often, vertical eye movements are not measured during positional testing because clinicians mistakenly assume that:

■ The incidence of vertical nystagmus is rare. (Some clinicians even mistakenly assume that it is a sign of severe central-nervous-system dysfunction.)

■ Vertical nystagmus cannot be irregular in shape, therefore any nystagmus-like movements cannot be considered significant.

After years of investigation, both of these assumptions were found to be in error. Furthermore, vertical positional nystagmus and nystagmus-like movements were found to be the most common indication of inner-ear dysfunction. Clearly, these vertical movements must be measured to ensure that diagnosis is complete and accurate.

In Phase I of ENG testing, vertical and horizontal eye movements should be recorded in each of the following positions:

■ **Position 1*:** Standing up straight, feet together, arms straight out in front, eyes open.
■ **Position 2*:** Standing up straight, feet together, arms straight out in front, eyes closed.
■ **Position 3:** Lying down flat on a table, nose pointing toward the ceiling, eyes closed.
■ **Position 4:** Lying down flat on a table, head turned all the way to the right, eyes closed.
■ **Position 5:** Lying down flat on a table, head turned all the way to the left, eyes closed.
■ **Position 6:** Lying down on your left side, eyes closed.
■ **Position 7:** Lying down on your right side, eyes closed.
■ **Position 8:** Lying down with your back and head elevated 20 degrees, eyes closed.

You will notice that in every position except the first, the eyes are to be kept closed. When a patient's eyes are open, he or she can usually stop nystagmus and other eye movements by focusing on a fixed point, such as a light fixture or a painting (using visual information to compensate for the lack of balance information). This ruins ENG testing. By concentrating hard, patients can sometimes suppress nystagmus and other eye movements even when their eyes are closed. For this reason, ENG technicians often try to disrupt the patient's concentration mechanisms by asking him or her to count backward or perform simple calculations.

As I said before, the presence of any nystagmus or nystagmus-like eye movements—vertical or horizontal—during positional testing is usually a clear sign of inner-ear dysfunction.

---

*Note to physicians: Clinical evidence of phobia-related and vestibular-related symptomatology produced in the eyes-closed Romberg position led to the addition of positions 1 and 2 in ENG testing.

Phase #2: Rotation Studies

In the rotational phase of ENG testing, nystagmus is intentionally induced by spinning the patient in a swivel chair. (Note that since only horizontal rotation is used, only horizontal eye movements need to be measured in these rotation studies.) When no inner-ear dysfunction is present, nystagmus patterns should have a normal, even beat. Therefore, in these rotational tests, the physician should be looking for signs of abnormal, irregular, or exaggerated nystagmus, or for an absence of nystagmus where it should be present. Any of these can be indicative of an underlying inner-ear dysfunction. Phase 2 of ENG testing should include the following tests:

- **Rotation Test #1:** Patient is spun clockwise in a swivel chair for ten rotations with eyes closed. The chair is stopped and ENG readings are taken. Eyes must remain closed until readings are completed since opening them can suppress nystagmus and affect ENG results.
- **Rotation Test #2:** Patient is spun counterclockwise in a swivel chair for ten rotations with eyes closed. The chair is stopped and eye movements are recorded. Once again, eyes must remain closed until readings are complete.

During the rotational tests, patients may feel mildly uncomfortable, dizzy, light-headed, nauseous, and even panicky. This is common, especially when inner-ear dysfunction is present, and should not make you frightened or alarmed. Typically, these symptoms dissipate as soon as the patient opens his or her eyes (because opening the eyes normally stops nystagmus).

Phase #3: Calorics

In the caloric phase of ENG testing, nystagmus is once again intentionally induced, this time by irrigating the ears with warm or cold water. As in the rotation studies, the physician should be looking for the absence of nystagmus where it should be present, or the presence of dysrhythmic, irregular, or abnormally excessive nystagmus.

In Phase 3, all tests are performed with the patient lying on a table with his or her back elevated 20 degrees. Due to the positioning of the head, only horizontal nystagmus is stimulated in the caloric tests. It is therefore unnecessary to measure vertical eye movements in this phase of ENG testing. Phase 3 includes the following tests:

- **Caloric Test #1:** Left ear is irrigated with cool water (~30°C) for thirty seconds. Irrigation is stopped and eye movements are recorded. Patient's eyes must be closed the entire time.

■ **Caloric Test #2:** Right ear is irrigated with cool water (~30°C). Irrigation is stopped and eye movements are recorded for thirty seconds. Eyes must be closed the entire time.

■ **Caloric Test #3:** Both ears are simultaneously irrigated with cool water (~30°C) for thirty seconds. Irrigation is stopped and eye movements are recorded. Eyes must be closed the entire time. (When both ears are irrigated simultaneously, the disruptive effects should cancel each other out, and little or no nystagmus should be present—but this does not necessarily hold true if CVS dysfunction is present.

■ **Caloric Test #4:** Left ear is irrigated with warm water (~44°C) for thirty seconds. Irrigation is stopped and eye movements are recorded. Eyes must be closed the entire time.

■ **Caloric Test #5:** Right ear is irrigated with warm water (~44°C) for thirty seconds. Irrigation is stopped and eye movements are recorded. Eyes must be closed the entire time.

■ **Caloric Test #6:** Both ears are irrigated with warm water (~44°C) for thirty seconds. Irrigation is stopped and eye movements are recorded. Eyes must be closed the entire time.

As in the rotation studies, irrigation may stimulate a variety of unpleasant feelings, including dizziness, light-headedness, nausea, and panic. Once the patient opens his or her eyes, these feelings should quickly subside.

For a more detailed discussion of ENG testing and interpretation, you may wish to read *A Solution to the Riddle Dyslexia* (Springer-Verlag, 1980).

Appendix B: Illustrations

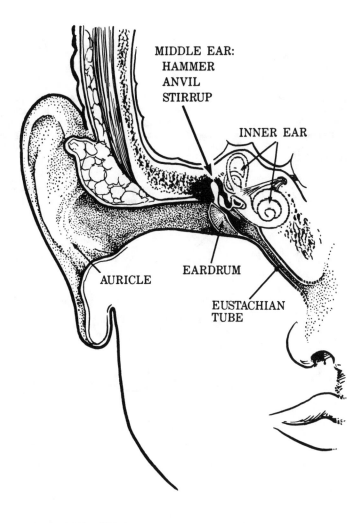

Figure 1. The Inner Ear and Middle Ear. (Harriet R. Greenfield, *The Harvard Medical School Health Letter*)

a.

b.

Figure 2. Blurring-Speed Test. In the Blurring-Speed Test, a series of moving objects (a) are projected on a wall and the speed of their movement is gradually increased. The point at which these objects appear to blur (b) is the patient's blurring speed. On the average, inner-ear impaired individuals have blurring speeds one-half that of nonimpaired individuals. (*A Solution to the Riddle Dyslexia*, Springer-Verlag 1980)

Figure 3. Bender Gestalt Drawing Test. Patients are requested to copy these eight figures to the best of their ability. (*A Solution to the Riddle Dyslexia*, Springer-Verlag 1980)

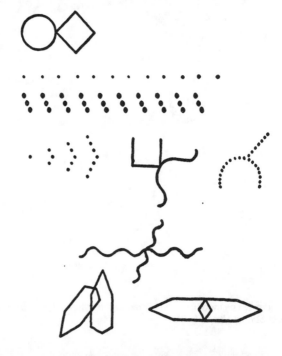

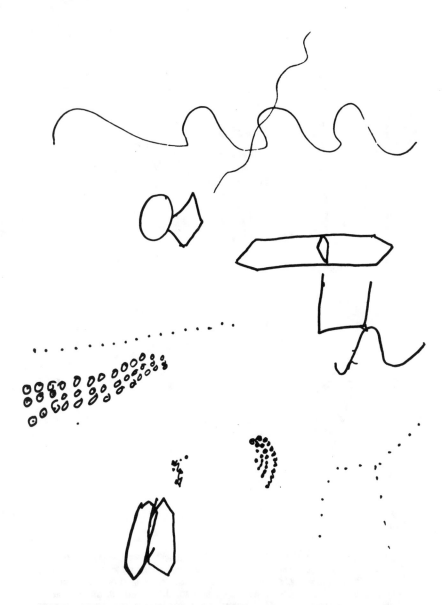

Figure 4. Bender Gestalt Drawings of a Ten-Year-Old Boy with Inner-Ear Dysfunction. Drifting, angular, rotational and directional errors like these are common when CVS dysfunction is present. Previously, these errors were believed to be psychologically determined.

Figure 5. Goodenough Figure Drawings of Patients with Inner-Ear Dysfunction. In the Goodenough Figure Drawing Test, patients are requested to draw a person. When CVS dysfunction is present, figures are frequently tilted or oversimplified, and details such as hands, fingers, feet, and facial features are often omitted. These characteristics reflect CVS-determined gyroscopic imbalance and/or poor fine-coordination skills. Previously, these characteristics were believed to be psychologically determined. (*A Solution to the Riddle Dyslexia*, Springer-Verlag 1980)

Bibliography and Recommended Reading

Agoraphobia. British Medical Journal 1 (1900):98.

Barber, H. O., and Stockwell, C. W. *Manual of Electronystagmography*. St. Louis, Missouri: The C. V. Mosby Company, 1980.

Bender, L. "A Visual Motor Gestalt Test and Its Clinical Use." New York: American Orthopsychiatric Association Research Monograph No. 3, 1938.

Benedikt, M. *Allgemeine Wiener medizinische Zeitung* 15 (1870):488.

Crabtree, N. Ototoxicity. "Proceedings of the Royal Society of Medicine." (1973):66, 189–193.

Eccles, J. C. "The Cerebellum as a Computer: Patterns in Space and Time." *Journal of Physiology* 229 (1973):1–32.

Eccles, J. C., Ito, M., and Szentagothai, J. *The Cerebellum as a Neuronal Machine*. New York: Springer-Verlag, 1967.

Eckstein, Gustav. *The Body Has a Head*. New York: Harper and Row, 1970.

Fenichel, O. *The Psycho-Analytic Theory of Neurosis*. New York: Norton, 1945.

Freud, S. *The Complete Psychological Works of Sigmund Freud*. Standard Edition, Vols. I–XXIV (especially Vol. X). Richards, A., ed. London: The Hogarth Press, 1962.

Freud, S. *An Outline of Psychoanalysis*. New York: W. W. Norton, 1939.

Goodenough, F. L. *Draw-a-Man Test: The Measurement of Intelligence by Drawings*. New York: World Book, 1926.

Gordon, A. G. "Perilymph fistula: a cause of auditory, vestibular, neurological and psychiatric disorder." *Medical Hypotheses* 2(1976):125–134.

Guye, A. "On Agoraphobia in relation to ear disease." *Laryngoscope* 6 (1899):219–221.

Jackson, J. H. *Selected Writings of John Hughlings Jackson*. J. Taylor (ed.). London: Hodder and Stoughton, 1931.

Jacob, R. G., Moller, M. B., Turner, S. M. and Wall III, C. W. "Otoneurological Examination in Panic Disorder and Agoraphobia with Panic Attacks: A Pilot Study." *American Journal of Psychiatry* 142 (1985):715–720.

Klein, D. F., Gittleman, R., Quitking, F., and Rifkin, A. *Diagnosis and Drug Treatment of Psychiatric Disorders: Adults and Children*. Baltimore: Williams Wilkins, 1980.

Lannois, M. and Tournier, C. "Les lesions auriculaires sont une cause determinante frequente de l'agoraphobie." *Annales des maladies de l'oreille, du larynx du nez et du pharynx*. 24 (1899):286–301.

Lentz, J. M., & Collins, W. E. "Motion sickness susceptibility and related behavioral characteristics in men and women." *Aviation, Space and Environmental Medicine* (1977):48, 316–322.

Levinson, H. *Smart But Feeling Dumb*. New York: Warner, 1984.

Levinson, H. *A Solution to the Riddle Dyslexia*. New York: Springer-Verlag, 1980.

Liedgren, S. R., Odkvist, L. M., & Frederickson, J. M. "The effect of marihuana on vestibular, cerebellar, and oculomotor function." *Canadian Journal of Otolaryngology* (1974):3, 291–301.

Marks, I. and Bebbington, P. "Space phobia: syndrome or agoraphobic variant?" *British Medical Journal* 2 (1976):345–347.

Marks, I. "Space "phobia": a pseudo-agoraphobic syndrome." *Journal of Neurology, Neurosurgery and Psychiatry* 44 (1981):387–391.

McCabe, B. F. "Some remarks on vestibular compensation." *Canadian Journal of Otolaryngology* (1974):3, 343–347.

Minkler, Margaret. 1982 personal communication relating agoraphobia to an inner-ear dysfunction.

Page, N. G. R. and Gresty, M. A. "Motorist's vestibular disorientation syndrome." *Journal of Neurology, Neurosurgery and Psychiatry* 48 (1985):729–735.

Palay, S. L., and Chan-Palay, V. *Cerebellar Cortex: Cytology and Organization*. New York: Springer-Verlag, 1974.

Pitts, F. N., and McClure, J. N. "Lactate Metabolism in Anxiety Neurosis." *New England Journal of Medicine* 277 (1967):1329–1336.

Rabiner, C. J., and Klein, D. F. "Imipramine Treatment of School Phobia." *Comprehensive Psychiatry* 10 (1969):387–390.

Sekitani, T., McCabe, B. F., & Ryu, J. H. "Drug effects on the medial vestibular nucleus." Archives of Otolaryngology (1971):93, 581–589.

Selye, H. *The Stress of Life*. New York: McGraw-Hill, 1978.

Sheehan, D. *The Anxiety Disease*. New York: Charles Scribner & Sons, 1983.

Sherrington, C. S. *The Integrative Action of the Nervous System*. New York: Charles Scribner & Sons, 1906.

Shuster, A. R. "The psychotropic drugs: Considerations relative to the vestibular pathways and testing." *Laryngoscope* (1965):75, 707–749.

Snider, R. S. "The Cerebellum." *Scientific American* 174 (1958): 84–90.

Snider, R. S., and Stowell, A. "Receiving Areas of the Tactile, Auditory and Visual Systems in the Cerebellum." *Journal of Neurophysiology* 7 (1944):331–357.

Von Uexkull, J. "A Stroll Through the Worlds of Animals and Men." In Schiller, H. (ed.) *Instinctive Behaviour*. New York: International Universities Press, 1957.

Index